The **COMPLETE**

IDIOT'S

GUIDE TO

Buying or Leasing a Car

by Jack R. Nerad

EAST CHICAGO PUBLIC LIBRARY
EAST CHICAGO, INDIANA

Macmillan Spectrum/Alpha

A Division of Macmillan General Reference
A Simon and Schuster Macmillan Company
1633 Broadway, New York NY 10019-6705

This book is dedicated to my lovely wife, Sandi, for saying, "You better get up off the couch and work on your book," and for the wonderful, kind, generous things she does for me each day. I also dedicate this book to my new daughter, Madeleine, who arrived in this world in the midst of my author review. I hope that after she reviews this author, she'll decide to keep him as her father.

©1996 by Jack Nerad

All rights reserved. No part of this book shall be reproduced, stored in a retrieval system, or transmitted by any means, electronic, mechanical, photocopying, recording, or otherwise, without written permission from the publisher. No patent liability is assumed with respect to the use of the information contained herein. Although every precaution has been taken in the preparation of this book, the publisher and author assume no responsibility for errors or omissions. Neither is any liability assumed for damages resulting from the use of information contained herein. For information, address Alpha Books, 1633 Broadway, 7th Floor, New York, NY 10019-6785.

International Standard Book Number: 0-02-861274-4

Library of Congress Catalog Card Number: 96-084589

98   4

Interpretation of the printing code: the rightmost number of the first series of numbers is the year of the book's printing; the rightmost number of the second series of numbers is the number of the book's printing. For example, a printing code of 96-1 shows that the first printing occurred in 1996.

Printed in the United States of America.

This publication contains the opinions and ideas of its author and is designed to provide useful advice on the subject covered. The author and publisher are not engaged in rendering legal or other professional services in this publication. Laws vary from state to state, as do the facts and circumstances of various transactions, and this publication is not intended to provide a basis for action in particular circumstances without consideration by a competent professional. The author and publisher expressly disclaim any responsibility for any liability, loss, or risk, personal or otherwise, that is incurred as a consequence, directly or indirectly, of the use and application of any of the contents of this book.

629.222
N443c

Publisher
Theresa H. Murtha

Managing Editor
Michael Cunningham

Development Editor
Lisa A. Bucki

Production Editor
Phil Kitchel

Technical Editor
B.J. Killeen

Copy Editors
Kate Givens
Brian Robinson

Illustrator
Judd Winick

Designer
Kim Scott

Cover Designers
Dan Armstrong
Barb Kordesh

Indexer
Chris Wilcox

Production Team
Heather Butler
Angela Calvert
Aleata Howard
Daniela Raderstorf
Beth Rago
Megan Wade
Christy Wagner

Contents at a Glance

Contents

Introduction

Car buying should be fun.

I know what you're thinking: What? Is he crazy? Car buying is as much fun as body waxing, keel-hauling, or do-it-yourself surgery. Sure, buying or leasing a new vehicle can be frustrating and expensive, but I'm here to tell you it doesn't have to be.

When you think about it, getting a new vehicle should be a *lot* of fun. After all, few things give your ego a bigger boost than several thousand dollars' worth of shiny paint, sparkling glass, and polished chrome. Even people who aren't dyed-in-the-wool automobile fans have to admit that, as consumer products go, new cars are pretty cool.

Sadly, many people dwell on the frustration, uncertainty, and expense. And of these three, I venture a guess that the uncertainty troubles people most of all. The uncertainty comes in two forms: People don't know what to buy, and they don't know what to pay.

You don't need a short course in purchasing snack foods or headache remedies or hand tools. That's all pretty straightforward—you walk in the store, find the right aisle, read the label and the price, and proceed to the cash register. You don't need the steel-trap mind of a bowling-ball driller to figure that one out. But buying a vehicle is different. There are a lot of choices, and the price marked is usually not the price you want to pay.

That's just for openers. You can also stumble in acquiring financing (the ever-popular auto loan), trading in your current ride, signing a lease contract...the list is lengthy, if not quite endless.

It's a jungle out there, or seasoned guides are few and far between. But now that you have this book, let me encourage you a bit. First of all, I bring a little bit of experience with me. As the Editor of *Motor Trend*, Director of Publications at J.D. Power and Associates, and the co-host of the Mutual Radio Network program *America on the Road*, I've helped thousands of people choose the right vehicle, and answered their automotive questions for years, and that experience gives me a unique perspective on what car buyers want and need to know.

Which is why I wrote this book. There is a way to crawl through this maze of obstacles unscathed, unhurt, and unbowed and, at the end of the day, emerge with a well-built, high-quality vehicle that suits your needs—for a price you can afford. I'm here to help.

How to Use This Book

The Complete Idiot's Guide to Buying or Leasing a Car is divided into five different parts. Maybe that sounds complicated, but it's not.

Part 1 places you in the context of the automotive world at large, helping you with the big choices (like whether you should buy an import or a domestic), assessing the real costs of owning a car, and informing you that you, the vehicle buyer, are crucial to the success of the giant automobile manufacturers. It will give you some hints on picking the right vehicle and warn you about two giant potential potholes in your route to new wheels.

Part 2 helps you get serious about shopping. It discusses crucial safety issues, gives you hints on affordability, and walks you through list-building. If you'd like to shop for a vehicle from the comfort of your own armchair, read Part 2.

Building on the research outlined in Part 2, Part 3 is all about using that research to narrow your choices. It helps you choose the vehicle that's best for your particular needs, and helps you equip that vehicle with the right options. On top of that, if you currently own a vehicle, this part tells you whether selling it yourself or trading it in is your better option.

If you've already chosen a vehicle and know how you're going to dispose of your current chariot, you might want to skip directly to Part 4, which helps you set the stage for the best deal possible. This section describes crucial preliminary steps like lining up financing, and tells you the best days, weeks, and months to buy a vehicle.

If you're currently shopping for a vehicle, you'll want to take a long look at Part 5. This section of the book demystifies vehicle pricing, decoding threatening terms like *MSRP* and *dealer invoice prices*. Does auto leasing sound intriguing? You'll get an in-depth look at this wildly popular phenomenon in this section, plus a side-by-side comparison of leasing versus buying. This section will also help sharpen your showroom bargaining tactics and give you other alternatives to the typical dealer dance.

Finally, don't think the process is over when you come to an agreement with the salesperson. You get hints on the vagaries of add-on sales, the province of the F&I manager, how to take delivery of your new vehicle, and sound advice on what to do if something goes wrong with your newly bought gem.

Extras

In addition to the main text of the book, you'll also encounter special boxes brimming with information that look like this:

Bet You Didn't Know

These boxes contain tasty tidbits of information, more or less on the subject, that can enhance your understanding of the topic at hand.

Money-Saving Tip

Within these boxes are especially important flashes of information—important because they can save you hard-earned cash.

Let's Talk Terms

Boxes like this contain...well, this should be obvious, but they contain a definition of an important **term** or **concept**.

Lemon

Boxes like this contain warnings about bad advice and bad deals. Heeding these warnings can save you cash and heartaches.

Acknowledgments

No book like this is done in a vacuum. There's not enough air in a vacuum to sustain life long enough to write a book. No book is done without the help of others, either, so I'd like to acknowledge them for their help.

Thanks to John Rettie of J.D. Power and Associates for his assistance in procuring information from the vast resources of his firm and helping me share it with the readers of this book.

Thanks to Bob Esco, professional car salesman par excellence, for sharing with me some behind-the-scenes dealership dynamics. I'm sure his time could've been more profitably spent putting somebody into a new Ford, so I appreciate his help all the more.

Thanks to Greg Coppock of Consumer Research Bureau for his helpful comments, particularly on the chapters in this book dealing with leasing.

Thanks to B.J. Killeen, this book's technical editor. B.J. served as the assistant managing editor at *Motor Trend* during my tenure as editor there (and several years after, for that matter), so I knew she would do a terrific job keeping me on my toes as tech editor. And of course, she did. Thanks, B.J.

I would also like to extend my sincere thanks and appreciation to Lisa Bucki, this book's development editor, who was tireless in her efforts to keep this book on track. Lisa, thank you very much for your helpful advice and your attention to details. It helped make this book better.

And by all means, thanks to the editorial staff at Macmillan Publishing, including Phil Kitchel, production editor, and Brian Robinson and Kate Givens, copy editors.

And a Final Thanks...

To you, the reader. You are about to embark on a difficult task. (No, I don't mean reading my writing; I mean buying a vehicle.) But it's far from impossible, and it is certainly one that can be performed to a satisfying conclusion. That's exactly what I hope for in your case. Thank you for your attention and best of luck in your search for the right vehicle.

Special Thanks from the Publisher to the Technical Reviewer

The Complete Idiot's Guide to Buying or Leasing a Car was checked by an expert who reviewed the technical accuracy of what you'll find here.

Special thanks to B.J. Killeen, one of a handful of female automotive journalists in the country. Now freelancing as a writer for magazines such as *Mustang Monthly*, *Petersen's Specialty Publications*, *Chevy High Performance*, and *Drag Racing and High Performance Illustrated*, as well as doing new-vehicle product presentation tours for domestic and import manufacturers, B.J. is also the editor of *American Woman Motorscene* magazine, a publication for women interested in automobiles and motorcycles. B.J. is a frequent co-host of the radio programs *America on the Road* and *In The Driver's Seat*, and makes guest appearances on television shows such as *The Home Show*.

Trademarks

All terms mentioned in this book that are known to be or suspected of being trademarks or service marks have been appropriately capitalized. Alpha Books and Macmillan General Reference cannot attest to the accuracy of this information. Use of a term in this book should not be regarded as affecting the validity of any trademark or service mark.

Part 1
You and the Automotive World

You may not realize it, but you are a VIP in the automobile industry. Why? Because you are a potential customer (in industry lingo "a prospect") and they need all the prospects they can find. The business of manufacturing and selling cars, trucks, and vans used to be a growth business. Vast fortunes were made on the booming expansion of the industry. These days, though, growth has slowed considerably. Today most people buying a new vehicle are simply replacing an old vehicle.

That means the 40 brands of cars and trucks in the U.S. market will battle tooth-and-nail for your business. They will offer you discount financing, subsidized leasing, vehicle maintenance, roadside assistance, and even cold hard cash to win your business.

This part tells where you stand in the automotive scheme of things and offers some suggestions on where you go from here.

What Are You Getting Yourself Into?

In a nation that can't agree on much of anything, one thing we all seem to agree on is that we love cars. From TV game shows to magazine sweepstakes to the fund-raiser at the local Elks Lodge, the grand prize is almost always a shiny new automobile. Americans' love affair with the four-wheeled species has been documented on stage and screen, in books, magazines, and popular music. Nobody has ever written a hit song about a toaster, toothbrush, or bowling ball, but we've hummed the praises of the automobile from the days of "In My Merry Oldsmobile" to "Little Red Corvette."

And why not? Everybody likes new cars. The bright shine of the fresh paint and the evocative aroma of the interior are American aphrodisiacs. They seem to get everyone's juices flowing.

Isn't it ironic, then, that most people love *having* a new car, but few people love *buying* one? For most of us, buying a vehicle is a stress-filled experience. For one thing, we all know that, in hard-earned dollars and cents, a car, van, pickup, or sport utility vehicle is a big investment, probably the largest investment (after our home) most of us will ever make. Fumble this choice, and you immediately blow a big wad of money. You could be stuck with a car that's more of an enemy than a friend, a payment book that reminds you every month how stupid you've been, and no hope of unloading the terrible burden without suffering a huge financial and psychological loss.

Failing to choose the right vehicle can cost you big in two ways—dollars and headaches. Because most people rely on their cars as an essential part of their day-to-day lives, a vehicle failure can be devastating to the wallet and the psyche. A recent survey showed that most people would rather do without their morning coffee, their favorite TV show, or even a romantic interlude with their significant other than be without their car for a day. If you have to get from Point A to Point B and your car isn't cooperating, you've got a major problem.

Dances with Wolves

Considering an encounter with a car salesman is yet another reason to reach for the Pepto-Bismol. Because we're used to paying posted prices for virtually everything we buy, the journey to the Arabian bazaar that is the automobile showroom can be a stomach-turning prospect. Who among us knows what price we should really pay for that nice new Miata, the low-mileage 1993 Explorer, or the ratty-but-runs-good '82 Tercel? The guy in the polyester sportcoat does this dance four times a day—you do it once every four years. Who do you think is going to come out on top?

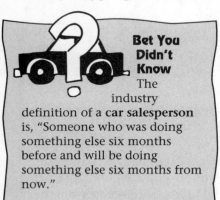

Bet You Didn't Know The industry definition of a **car salesperson** is, "Someone who was doing something else six months before and will be doing something else six months from now."

Choosing the right vehicle and paying the right price for it isn't as difficult as channeling the dead. Knowing the territory can make the difference between a blissful experience and being stranded by the side of the road in a downpour. The step-by-step guide you hold in your hands can make the search and acquisition easy and, dare I say it, fun, instead of the equivalent of a trip to the oral surgeon.

Today's Automotive Landscape

This year, between 12 and 15 million individuals will buy new cars, vans, pickups, and sport utilities. Another 25 million or so will buy used cars and trucks. These 40 million people have a common fear—they're afraid of getting a lemon. For all the strides the auto industry has made since the dawn of the consumerist era, there are still plenty of bad cars out there: plenty of transmission fluid leakers, paint chippers, and steering-pump squealers. Further, cars and trucks are sold by people with an often well-earned reputation for prevarication, puffery, and flim-flam. The consumer is fearful of getting stuck, and rightly so.

Each year hundreds of millions of Americans deal with the difficulties of vehicle selection and acquisition. And it's not a simple process. Most people are afraid of making a colossal mistake. They're terrified by technical terms like "multi-valve engines" and "sequential fuel injection." They're confused by manufacturers' pricing strategies. They're unsure whether to buy or lease. They don't trust the salespeople they'll deal with. They're worried about how much they should pay. They don't know what options are worth buying and which ones they should pass on. They're not certain which of their many financing options is the best one. Just about every phase of choosing and acquiring a car can be fraught with anxiety and difficulty.

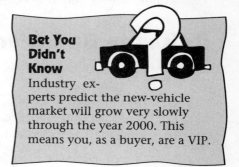

Bet You Didn't Know

Industry experts predict the new-vehicle market will grow very slowly through the year 2000. This means you, as a buyer, are a VIP.

There Are a Lot of Choices Out There

There's good reason for this fear. Never before have car buyers been confronted with so many choices. Forty years ago, almost everyone in America purchased a car from the American Big Three automakers—General Motors, Ford, and Chrysler. There were fewer than a dozen brands to consider. Now the customer must winnow his or her pick from 41 separate brands and more than 250 individual models. It's what members of the auto industry refer to as "market clutter." I bet you'd be hard pressed to name even half of the car brands out there, much less name even a quarter of the models in your price range.

Bet You Didn't Know

Today's Chrysler Corporation is built on the heritage of several now-deceased car manufacturers, including Hudson and Nash, which combined to form American Motors in the Fifties and was subsequently acquired by Chrysler in the Eighties. The Jeep brand was started by Willys, acquired by American Motors, and then became a Chrysler brand with the AMC acquisition.

At the same time, the stakes for you, the individual buyer, are going up. Cars, vans, pickups, and sport utilities cost more now than they ever have. The average new car purchased last year cost more than $20,000, according to the U.S. Commerce Department, and other sources say the figure was even higher. The average used car purchased last year averaged more than $12,000, also the highest level ever. More important, those prices represent the highest proportion of the average consumer's annual income in history. People are devoting a substantial share of their monthly pay to their wheels. No wonder they're very concerned about making a costly mistake.

It Used to Be Easier to Choose the Right Car

If you look back to the Fifties, it was much easier to choose a car than it is today. First of all, unless you were a pinko or one of those weird sports-car fanatics, you bought American. That was simply a given. Sure, a few anti-establishment types opted for MGs, Jaguars, or Volkswagen Beetles, but more than nine out of ten Americans purchased a car from one of the Big Three U.S. manufacturers.

Second, not only were there fewer brands, those brands offered fewer individual models. You didn't have to choose from a dozen Fords or Chevrolets of half a dozen Cadillacs or Chryslers. These days every car brand has become a mini-General Motors, with many models to choose from. To further confuse the situation, these models may come from different factories and may differ significantly in quality.

Finally, in the halcyon days of the Fifties, many customers showed strong loyalty to their brands. Those of us who are old enough to remember Howdy-Doody also remember "Ford families" and "Chevrolet families" and, at the top of the economic food chain, "Buick" and "Cadillac families." These class distinctions helped buyers choose their vehicles, because they could see where they fit on the personal income ladder and then pick from among the three or four brands that matched their circumstances.

That's all gone out the window. Today you can buy a Chevrolet that costs $10,000 or a Chevrolet that costs $40,000. Ford, Toyota, Nissan, and Mazda offer price spreads nearly as wide. While additional choice is great, this is another factor that makes choosing the right vehicle much harder than it was when your parents first entered the car market.

Bet You Didn't Know Fewer than 40 percent of car buyers will replace their current car with a new car of the same brand.

Now, I'm not saying cars were better in those days. Much as I like the wild excesses and idiosyncratic styling of years gone by, empirical evidence suggests that today's vehicles are, by most measures, far superior to those of 30 years ago. But there is no doubt that in the dim Dark Ages of the Sixties, sorting through the choices was definitely easier.

Today's Complicated Choices Can Work for You

It's a complicated world out there. More choices can lead to indecision, stress, and outfits that don't match. But on the other hand, it's also good to have choices.

Before you become overwhelmed by the whole process, it's important to realize that virtually every car buyer in America needs help when it's time to buy a new vehicle. In addition to the hundreds of choices a buyer must wade through, there are other swamps to navigate.

Dealers and their salespeople are notoriously shifty. Manufacturers' Suggested List Prices (the much-misunderstood window stickers) are paper tigers: confusing and treacherous. Finalizing the deal with the dreaded F & I (Finance and Insurance) manager is a booby trap waiting to be sprung. And there are so many questions. Should I buy the extended warranty? Should I buy rust-proofing? Fabric protector? Credit life insurance? What options should I buy? Which options aren't worth the money?

Making Your Choices Work

If all the choices have you experiencing Excedrin headache #6, and your brain has gone numb from trying to decide between the four-wheel-drive sport utility, the two-seat sports car, or adding a fourth bedroom to your house, there is a flip side to all these complications. Each and every car manufacturer is stuck in the same environment you are. And even though, if you're like me, it's difficult for you to make your monthly nut for food, shelter, clothing, and video rentals, pity the poor car company that must keep its dealers happy, its factories running, its payroll and health care benefits paid up, and, most important of all, pay the tab on its fabulously expensive product-development process and production plants.

The fact is, in the eyes of most industry experts, there are simply too many car companies out there. There are too many factories, too many development engineers, too many stylists, too many regional sales managers, too many advertising agencies, and, yes, too many car dealers in the world to serve the people who want and need to buy cars. In many ways, the car business isn't what it used to be.

These days, in the good ol' USA, most people buying new cars are simply replacing an old one. Relatively few new buyers are coming into the market, and their numbers are almost matched by old buyers who are leaving it (many by hearse).

What does this mean to you, the new-car buyer?

To the car companies of the world you are a very precious resource. In their eyes, there simply aren't enough of you to go around, so they will bash each other six ways to Sunday to obtain your business. They will spend millions of dollars on advertising campaigns just to get your attention. They will keep updating their products (at huge expense) both stylistically and technically to retain their competitive edge. They will offer big incentives, like cash and loss-leader financing, to persuade you to buy their vehicles. And they will provide lengthy warranties on their vehicles to induce you to put your name on a sales contract.

In simple terms, Ms. and Mr. Buyer out there in ConsumerLand, you are in the driver's seat. The car manufacturers and dealers need you a lot more than you need them. You can provide them with something they crave desperately—a willing buyer with the financial wherewithal to spend. Like I say, you're a rare commodity, so use this to your advantage.

How? Remember that hit tune "Shop Around" and its pithy lyric, "Don't ya be sold on the very first one?" Well, that songwriter was right on when it comes to car shopping. Do your homework. Get some price quotes. Talk to several salespeople. All of this will help you find your comfort zone.

You might not be aware of it, but you are equipped with two of the most powerful deal-making tools in the world—your feet. If, at any time, you don't like the way the proceedings are going when you negotiate with a salesperson, simply walk away. Never fear that the terrific deal you're offered "for today only" by a hungry salesperson will never be matched. More than likely you can match or better the deal any day of the week.

Bet You Didn't Know Experts predict that the major growth in the automobile business in the next few years will come in Asia. Countries like Singapore, Thailand, and China will enjoy boom times, while sales in America will be slow.

I'm certainly not advising arrogance or discourtesy toward salespeople. What I do advise is that you stand up for yourself and expect, in fact, *demand* to be treated with respect. Shop around, not only for the best deal, but for the best treatment. And don't buy until you feel comfortable with the car, the deal, the salesperson, and the dealership.

How do you reach that comfort level? Read on, and I'll tell you in the next few chapters.

The Least You Need to Know

➤ People love new cars, but they don't love buying them.

➤ It used to be easier to choose a car.

➤ Choosing the right car or truck and paying the right price *is* possible.

➤ A rational buying process is crucial to getting the best deal.

➤ The intense competition between car manufacturers can help you get the right vehicle and the right deal.

Chapter 2

The Big Choices

> **In This Chapter**
>
> ➤ America versus the world
>
> ➤ Transplant vehicles
>
> ➤ Getting the best quality
>
> ➤ Trend to trucks and minivans

If today's vehicle market gives you one thing, it's choices. Do you want an American-made vehicle or an import? If it's an import you're after, should it be from Japan, Germany, Britain, Sweden, or Korea? What kind of vehicle do you want? A family sedan? Sports car? Pickup truck? Minivan? Sport utility? Luxury car?

As you look over the vast automotive landscape, you will be confronted with unfamiliar terms like *transplants* and *customer satisfaction indices*. This chapter is designed to define those terms and put them in context to help you make the important choices you need to make as you move toward a vehicle acquisition. This chapter will discuss the quality issue as well, and you'll find it more complex than it might seem on the surface. But to predict the future we first must learn a little about the past.

USA versus the World

Some of us are old enough to remember when the term "Made in Japan" was a sign of poor quality and shoddy workmanship. Obviously, that is true no more, and one of the Japanese industries responsible for that remarkable turnabout is the automobile industry. In the course of one generation, the Japanese were able to transform their design and manufacturing operations from little better than a joke to the leading edge.

Thirty years ago, the cars that emerged from Japan's factories were almost laughable by American standards. To our eyes at least, the cars were too small and the styling too oddball—Godzilla movies on wheels. Even worse, the quality and reliability were not up to American standards.

The Japanese quickly found this out when they first tried to market their cars here in the 1960s. But, to their credit, they didn't bury their heads in the sand and claim they didn't have a problem. Instead, the took the novel approach of actually asking people what they liked and didn't like. They enlisted market-research techniques that included customer surveys, focus groups, and consumer clinics to determine consumer preferences.

What they discovered wasn't nuclear science. When the research was over they concluded that American car buyers put a high priority on quality and reliability. Because Americans depend on their cars, they told the research firms they needed cars that start every time and run without incident—mile after mile after mile.

Well, no chit, Cherlock! You might have guessed that's what they'd find. But the important thing is not what they discovered through their research, but what they did about it. They turned quality and reliability into a religion. They worked overtime to find ways to make their cars run better and last longer. They investigated new management and production techniques that would help them build cars better. And they used the close-knit group dynamics of Japanese society to enforce these ideals within their workforces. The result: Japanese cars got a lot better very quickly.

Never Discount Good Luck

While the cars the Japanese sold in the United States definitely improved at a rapid rate, the Japanese manufacturers also benefited from some luck in their efforts to conquer the American car market. Remember the old saw "Timing is everything"? Well, timing certainly worked to Japan's advantage when two mammoth oil crises hit the developed world.

The first oil crisis in 1973-74 persuaded many buyers to consider Japanese cars for the first time. After all, the Japanese were skilled at building small, highly fuel-efficient cars, because that's exactly what their domestic market required.

Bet You Didn't Know

More than 25 percent of the car market in Japan is made up of tiny vehicles with engine displacements of 1 liter or less, smaller than most American motorcycle engines.

By the time the second oil crisis rolled around in 1979, the Japanese had established a strong beachhead in the United States, and the second oil crunch helped them consolidate and expand quickly. The Big Three U.S. manufacturers—General Motors, Ford, and Chrysler—had not yet fully accepted the need for more fuel-efficient vehicles. Their attempts to adapt their full-size cars to the fuel-conscious environment resulted in lumbering behemoths that were so underpowered they could barely clear a freeway on-ramp without white-knuckling their drivers. And the U.S. manufacturers' first attempts at lighter, front-wheel-drive cars resulted in such lame excuses as the Chrysler Omni/Horizon twins and the GM X-cars. Many buyers saw them and said, No Way! Both Ford and Chrysler teetered on the edge of bankruptcy, and GM suffered mightily as well.

As the Eighties dawned, Americans snapped up Toyotas, Hondas, Datsuns (soon to become Nissans), Mazdas, and Subarus in ever-increasing numbers. Mitsubishi, which had been selling cars and small pickup trucks through Chrysler since the early Seventies, opened up its own dealership network, as did Isuzu. Daihatsu and Suzuki, two smaller-scale Japanese manufacturers, would soon follow suit.

Well, there was little doubt that American car companies were losing more than a piece of the car market to the Japanese. Starting from ground zero in about 1970, Japanese-built cars grabbed more than 10 percent of the U.S. car market by the early Eighties. Prognosticators suggested that the percentage might reach 20 percent within five years and 30 percent by the end of the decade.

These dire predictions got the politicians into action. Behind closed doors, they hammered out what came to be known as the Voluntary Restraint Agreement (or VRA). Under terms of the agreement, to be enforced by Japan's powerful Ministry of Trade and Transportation (MITT), Japanese manufacturers were required to limit their shipments of vehicles to America, thus putting a limit on the Japanese share of the market as a whole. Further, each manufacturer was assigned a quota based on its percentage of sales in America. Toyota, the market leader, got the highest allocation; Nissan and Honda were next; Mazda, Mitsubishi, and Subaru received relatively sizable pieces of the pie; and the remaining Japanese manufacturers had to struggle for the crumbs.

While not officially a quota, the VRA effectively limited the importation of Japanese-built cars into America. Since the agreement did nothing to eliminate the continued demand for Japanese cars by American buyers, this had several immediate effects:

1. It limited the Japanese share of the American car market.

2. It drove up the price of Japanese cars in the U.S.

3. It made many dealers of Japanese cars rich.

Did the Voluntary Restraint Agreement rescue the American auto industry? The answer to that question isn't crystal clear, but what *is* clear is that the VRA immeasurably changed the auto industry, not just in the United States, but in the world.

Transplant, What's a Transplant?

A *transplant* is a vehicle manufactured in a country, such as the U.S., but designed and sold by a company from another country, such as Japan. One success you can claim for the VRA is that it put thousands of Americans to work in the auto industry. But ironically, those thousands work for Japanese bosses in Japanese-owned manufacturing plants here in the United States. It put thousands of others to work in Japanese-owned plants in Canada and Mexico.

Where did these factories come from? They were the Japanese manufacturers' response to the VRA. As part of the "voluntary" agreement, Japanese manufacturers were prohibited from importing more than their quota of vehicles into the United States. But they were not prohibited from building cars in the U.S. So several Japanese manufacturers, led by Honda, quickly erected U.S. factories (as well as factories in Canada and Mexico, which were also unaffected by the terms of the VRA). In less than five years, the Japanese had the capacity to build several hundred thousand cars and trucks on U.S. soil.

The American manufacturers and many pundits scoffed at all this. They believed a key reason for the quality of Japanese vehicles was the quality and work ethic of the Japanese workforce. They were convinced that American workers wouldn't put up with Japanese-style management techniques, and, sadly, they just didn't believe that Americans could build vehicles as well as the Japanese could.

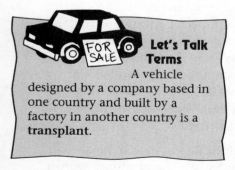

Let's Talk Terms
A vehicle designed by a company based in one country and built by a factory in another country is a **transplant**.

But they were wrong. When the Japanese-owned and managed factories began to crank up production in Marysville, Ohio; Georgetown and Smyrna, Tennessee; Fremont, California; and several other cities and towns in North America, the quality of the cars and trucks they built was as good, and sometimes better, than the quality of the same vehicles built in Japan. Americans not only accepted the Japanese-style team techniques, they flourished in them. Today the Japanese have the factory capacity to build more than half a million cars here in North America.

The establishment of American factories brought with it another benefit as well: It allowed the Japanese a hedge against value fluctuations between the dollar and the yen. That hedge has proved a lifesaver to several of the Japanese manufacturers when the dollar weakened considerably against the yen in 1994-95. Had it not been for the North American production capacity, the Japanese might have found themselves priced out of the U.S. market.

In fact, the Japanese experience in the United States has been so positive that two vaunted European manufacturers—BMW and Mercedes-Benz—have recently constructed factories here as well. Their goal is to use relatively low-cost, high-quality American labor to build cars for the U.S. and the world. They, too, are hedging their bets against wild currency swings, which could otherwise cost them dearly.

Getting the Best Quality

So much for the historical perspective. The question you probably have on your lips is, who makes the highest quality cars? The Japanese? Americans? Europeans? Or the Koreans?

Well, if you want a simple answer, it's the Japanese. The bulk of data from J.D. Power and Associates, *Consumer Reports*, and other research entities suggest that the best quality vehicles still come from Japanese manufacturers. But if you jump to conclusions from this simple answer, you may jump right out of the boat and into deep water. As it affects your buying or leasing decision, the answer you need isn't simple.

First off, what is "quality"? Certainly that word means different things to different people. In the auto industry, largely because of the huge influence of J.D. Power and Associates, the term *quality* has come to mean the absence of defects. In its highly publicized New-Car and Light Truck Initial Quality Studies, which are conducted every year, J.D. Power and Associates asks owners who have driven their new cars for about 90 days to report on the problems they've experienced. The research company then folds this data into reports that rank car companies, brands, and individual models on the basis of problems per 100 vehicles (see Tables 2.1 and 2.2). The industry has come to refer to these studies as indices of "things gone wrong."

J.D. Power and Associates also takes this approach in its famous Customer Satisfaction Index studies. In these studies, the research firm questions owners of automobiles after about one year of ownership about their experiences with their vehicles and their dealer (see Table 2.3). Again, the questions revolve around problems—things gone wrong.

Bet You Didn't Know

According to J.D. Power and Associates' most recent Customer Satisfaction Index Study, Japanese and European manufacturers provided better satisfaction than domestic car makers despite the fact that import car buyers are more difficult to please.

Consumer Reports magazine, run by the nonprofit Consumers Union, bases its well-known Reliability Reports on the same premise. The organization asks the readers of its magazine to tally and report on problems they have had with their vehicles to assemble its Frequency of Repair data.

Table 2.1   J.D. Power and Associates' Top 10 Manufacturers in Initial Product Quality

Manufacturer	Problems	Manufacturer	Problems
Lexus	54	Saturn	81
Infiniti	67	Nissan	82
Volvo	71	Mazda	83
Honda	78	Mercedes-Benz	83
Toyota	80	Saab	84

Source: J.D. Power and Associates 1996 New Car Initial Quality Study
*per 100 vehicles; Lower = Better

Table 2.2   J.D. Power and Associates Top 10 Models in Initial Product Quality

Model	Problems	Model	Problems
Lexus SC 300/400	45	Mazda Millenia	61
Lexus LS 400	52	Infiniti J30	62
Lexus ES 300	54	Mazda Protégé	64
Subaru Impreza	57	Chrysler New Yorker	67
Infiniti Q45	58	Infiniti I30	67

Source: J.D. Power and Associates 1996 New Car Initial Quality Study
*per 100 vehicles; Lower = Better

Table 2.3   J.D. Power and Associates Above Average Manufacturers in Customer Satisfaction

Manufacturer	Index	Manufacturer	Index
Infiniti	168	Volvo	148
Lexus	166	BMW	144
Acura	159	Buick	144
Mercedes-Benz	158	Jaguar	143
Saturn	158	Oldsmobile	142
Honda	154	Subaru	141
Cadillac	151	Toyota	140
Lincoln	150	Nissan	138
Audi	149	Porsche	138

Source: J.D. Power and Associates 1996 New Car Customer Satisfaction Index Study.
Index numbers based on statistical formula for determining customers' satisfaction levels with their vehicle and dealer service after one year of ownership.
Higher = Better

Certainly, there is nothing wrong with the methodology of adding up problems. Of the two organizations, I'd say J.D. Power and Associates' method is a bit more scientific (and note, I may be a bit prejudiced since I once worked for the organization) because it takes a random sample of all owners of each model. *Consumer Reports*, on the other hand, relies on the responses of its readers. In any case, there is little doubt that both organizations provide valuable data and that both organizations have forced auto manufacturers to clean up their acts and build better cars.

Things Gone Right

If your idea of a good vehicle is a vehicle that doesn't cause you any problems, then you've found keys to help you unlock that vehicle in the J.D. Power and Associates Initial Quality Studies and in *Consumer Reports* reliability ratings. But many of us associate quality not just with the absence of defects, but with the presence of positives.

Let's take a simple example. Pretend you're shopping for something pretty rudimentary—say, a new doormat. You examine one in the store, and it has no defects: It's woven of sturdy material, the stitching is strong; you can't see anything wrong with it. Will you buy it because of its absence of defects? Or will you continue to look for one that not only lacks defects, but also catches your fancy? Maybe one that says "WELCOME" on it, or one with your family name; or, if you're more reclusive, one that says "GO AWAY."

What we're discussing here is not just "things gone wrong," but also "things gone right." One could make the case that real quality is a complex interaction of the absence of "things gone wrong" and the presence of "things gone right." The Japanese have become the past masters of eliminating defects, but are they as strong at building in positives? And how do we find that out?

In the last two years, J.D. Power and Associates and a San Diego-based market research firm called Strategic Vision have both taken runs at it. Strategic Vision, a firm founded by clinical psychologists, conducts what it calls its Total Quality survey of owners who have owned their vehicles for about 90 to 120 days. The survey measures both problem incidence and positive attributes, and from this information the firm derives its "Total Quality Index."

From the Total Quality study Strategic Vision publishes a list of what it refers to as "The Best-Loved Cars and Trucks in America," listed in Table 2.4.

Table 2.4 The Best-Loved Cars and Trucks in America

Vehicle Type	Make/Model
Small car	Saturn SL Sedan
Compact car	Honda Accord
Mid-Size car	Dodge Intrepid
Large car	Pontiac Bonneville
Lower-price sports car	Ford Mustang
Mid-specialty car	Chevrolet Monte Carlo
Near luxury car	Oldsmobile Aurora
Luxury car	Mercedes-Benz E320
Minivan	Chrysler Town & Country
Mid-size sport utility	Jeep Grand Cherokee
Full-size sport utility	Chevrolet Tahoe
Compact pickup	Toyota Tacoma
Full-size pickup	Dodge Ram

Source: Strategic Vision's 1996 Total Quality Survey

The research firm also releases a list called the "Top Quality Best of the Best," (see Table 2.5). This list reveals the top two or three "winners" in each of 13 car and truck market segments. For example, in the "Small Car" class in the 1996 survey, the most recent available, the Saturn SL Sedan was at the top; the Honda Civic ranked second; and the Volkswagen GolfIII was third. The last is a particularly interesting result, since the VW Golf was well down the list in the J.D. Power and Associates 1996 Initial Quality Study. What one might infer from this is that the Golf's positive attributes—styling, fun-to-drive, and so on—helped outweigh some defects in build quality and reliability.

Table 2.5 Top Three Best of the Best by Segment

Market Segment	Make/Model	Total Quality Index
Small car	Saturn SL Sedan	822
	Honda Civic	813
	Volkswagen GolfIII	812
Compact car	Honda Accord	815
	Toyota Camry	807
	Ford Contour	802
Mid-size car	Dodge Intrepid	825
	Ford Taurus	812
	Mercury Sable	806
Large car	Pontiac Bonneville	827
	Buick LeSabre	816
	Chevrolet Caprice	812
Lower-price sports car	Ford Mustang	835
	Dodge Avenger	827
	Saturn Coupe	814
Mid-specialty car	Chevrolet Monte Carlo	817
	Ford Thunderbird	811
	Pontiac Grand Prix	789
Near luxury car	Oldsmobile Aurora	852
	Chrysler LHS	844
	Volvo 850	842
Luxury car	Mercedes-Benz E320	892
	Lexus LS 400	877
	Infiniti J30	845

continues

Table 2.5 Continued

Market Segment	Make/Model	Total Quality Index
Minivan	Chrysler Town & Country	811
	Dodge Caravan	798
	Plymouth Voyager	774
Mid-size sport utility	Jeep Grand Cherokee	830
	Ford Explorer	818
	(Two winners named)	
Full-size sport utility	Chevrolet Tahoe	847
	Toyota Land Cruiser	841
	(Two winners named)	
Compact pickup	Toyota Tacoma	762
	Chevrolet S-10	754
	(Two winners named)	
Full-size pickup	Dodge Ram	816
	GMC Sierra	788
	(Two winners named)	

Source: Strategic Vision's 1996 Total Quality Survey
Higher = Better

Not to be outdone, J.D. Power and Associates has recently introduced a new study called Automotive Performance, Execution and Layout (APEAL) that also addresses "things gone right." It examines positive attributes vehicles exhibit, things like ride comfort, fun-to-drive, and styling—those things that make people fall in love with their cars. The consumer survey data goes through the firm's statistical wringer and out comes a study that ranks vehicles by how much their drivers like them. Further, the study also addresses why consumers *didn't* purchase the other vehicles they considered at the time they bought a car or truck.

In the initial J.D. Power and Associates APEAL study (see Table 2.6), the vehicles that did well were very different from those that traditionally do well in the Initial Quality and Customer Satisfaction studies. This indicates that the product positives—styling, comfort, power, and handling—can outweigh the simple absence of defects. In fact, because vehicles on the whole are so largely trouble-free these days, these positive attributes of style, comfort, and fun will be the only way to discriminate between vehicles.

Table 2.6   J.D. Power and Associates APEAL Study Leaders by Segment

Market Segment	Make/Model	APEAL Score
Luxury car	BMW 7-Series	763
Sports car	Chevrolet Corvette	710
Mid-Size car	BMW 325i Sedan	689
Sport utility	Chevrolet Tahoe	685
Pickup	Dodge Ram	676
Van	Honda Odyssey	645
Small car	Volkswagen Golf/GTI	643

Source: J.D. Power and Associates 1995 APEAL Study

The Bottom Line on Quality

So back to that difficult question: Which manufacturer makes the highest quality cars? If by quality you mean the absence of defects, the answer is the Japanese, and, despite the fact that many vehicles built by Americans in Japanese-owned and -operated plants rate very well in terms of absence of defects, the best of the best are still built in Japan.

Don't think for a moment, however, that just by acquiring a car or truck sold by a Japanese manufacturer, you'll get a largely problem-free car. That's just not the case—for several reasons:

1. The relative absence of defects varies widely from manufacturer to manufacturer.

2. The relative absence of defects varies widely from model to model within a manufacturer's lineup.

3. Some vehicles sold under Japanese nameplates are not built by the manufacturer who builds most of the vehicles sold under those nameplates. (For example, Mazda compact pickup trucks are currently built by Ford; Honda sport utility vehicles are currently built by Isuzu.)

4. The relative absence of defects can vary widely vehicle to vehicle even among cars and trucks built in the same factory. (In essence, there are still lemons out there.)

What's a Car Buyer to Do?

Okay, I realize I'm not making it easier for you, but if absence of defects is your aim, your best bet is to first consider vehicles from Lexus, Infiniti, Toyota, Honda, Nissan, Saturn, and Acura. If, on the other hand, you're looking for vehicles that provide a high level of quality and positives like expressive styling and fun-to-drive attributes, you can widen your sights a bit. Based on the research data I've reviewed and thousands upon thousands of hours testing cars over the last dozen years, among the first tier of these additional brands you can include are Volvo, Mercedes-Benz, BMW, Mazda, Lincoln, Subaru, Cadillac, and Porsche.

After that comes what I describe as the "if you really love it" group. This includes selected models from virtually every other brand of vehicles out there. For example, if you really want to drive a Chevrolet Camaro or a Dodge Avenger or a Land Rover Discovery, I won't tell you to change your mind, even though there are more defect-free vehicles in each category.

I look at it this way: Should you choose a spouse because he or she is "problem-free" or should you look for positive attributes that might far outweigh any negatives? I've been lucky enough to find a spouse with infinitely more positives than negatives and, with luck, she feels the same way about me. My basic recommendation is this: Don't try to sift all the emotion out of your vehicle purchase. That's part of the fun.

A Look at Various Vehicle Types

Those who think Americans' cars are just transportation are very wrong. Here in the United States, as in many countries of the world, your vehicle is an emblem of who you are and how you see yourself. There's a reason college professors seem to prefer Saabs and nightclub bouncers run to Pontiac Firebirds: Just as people dress the role that they live, so do they buy a car or truck that represents how they see themselves.

A lot of terms are used to divide the daunting array of new vehicles into smaller, more rational categories. The Environmental Protection Agency divides vehicles by interior volume and weight categories. The industry also loosely classifies vehicles as sub-compact, compact, mid-size, full-size, near-luxury, and luxury. There are full-size sport utilities and compact sport utilities, full-size pickup trucks and compact pickup trucks, full-size vans and minivans. *Consumer Reports* classifies vehicles using one system; J.D. Power and Associates uses another; *Automotive News* uses still another. What this means is, the classifications that are supposed to help make your decision clearer only seem to confuse it.

In Appendix B of this book, I list my personal choices as "Best Bets" in 11 different product categories. These categories don't correspond to any EPA guidelines or governmental regulations, but they do divide the market into areas that are relatively easy for the woman or man on the street to understand. These categories are listed in Table 2.7. Certainly, there are no hard-and-fast rules defining these categories. For instance, a "large domestic car" to one person might be a "domestic luxury car" to another, but categorizing vehicles, in at least a general way, should help you narrow your search.

Table 2.7 Various Vehicle Types

Category	Example
Family cars	Honda Accord
Small cars	Geo Prizm
Sporty cars	Toyota Celica
Large domestic cars	Buick
Domestic luxury cars	Cadillac DeVille
Import luxury cars	Lexus LS400
Compact sport utilities	Ford Explorer
Full-size sport utilities	Toyota Land Cruiser
Minivans	Dodge Caravan
Compact pickups	Ford Ranger
Full-size pickups	Chevrolet C/K

Sport Utilities: Today's Hottest Segment

The American automobile market is also a market of fads. Types of vehicles come into favor and go out of style. As this is being written America is in the midst of a sport utility vehicle craze. Manufacturers can't seem to build enough sport utilities to satisfy the huge demand out there.

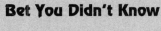

Bet You Didn't Know

In 1980 fewer than 40,000 sport utility vehicles were sold in the United States. This year, the total will be more than 1.5 million.

Sport utility vehicles are very popular today because of the two words that make up the name of the segment. They are perceived by many as "sporty," certainly much sportier than a station wagon, and they provide a great deal of utility. Though usually not as large as the interiors of minivans and full-size vans, most sport utility vehicles, especially in four-door versions will hold a lot of stuff, and, because they are often equipped with four-wheel-drive, they can transport that stuff to many out-of-the-way places.

At least that's the romantic notion that has fueled the sport utility craze. The fact is, many of them will never set a wheel off the pavement. Most often they will be used for duties remarkably similar to those of the old, mundane station wagon of yore. In addition, they are relatively expensive, complicated, more difficult to maintain than a traditional car, and often more expensive to insure. Not only that, but their generally poor fuel economy has members of the Sierra Club on edge.

All that said, however, there's a lot to like about sport utility vehicles, from their "command-of-the-road" driving position to their rugged construction. In you live in the snow belt or just love winter sports, a sport utility might be worth the added expense the breed can require.

Should Your Next Car Be a Truck?

So far the 1990s have been the decade of the truck. As recently as 15 years ago, most trucks were sold for commercial purposes or to individuals who used them for both work and play. Contractors, tradesmen, ranchers, and farmers were the primary buyers of trucks.

But over the last two decades, there has been a slow evolution toward trucks, fueled by the advent of the minivan in the early Eighties and by the sport utility boom. For 1996, industry experts estimate that nearly 45 percent of the light-vehicle sales will be trucks, which includes traditional pickups as well as vans and sport utility vehicles.

This is a massive change in the market, and one that most manufacturers failed to predict. Why do people like trucks? There are several reasons:

1. Many people feel they are more stoutly built than passenger cars.

2. They are very utilitarian, allowing the transportation of a large amount of stuff (in the case of pickups) or people (in the case of minivans).

3. They offer good visibility and a "command of the road."

4. They are more "status neutral" than passenger cars, whose brands immediately call up associations, good or bad.

5. Many people feel they are safer than passenger cars.

In fact, there is a grain of truth in each assumption. Some trucks, particularly pickups and sport utilities, do offer beefier construction than passenger cars, largely because of the jobs they must perform. On the other hand, trucks lag behind passenger cars in the J.D. Power and Associates Initial Quality studies, so the claim they are "better built" seems rather cloudy.

There's no doubt that trucks are more utilitarian than most passenger cars, and, because they are generally taller than most cars, they do offer better forward visibility. That's very valuable when you're trying to wend your way through thick traffic.

In the old days trucks offered little status; nowadays you see everyone from a counter person at a fast-food joint to an oil millionaire driving a truck, so their status remains pretty nebulous. Many people find that to be a positive, but that's changing as well. Upscale sport utility vehicles are hitting the market in prodigious numbers right now, and even a couple upscale minivans are vying for the well-fixed family market.

During the early Nineties, luxury car makers saw many of their potential buyers opt instead for sport utility vehicles, so now they are beginning to compete in that segment in earnest.

Minivans Aren't Just for Families Anymore

If the station wagon was the vehicle of choice for the prototypical mom in the 1950s, then the minivan has become that vehicle for the 1990s. Chrysler Corporation's invention of the early Eighties has spawned a market of more than one million units per year. But these days, minivans are simply Cleavermobiles, meant for toting Mom, Dad, and their 1.7 children.

Several other groups of buyers have also gravitated to minivans. In Las Vegas, the new trend in taxicabs is to minivans. Young outdoor adventurers who can't pay the freight for a sport utility are taking a long look at minivans. And of course tradesmen and commercial enterprises like the relatively low purchase price, good ride comfort, reasonable fuel economy, and lockable storage that minivans provide.

Still, the family market is where the minivan shines. The vehicle's capability to haul up to eight passengers in reasonable comfort with car-like amenities is the big reason. And minivans are getting more stylish than ever.

Who Builds the Best Luxury Cars?

Speaking of style, a good question is which manufacturer is turning out the best luxury cars these days? Unfortunately, that's a trick question, hinging on the word "best."

If by "best" you mean luxury cars with the fewest defects and problems (the "things gone wrong" that I discussed earlier), there's little doubt that the Japanese lead the way. And leading the way among the Japanese are Lexus and Infiniti, followed closely by Acura.

If, on the other hand, your idea of "best" extends to positive attributes that generate enthusiasm for the vehicle from its drivers, then the German luxury machines from BMW and Mercedes-Benz also hold sway. In the luxury arena, you pay for quality and, from virtually all sources, you get it. It is your choice whether you opt for the flawless (but somewhat bland) perfection of the Japanese luxury cars or the perhaps less-perfect but more exuberant style of the German luxury models.

How do you decide what's best for you? I'll tell you some good ways to help make a positive decision in Chapter 5.

The Least You Need to Know

➤ Despite strong progress by the American manufacturers, the Japanese still build the vehicles with the fewest defects.

➤ There is more to quality than just lack of defects; quality is a complex interaction of the relative absence of defects and the presence of positive attributes.

➤ Vehicle quality varies significantly by manufacturer, by model, and by individual vehicle. Choosing a vehicle from a manufacturer with a "high quality" or "low defect" reputation limits your chance of getting a lemon, but it's no guarantee.

➤ At any given time some vehicle types are more in demand than others as styles and tastes shift.

➤ Each vehicle type has pluses and minuses.

Chapter 3

Money Talks

In This Chapter

➤ Why a new car isn't a good investment

➤ Looking at real costs

➤ The skinny on insurance

➤ Proper maintenance

➤ Glancing at warranty coverage

There's more to a vehicle purchase than meets the eye—or shows up on the checkbook register. The fact is, owning and operating a motor vehicle comes with a wide variety of costs, and only one or two are obvious when you saunter into the showroom to look at a new car, truck, or van.

This chapter is all about bringing these costs into the open. I'll tell you why buying a new car is a poor investment, but not necessarily a bad idea. I'll spell out all the costs of owning a vehicle—not just the obvious ones. I'll give you the low-down on auto insurance. And I'll walk you through the maintenance steps that will keep your new wheels looking and acting new, and look at the manufacturer's warranty terms that can help.

It's an Expense, not an Investment

Well, all other things being equal, a house, well-located vacant real estate, and the stock of healthy companies can be expected to appreciate, or increase in value over time. On the other hand, even the highest quality new vehicles on the market will lose value over time, and the value of some new vehicles will sink like a stone after their initial purchase. The typical car or truck will often lose up to 25 percent of its value in the first year after the buyer takes delivery.

Without resorting to an Adam Smith short course on capitalism, the reason for this is simple supply and demand. With very rare exceptions, the minute you buy a new vehicle, the manufacturer can supply the dealer of that vehicle with another one just like it. The typical consumer says to herself, "Why should I buy used when I can buy new?" And this has a chilling effect on the price of used vehicles.

As I told you earlier, too many car manufacturers are chasing too few customers. Overall, that's good for the consumer, because car companies are willing to go to great lengths to compete with one another. But it also means that, as an investment, new cars, trucks, and vans are fairly weak. Look at it this way: How would you like your new house's value to plummet by 25 percent a year after you ponied up for the down payment?

Does that mean you shouldn't buy a new car? Not at all—although if you're not hung up on new car smell and the virginal feel of a pristine motor car, you might find a used car is a better bargain. If you have your heart set on a new car, by all means buy one; just remember that a new car is an expense, not an investment. What this means is simply that over a fairly short time—10 years tops—its useful life will be exhausted. By owning (or leasing) a new car, you'll obtain transportation, an ego boost, and identity on a pay-as-you-go basis. You will not be creating an inheritance for your grandchildren.

The Real Costs of a New Car

Many buyers get hung up on the purchase price of the car. They'll do anything they can to shave a hundred bucks here or there by playing one dealer against another, driving across town, across the county, or even out of state. But many of those same "bargain hunters" won't pay any attention at all to the historical resale value of the model, its quality record, or the cost to insure it. This is a prime example of "penny-wise, pound-foolish."

If your idea of smart buying consists of simply comparing purchase prices of various models, you're not doing yourself any favors. You'll quickly find which car you can get for the least money, but that won't tell you which car is the best bargain. To arrive at that, you have to do a little more homework, because all cars, trucks, and sport utilities are not created equal. Since you'll be using your new vehicle for several years, you should really be interested in ownership expense, not initial purchase cost. Only by looking at ownership expense can you really determine which vehicle is your best bargain.

Let's map out exactly what those ownership costs are. First, there is the *retail price* of the new vehicle. This isn't the "sticker price" you see on the Monroney label on the car's side window; this is a negotiated price usually somewhat lower than that "sticker" or "list" price. Today this average price is over $20,000.

Since few of us have the financial wherewithal to come up with 20 grand or more in cash for a vehicle purchase, you also have to factor in the cost of *auto financing*. This includes your interest on the car loan plus any fees you must pay to acquire that loan. These fees can include document searches, credit reports, and fees charged for doing the loan paperwork.

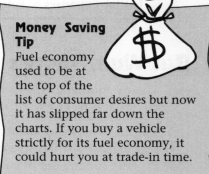

Money Saving Tip
Don't expend all your efforts trying to drive down the price of the model you decide on. First, do your homework on quality and resale value to make sure the model you pick is worthy of consideration.

As I said, you also have to insure the vehicle. Many states require that you have *auto insurance*, and, even if your state doesn't, you're courting financial disaster if you decide to forego insurance. All it takes is one errant driver to turn your pride and joy into a smoldering pile of scrap metal.

In addition to insurance, you'll be faced with state, and perhaps local, *licensing fees*. Many states base these licensing fees on the value of the car or the horsepower of the engine, with owners of bigger, more powerful vehicles paying more.

State and local *vehicle inspections*, mostly for exhaust emission compliance, are becoming commonplace in many areas, so add these to your list of expenses.

Most states also sock you with *sales tax* on your automotive purchase, as do several localities. Add this cost to the list and note that you might save money by purchasing your vehicle in another county or even another state that has lower sales-tax rates.

Money Saving Tip
Fuel economy used to be at the top of the list of consumer desires but now it has slipped far down the charts. If you buy a vehicle strictly for its fuel economy, it could hurt you at trade-in time.

Of course there's the obvious expense—*fuel*. Your new vehicle won't be very useful if you don't put gas in it, so add that item to the expense list as well.

Next on the list is *maintenance*. Just as your body thrives on preventive medicine and regular exercise, so your vehicle thrives on regular maintenance. Remember the old saying, "A stitch in time saves nine?" Well, that certainly applies to your new vehicle.

Going hand in hand with maintenance is the cost of *repairs*. If you fail to maintain your car properly or if you choose a car with a poor service record, this expense will grow substantially. On the other hand, in this day of long, manufacturer-backed warranties, repair costs shouldn't cause a pang of dread to shoot up your backbone.

The worksheet that follows will help you examine in detail the wide range of expenses involved in buying and owning a vehicle. By filling in a sheet for each vehicle you are considering, you'll get a good picture of the model that is the best overall buy.

Auto-Related Expenses Worksheet

Initial Expenses:

1. Purchase price   _____

2. Financing costs   _____

3. State and local sales taxes   _____

   Initial Expenses Subtotal   _____

Annual Expenses:

4. Insurance   _____

5. State and local licensing fees   _____

6. Vehicle inspection fees   _____

7. Fuel   _____

8. Maintenance   _____

9. Repairs   _____

   Annual Expenses Subtotal   _____

Total First Year Expenses:

Initial Expenses + Annual Expenses = _____

But Wait, There's One More

There's another expense you have to look at—and most often, it's the biggest expense of all. What is it? *Depreciation.*

The insidious thing about depreciation is that it's a nearly invisible cost. For the first nine expenses, you write out a check or whip out a charge card—you can see and feel the expense coming out of your checking account. But depreciation is a different animal.

Depreciation is a measure of the decline in value of your vehicle over the years you own it. That is, you almost always sell a car for less than you paid for it, and the difference is depreciation. The bad news is, for those who purchase new cars, it will likely be the biggest expense they encounter. In the next chapter we'll look at depreciation a little closer, but for now, make sure you put it on your list of ownership expenses.

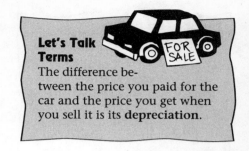

Let's Talk Terms
The difference between the price you paid for the car and the price you get when you sell it is its **depreciation**.

Now for a little more detail on some of the other expense categories I just described.

The Ones You Can Do Nothing About

My father once told me it's pointless to worry about things you can't do anything about. That was very good advice, and it applies directly to the process of making the most intelligent automotive purchase. Of the ownership costs I outlined earlier, three are categories you can't do much about. As you might expect, these are the three that are most closely tied to the government. Death is virtually impossible to escape, as are state and local licensing fees, vehicle inspection fees, and state and local sales taxes. As I mentioned, you might think about crossing city, county, or state lines to avoid higher sales taxes. This might save you a few bucks, but it can complicate the licensing procedure and, in many cases, isn't worth the trouble it will cause you.

Your dealer should be able to give you a good idea of the license fees associated with a vehicle. Or you may want to phone your state Department of Motor Vehicles or Secretary of State's office for that information. In most instances, similar vehicles will have similar associated license fees.

Insurance: An Ugly Necessity

For the vast majority of us, automobile insurance isn't just a good idea; it's a necessity. Several states require all vehicle owners to buy insurance and be able to prove that they are insured at every routine traffic stop. And even in states where automobile insurance isn't required, it's a *very* good idea for any of you who own real assets like equity in a home or a business.

In the overall scheme of auto insurance, your vehicle isn't the most costly part of the program; it's the harm to you and others that your vehicle can cause.

Think of it this way. If your vehicle is stolen and not recovered, or if it's a total loss after a collision, the most that will come out of your pocket (or your insurance company's

Let's Talk Terms

Collision insurance covers accident damage to your vehicle. **Comprehensive** covers damage from causaes such as windstorm, hail, fire, flood, theft, or vandalism. **Personal liability** pays claims and legal judgments if your vehicle injures or kills another person, or damages property. **Uninsured motorist** covers you and your passengers if injured by uninsured drivers. **Medical** covers medical expenses of the driver and passengers in your vehicles caused by an accident.

pocket if you're insured) is the total cost of the vehicle. Even in these days of high-priced automobiles, that's usually $30,000 or less.

Now compare that $30,000 with the colossal cost of medical care or a legal judgment of wrongful death if you or someone else driving your vehicle should hit and injure another driver or pedestrian. This crucial portion of your insurance is called *personal liability*, and if you skimp on this it could come back to haunt you. With judgments for injured victims often running a million dollars or more, an unfortunate accident could easily wipe you out financially.

Further, don't forget to purchase coverage against uninsured drivers. Despite the fact that many states require all motorists to have insurance coverage, many don't, and the odds of being involved in an accident with one of these irresponsible drivers is great.

Bet You Didn't Know

Experts estimate that one in 10 drivers does not carry auto insurance. Not only that, an even higher percentage of motorists are underinsured, meaning they are not carrying enough insurance to cover them in the event of a major accident. These motorists are risking their homes and financial well-being for the sake of a few hundred dollars a year.

Tips for Limiting Your Insurance Costs

All right, you're resigned to the fact that you'll have to pay for automobile insurance (and pay and pay and pay). How do you limit this significant expense? Here are a few simple ways:

➤ **Choose your vehicle wisely.** Some vehicles, primarily sports cars and performance cars, are more likely to be involved in accidents and are more frequently stolen. This means they will be more expensive to insure. Cars and trucks with powerful engines, particularly if they are turbocharged or supercharged, command high rates. The best bet: Check with your insurance agent *before* you buy.

- ➤ **Shop around.** Insurance rates vary widely, so check with several insurance providers before you sign up; but remember, a low rate might also mean a low level of service, so check with your state insurance commission or local consumer groups before buying from a "bargain" company.

- ➤ **Insure all your vehicles and your home with one company.** Package deals can lower your premiums by as much as 25 percent.

- ➤ **Avoid encounters with the law.** Traffic tickets can send your premiums skyrocketing, so don't give the gendarmie reasons to pull you over. If they do, see if traffic school will expunge the offense from your record.

- ➤ **Buy vehicles with state-of-the-art safety and security equipment.** Some insurers offer discounts for vehicles equipped with airbags, antilock brakes, and alarms.

- ➤ **Opt for a high "deductible," the amount of damage you pay for before your insurance kicks in for the remainder.** Choosing a $500 or even $1,000 rather than a $100 deductible could save you hundreds of dollars over the life of the policy.

- ➤ **Get married.** Sure, it might limit your personal freedom, but insurance companies have found us old married codgers are better risks.

- ➤ **Quit smoking.** Not only is it a healthy idea, but several insurers have found that non-smoking drivers are safer drivers.

- ➤ **Be older.** It's a tall order, I know, but insurance companies offer lower rates to older drivers based on their better loss histories.

Maintenance: Not What It Used to Be

There was a time when maintaining a car was a very complicated and difficult task. Back in the Dark Ages of the 1950s and 1960s vehicles needed maintenance almost constantly. It seemed there were always mufflers to be replaced, valves to grind, points and plugs to be changed and air filters to be unclogged.

Now things are simpler because car manufacturers have learned over the years that many of their customers do little more to maintain their vehicles than putting gas in and giving them an occasional oil change. When these poorly maintained cars then break down, the customers don't blame their own slovenly maintenance habits; they blame the automobile manufacturer. So, in self-defense, auto makers have made their vehicles much less maintenance-dependent than before.

Electronic ignition systems have largely eliminated the need for a traditional tune-up that required new points, spark plugs, and condenser. The typical distributor has gone the way of the dodo bird and with it many problems that revolved around this mechanism that provided spark to each cylinder at the appropriate time to fire the gasoline inside.

The introduction of electronic fuel injection has eliminated similar problems that formerly were associated with carburetors. Adjusting the various carburetor jets for a smooth idle and brisk acceleration used to be one of the mechanic's best-known loves and/or curses depending on his skill and the quality of the products he was working with. While fuel injection isn't trouble-free, it is a system that, in general, either works well or doesn't work at all, and its electronic engine sensors adjust its operation as you drive, none the wiser.

All this doesn't mean that your new vehicle doesn't require maintenance. It simply means that the maintenance schedule is far simpler than in years past. Use the Maintenance Checklist to remind you of maintenance items.

Though the Maintenance Checklist might seem like a long laundry list of things to do, a complete check (of the items that require visual inspection) shouldn't take you more than 15 minutes. If you perform these simple procedures every month, you'll be able to keep your vehicle in top condition and recognize problems before they become major hassles.

The best news is that performing these procedures should cost you next to nothing. Compared to the overall cost of your car, the cost of maintenance items is minuscule. Paying a few dollars in routine maintenance can save you hundreds of dollars in repairs, towing, and all the inconvenience that entails.

Why You Don't Have to Fear Repairs

These days the warranties offered by new-car manufacturers have changed for the better. Ironically, the driving force for this change came from Chrysler Corporation. In the early Eighties, when it looked as if the company might fail in the face of foreign competition and poor product quality, Chrysler decided to fight back with a five-year/50,000-mile warranty. It made for good ad copy and offered some peace of mind to those brave souls willing to take a chance on the iffy quality of Chrysler products in those days.

The gambit worked for Chrysler and soon a warranty battle erupted. When the smoke cleared and an unofficial truce was declared, the overwhelming majority of auto manufacturers had settled on three-years/36,000 miles as the magical warranty formula.

Manufacturers have also added other warranty coverage as well in their constant battle to remain competitive. One warranty offered by many car makers is extended coverage of the powertrain components. These warranties are a good deal because they insure you against failure of the most expensive parts on the vehicle—the engine and transmission. This coverage can extend up to four years beyond the three-year/36,000-mile standard warranty.

Maintenance Checklist

❏ **Oil**   While 3,000 miles was considered the optimal oil-change schedule in the 1950's many manufacturers today specify 7,500 miles as an appropriate interval. Letting your vehicle go that long without changing the oil and installing a new oil filter might be okay, but my advice is this: oil is cheap; engines are expensive. Change that oil and filter every 3,000 miles and specify high-quality brands.

❏ **Coolant**   Check your coolant level, because if you lose coolant the resulting heat might well destroy your engine. Replace the coolant with a quality brand and have the radiator flushed every year or so to make sure your cooling system can do the job when it has to.

❏ **Belts and hoses**   Check your vehicle's belts and hoses monthly for signs of stress, leaks, and other wear. Losing a belt or hose can leave you stranded by the side of the road, so pay attention to them and replace them if you have any questions about their integrity.

❏ **Tires**   This is truly where the rubber meets the road, and every day a significant percentage of vehicles in America are riding on under- or over-inflated tires. The result of this is poor fuel economy, premature tire wear, and poor handling that can lead to accidents. Buy yourself a tire gauge and use it frequently. You can usually find the correct tire pressure in your owner's manual or sometimes on the driver-side doorpost.

❏ **Battery and electrical system**   In this era of sealed batteries, maintenance of the electrical system has become easier. There's no need to add distilled water to most batteries any more. But a failing battery or short in the electrical system can stop your car dead, so check your wiring for bad connections and have your mechanic run a battery check now and then to see that you have sufficient battery capacity. Also check your lights monthly to see that your headlights, taillights, brake lights, and turn signals are operable.

❏ **Windshield wipers**   The cost of windshield wipers is minimal, but worn wipers can cost you your vehicle or even your life, so replace them frequently, at least every six months.

Bet You Didn't Know

The so-called "extended warranties" you can purchase from most dealers, covering mechanical problems occurring after the manufacturer's warranty has expired, are nothing more than insurance policies. Your payment is the premium. If you want this coverage, buy an extended warranty that is backed by the manufacturer. "Third-party" warranty insurers have shown a nasty knack for going out of business.

Some manufacturers also offer "rust-through" or "perforation" warranties that insure you against corrosion that puts holes in your precious vehicle. They can do this because production techniques have improved so much that "rust bucket" vehicles are largely a thing of the past.

Finally some manufacturers, particularly those heavily involved in new-car leasing, now offer warranties on their used vehicles, usually after those vehicles go through some type of certification program. You might well find that you can purchase a two-year-old vehicle that will be covered by a three-year manufacturer-backed warranty—quite a good thing in the "peace of mind" department.

What this means to you as a car buyer is that it's much more difficult, though certainly not impossible, to be burned financially by buying a lemon. Sure, there are still bad cars and trucks out there, but the manufacturers are doing a much better, if hardly perfect, job of standing behind their vehicles. At the very least you have three years to figure out whether you have a lemon before the major bills start coming in.

The Least You Need to Know

➤ A new car isn't an investment; it's an expense. You use it up over time.

➤ Looking strictly at the purchase price is a fool's game. Many other factors figure into the process and only by looking at all of them can you determine if you're making the best deal for yourself.

➤ Depreciation—the loss in value your vehicle experiences as you own it—will likely be your biggest expense as a new-car buyer.

➤ Insurance is a cost that must be examined closely before you buy, because the vehicle you decide to purchase can affect your insurance costs significantly.

➤ Longer warranties have taken much of the financial worry out of owning a new car.

Chapter 4

A Pair of Budget Busters

In This Chapter

➤ Avoiding financial hell

➤ Car loan ABCs

➤ The depreciation trap

➤ Choosing high-resale models

➤ The used car alternative

➤ Certification programs

In the last chapter, I told you the purchase price is not the real cost of owning a vehicle. At best, it is simply an indicator of the real cost that's essentially intuitive; namely, a vehicle with a big purchase price will generally be more expensive to own than a vehicle with a more modest purchase price.

The real cost of vehicle ownership is comprised of a number of elements that include: initial cash outlay (down payment or lease initiation fee), insurance, state and local licensing fees, vehicle inspection fees, state and local sales taxes, fuel, maintenance, repairs, depreciation, and financing. Each of these is worth a quick look, but the two factors most worth ruminating over are depreciation (the flip side of "resale value") and financing.

Nothing can screw up a good deal like bad financing. Yet the most intense analysis many car buyers give their finance deal is a quick check to see if they can make the monthly payment. They apparently figure if they have the down payment (in cash or in their trade-in) and can afford the payment each month, what else do they need to worry about?

Money Saving Tip
The two key cost elements you should concentrate your attention on are financing and depreciation. Each can make what seems like a good deal turn sour.

Well, if they like mimicking Alfred E. Newman, *Mad* magazine's "What—me worry?" kid, there isn't anything else to worry about. But if they're interested in getting the most vehicle for the least amount of cash, a few other items are worthy of their attention. Paramount among these are financing costs and depreciation expenses.

Types of Transactions

Let's go back to the basics for a moment and look at the ways you can go about buying things. Certainly the simplest transaction is a cash purchase. You see an item on a store shelf, note the price, take it to the cash register, and pay for it with cash. No muss, no fuss, no hidden costs.

If you pay for that same item with a check or a debit card, which automatically withdraws money from your checking account, it seems almost as simple, but there are a few added fillips. First, in addition to the purchase price, there is one additional cost—the cost of the check or the cost your financial institution and/or the merchant might charge you to use your debit card.

Let's Talk Terms
The price you pay to borrow money is called **interest**, and it is generally expressed as a percentage of the amount borrowed, charged annually. For example, if you borrow $100 at 10 percent interest for one year, at the conclusion of the loan period you will pay back the $100 plus an additional $10 in interest.

Things get a bit more complicated if you pay for that item with a credit card. Of course, whenever you use a credit card, you are essentially borrowing money. Depending on the terms of the particular card you use, you might begin to pay interest on that borrowed money the second you make the transaction.

The card more likely has a "grace period," which means that if you pay the credit card company before the expiration of that time period, you are not charged interest on the money you borrowed. If you exceed the grace period, you pay interest on the charges you've made. The interest rate might be as low as about 8 percent or as high as over

20 percent, again depending on the credit card and terms of your agreement with the credit card company.

You're probably aware that there are vast differences in the terms and conditions offered by various credit card companies. Further, those terms and conditions, most notably interest rates, can fluctuate widely and rapidly. Carry a balance on your card and you'll pay interest on it—that's for sure. If you're not among those frugal few who pay off their credit card purchases every month, you can pay a pretty penny.

Finally, another way to make a purchase is to obtain a loan from a friend, relative, or financial institution to pay for the item or service. The most basic example of this is, "Hey, Bob, lend me a couple of bucks for a beer, will ya? I'm a little short today." (To which Bob replies, "You're not just short; you're ugly, too.")

In this example, it's pretty unlikely that Bob will charge you interest on the two dollars you borrowed. In fact, it's pretty unlikely you'll even pay him back. And if you have kindly relatives with ample cash on hand, they might not charge you interest on a much larger sum. Financial institutions, however, are not so benevolent. They can't afford to be, since they earn their salt by lending money and charging customers for its use.

Let's assume you want to borrow $5,000 to remodel the baby's room. With proper collateral, a financial institution will lend you a lump sum of $5,000, charging you the prevailing market interest rate. This loan may take one of two forms, depending on the method of repayment.

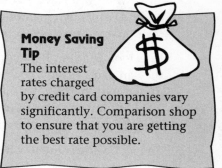

Money Saving Tip
The interest rates charged by credit card companies vary significantly. Comparison shop to ensure that you are getting the best rate possible.

If you repay the loan in a lump sum with interest at the conclusion of the loan period, it is referred to as a "term loan." If, on the other hand, you repay the loan bit by bit each month, the loan is referred to as an "installment loan."

Using a loan to make a purchase can be relatively simple (the "Hey, Bob" scenario), but generally it is the most complicated way to make a purchase. Why? Because it requires applying for a loan, obtaining the loan, and then making the purchase. To obtain the loan, your loan application and credit history must give the financial institution confidence that you will repay the loan—in full, on time. A variation of the loan model is the use of a "line of credit."

Let's Talk Terms
The assets you own that document your ability to pay back borrowed money (and that may be seized by the financial institution if you fail to pay) are referred to as *collateral*.

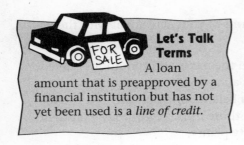

Let's Talk Terms
A loan amount that is preapproved by a financial institution but has not yet been used is a *line of credit*.

This is simply a method of applying for a loan before you have a reason to borrow. Lines of credit are becoming popular today, since many use the equity consumers have in their homes as collateral. Because of this, money borrowed using these credit lines is, by government definition, a "home mortgage," and thus the interest on the loan is tax deductible. (I'll tell you more about using a home equity line of credit for a vehicle purchase a little later, in Chapter 12.)

Cash versus Financing

As I just discussed, buying an item with cash is not just the simplest, but also the cheapest way to go. There are no hidden charges and no interest to pay, nothing but a simple clean, green transaction. Using a credit card that you pay off each month can be almost as cheap. (In fact, if you get "bonus" cash back or other "perks" that are valuable to you, the net cost might actually be lower than using cash, but this advantage quickly goes away when you leave an unpaid balance on the card and start paying interest.) Obviously, taking out a loan or using a line of credit are usually more expensive than paying cash.

Let's look at a simple example. Laura Frugal and Willie Spendthrift each have $20,000 in the bank and desire to buy cars that cost, quite coincidentally, $20,000. Laura decides to pay cash for her new wheels. She doesn't arrive at the dealership with a briefcase full of $20 bills, but she does write a check for $20,000. Can't get much more straightforward than that. Laura has a car; the dealer has $20,000. End of story.

Though Willie somehow has latched onto 20 grand in cash, he decides he will finance his car purchase. He puts down the recommended 20 percent ($4,000) and plans to pay the balance with a five-year installment loan. With a loan rate of 10 percent, over the course of the loan Willie will pay $340 per month or a total of $20,400. When you add that to his $4,000 down payment, Willie will have paid $24,400 for the same model that Laura bought for $20,000. It doesn't take a genius to see who made the better deal...except.

Except what?

Well, except that Willie takes the $16,000 in cash that he didn't put down on the car and invests it in South American pharmaceutical futures. In less than a year, Willie cashes in those futures for $32,000. Willie pays income tax on that windfall, but even after 28 percent is lopped off to the Internal Revenue Service, he still has a profit of around $11,500, which he keeps in his mattress. If you combine the two transactions, Willie Spendthrift is now the big winner, because, taking both deals into account, you could say his car cost him $12,900 ($24,400–$11,500).

Okay, I admit it, I threw you a curve there. What I'm demonstrating is the concept of *opportunity cost*.

Willie didn't spend all of his $20,000 on a car, so he was able to invest it in the futures market. He could have invested it in the stock market, real estate, or put it all on red at a roulette wheel in Las Vegas. Further, Willie doubled his money, a return of 100 percent—nice if you can get it. On the other hand, his $16,000 investment might have figuratively gone south, and he'd have been left with nothing.

What this example points out is if you're thinking of paying cash for a vehicle, look at the *opportunity cost* that represents. If you're currently collecting 4 percent interest in a bank account and the prevailing auto loan interest rate is 8 percent, you don't have to be John Kenneth Galbraith to grasp that you're better off using your cash rather than getting a loan; assuming, of course, that you'll keep enough cash on hand for that rainy day.

The simple rule of thumb is this: If your expected return after taxes of a projected investment is greater than the auto loan interest rate, you're better off taking the loan and financing your car purchase. (And by all means, don't forget to factor in taxes because your return on investment in most cases will be taxable.) If, on the other hand, your expected return after taxes on a projected investment is lower or equal to the auto loan interest rate, pay cash from your savings.

Let's Talk Terms
The potential advantage that could have been realized by using resources in one way that were not gained because the resources were used in another way is the **opportunity cost** of that transaction.

Let's Get Real Here

If we want to dwell in the land of reality, however, let's face facts. Most car buyers finance their vehicles not because they want to, but because they have to. Not many of us are lucky enough to have $20,000 sitting around. That doesn't mean we can't afford a new car. It simply means we'll have to use financing to buy it, and the wise consumer will shop for financing just like they shop for any other item or service.

If you want to get the best deal for yourself, you should consider all the possible sources of financing. The goal is two-fold. First, you want to see how the various sources stack up in terms of cost. Second, you'd like to see these sources actually compete for your business.

What are the sources of auto financing? (I thought you'd never ask.) Listed in descending order from those that are generally most expensive to those that are generally least expensive, they are

1. Finance companies.

2. Dealers.

3. Banks.

4. Credit unions.

5. Home equity loans or lines of credit (usually from banks or savings and loan institutions).

6. Borrowing against insurance, investments, and/or retirement funds.

7. Borrowing from family and/or friends.

Each has its advantages and disadvantages, so it makes sense to consider several alternatives before settling on the best one for you. In Chapter 12, I'll get much more specific about the benefits and liabilities of each of these finance sources. For now, however, I want you to remember that getting the least expensive financing is a key to getting the best deal. If you muff the financing, it has the potential to cost you a bundle of money.

The Financing Bottom Line

It makes no sense at all to shop long and hard for the right car, negotiate the right price on that car, and then settle for the financing terms offered by the dealer. The dealer's financing could well be the best deal available, particularly in these days of interest-rate promotions by the auto manufacturers and their affiliated finance companies. But you'll never know whether you're getting a good deal unless you comparison shop.

My advice is: Shop, shop, shop for your auto financing. Consider all the sources I listed. Make phone calls to several financing sources before you go on your buying mission and note their terms. And be certain that you're comparing apples to apples.

You want to examine two key areas: The interest rate you will be charged, which should be expressed in the standard *annualized percentage rate* (APR), and the length of the loan term. Remember, there are two ways to achieve a lower monthly payment:

1. Obtain a lower interest rate.

2. Agree to a longer loan term.

You should attempt to achieve number one, and be very wary of those who would lead you into agreeing to number two. Getting a lower interest rate saves you money in the long run. Getting a longer-term loan *costs* you money in the long run.

I'll give you an example. Let's say you want to borrow $20,000 to buy a new vehicle, and you want to pay for the vehicle in four years. You talk to your dealer salesperson about financing and find that the interest rate the dealer charges is 10 percent, which means your monthly payment will be $507. That 500 bucks a month seems a little too rich for your blood, so you ask the salesman about alternatives.

Dollars to lugnuts, the first thing he will suggest is lengthening the loan term. "Why don't you finance it over 60 months?" he'll ask you. "If you do that at the same interest rate the payment will only be $425."

"Wow!" you might say to yourself, "I'll be saving more than $75 a month."

With this naive thought rattling around in your head, it could seem like a very good deal to you. But you have to remember you'll be paying for your car an additional 12 months. Over the course of that five-year (60-month) loan, you'll pay $1,154 more in interest than you will if you take a four-year (48-month) loan.

Now, it may be worth $1,150 to you to have that extra $75 in your jeans each month, but, if it is, I want you to make that choice as a conscious decision. I don't want it to be the result of your failure to understand how financing works.

Let's take the example a little further. You want to borrow $20,000. You hear the dealer's two offers: 4 years or 5, both at 10 percent. But you've already shopped your credit union and know you can get a car loan there with a 7 percent interest rate. For a $20,000 loan, you'll pay the credit union $479 a month—more than the dealer's 5-year terms, but less than the dealer's 4-year loan offer.

Is it a good deal? It is if you can afford the $479 a month, because over the course of the loan, you will save about $1,350 in interest versus the 10 percent/ 4-year deal and a little more than $2,500 in interest versus the 10 percent/5-year deal.

I want to emphasize again, these are just hypothetical examples. In your circumstances, your dealer, bank, credit union, relative, you name it, might prove to be the low-cost source of your loan. But do yourself a favor and investigate various sources—or it could cost you.

> **Money Saving Tip**
> Lowering the interest rate saves you money in the long run; increasing the length of the loan costs you money in the long run.

That Ol' Devil Depreciation

The other fly in many car buyers' oatmeal is depreciation, and depreciation is even more insidious than financing, because it's a hidden cost that doesn't become obvious until you sell your vehicle. In fact, to many consumers, it isn't obvious even then, because they're too dazzled by the bright shine of their new vehicle to realize what a financial disaster their previous vehicle was.

As a matter of fact, if you asked most people to name the costs of owning their vehicle, only a few (most of them, like my wife, CPAs) would cite depreciation.

In the case of a vehicle, its depreciation is the purchase price minus the resale price—in the simplest terms, the price you paid for it less the price for which you sold it. A simple example: Jim Pickelmayer buys a new Withit 3000SE for $23,000 and four years later he sells it to his cousin Lewie for $13,000. The depreciation on his Withit 3000SE was $10,000.

As you can see, this is a difficult cost for you to estimate when you're buying a new car, because you won't really know what price you can sell your vehicle for until you actually sell it. And that won't happen, on average, until at least four years after you buy it. Without any doubt, depreciation is much more difficult to estimate than those costs that are apparent on a regular basis—financing, insurance, fuel and oil, state fees, and the like.

Let's Talk Terms
The amount you receive in payment for a vehicle you had purchased previously is its **resale value**. The amount an item declines in value over time is **depreciation**.

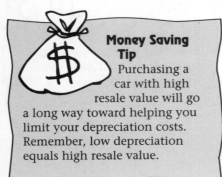

Money Saving Tip
Purchasing a car with high resale value will go a long way toward helping you limit your depreciation costs. Remember, low depreciation equals high resale value.

That's a shame, because over the first three to five years of new-car ownership, depreciation is likely to be your biggest cost. As I said in the previous chapter, vehicles are poor *investments* because their value plummets rapidly in the first few years of ownership. For instance, one expert source estimates that a popular domestic model with a purchase price right around $20,000 will decline in value (depreciate) nearly $4,000 at the completion of its model year—a drop of 25 percent. You don't feel that $4,000 coming out of your pocket, but it's a real cost nonetheless. And it's a big one. In contrast, the total interest on a typical loan for that car will cost less than $2,000.

That's why you hear so many people talking about "resale value" around car-buying time. However, to most consumers resale value is like the weather—everybody talks about it, but nobody does anything about it.

Some consumers will use resale value as one of their reasons for purchasing a particular model. ("I bought it because it has good resale value.") But if you press them on how they know the vehicle has good resale value, most of them shrug their shoulders.

Well, after reading this book, I want you to be able to do more than shrug your shoulders. Next in this chapter, you find some good methods to make certain you limit your cost of depreciation by getting a vehicle that is likely to have good resale value.

Tips to Choosing Low-Depreciation Models

My first bit of advice to you is this: Do some research. The best sources available to the consumer that spell out predicted depreciation for virtually every car, truck, van, and sport utility vehicle on the market are the *Complete Car Cost Guide* and *Complete Small Truck Cost Guide* from IntelliChoice, available at many libraries.

In its Annual Auto Issue, *Consumer Reports* also gives depreciation ratings for the various models on the market. The predictions are less concise than those from IntelliChoice. Models are rated on a five-point scale that runs from "much better than average" to "much worse than average." Unfortunately, both IntelliChoice and *Consumer Reports* decline to estimate depreciation on some new models, which limits their usefulness.

Beyond research, there are several industry "truisms" that will help you choose a vehicle that will limit your depreciation costs:

1. **Choose a mainstream, well-regarded model from a mainstream car company.** These models hold their value better than lesser-known vehicles because there is a ready market for them as used vehicles.

2. **Choose a model that is early in its life cycle.** In the Fifties and Sixties, car models used to change substantially each year, at least in appearance, but today car makers don't change models nearly as often. When they do change, though, the changes have a negative effect on the resale value of the older version. For example, if a new Whatsitz Leopold QT has just hit the market, it's more likely to hold its value than if the same model has been on the market three or four years.

3. **Choose a model from a manufacturer that doesn't change its models very frequently.** Some car companies—primarily the Japanese—change models completely every four or five years. Most European companies change their models much less frequently—some have life cycles of 10 years or longer, while the American auto makers are generally somewhere in between. Partly because their models are altered less frequently, European luxury cars have traditionally held their value better than most other models.

Lemon
An old rule of thumb is never buy a vehicle during its first model year. The fact is, you are often better off buying a first-year model from a high-quality manufacturer than a second- or third-year model from a poor-quality manufacturer. The key is to seek out high quality by perusing J.D. Power and Associates and *Consumer Reports* data.

4. **Choose a vehicle from a manufacturer that has a history of raising pric higher than the norm.** An increased price for a current model has a positive effect the price of used versions of that model. These increases are cyclical. Recently m ny Japanese makes have upped their prices frequently. In the 1980s, German car makers did the same. *Automotive News* is a good source of this information.

5. **Choose a model equipped with popular options.** In most cases, vehicles fitted with items like more powerful optional engines, automatic transmission and air conditioning will hold their value better than vehicles without these options.

6. **Finally (and this is a no-brainer), choose a model from a brand that has a reputation for good resale value.** As this is being written, some of those brands are Acura, Buick, GMC Truck, Honda, Lexus, Mercedes-Benz, Saturn, and Toyota. Chevrolet trucks also have a good resale history, but Chevy cars much less so.

Keys to Best Resale Value

Do:

❑ Buy a well-known model.

❑ Buy from a big manufacturer.

❑ Buy a model that has just undergone a big change.

❑ Buy popular options like automatic transmission.

❑ Buy from a manufacturer that traditionally raises prices often.

❑ Buy a model from a brand with a reputation for good resale.

Don't:

❑ Buy an obscure or discontinued model.

❑ Buy from a small or poorly regarded manufacturer.

❑ Buy a model in the last year before a significant change.

❑ Buy a base model without key options like automatic transmission, air conditioning.

❑ Buy a fully loaded model with every bell and whistle available.

❑ Buy a model from a brand with a history of poor resale value.

Final Thoughts on Depreciation: Used Cars and Your Car

One of the best ways to avoid a large part of the depreciation cost is to let someone else pay it. No, I'm not suggesting you bill your father-in-law. I do suggest that you consider the cost advantages of buying a used car.

I know what you're thinking—why should I buy somebody else's troubles? Well, I'm here to tell you there's been no better time than now to buy a used vehicle. For one thing, the leasing craze has sent millions of low-mileage two- and three-year-old vehicles into the used market. Daily rental companies like Hertz, Enterprise, Avis, National, and Budget add hundreds of thousands more relatively new, low-mileage vehicles into the mix.

Finally, car manufacturers are supporting the sale of used vehicles like never before. Many of them currently offer used-vehicle certification programs, complete with warranty coverage that could extend as long as three years from the date you purchase the vehicle. Vehicles that undergo the certification process are thoroughly inspected and receive required repairs and maintenance before they go on the market.

The fact is that the bulk of depreciation on most vehicles occurs in the first two or three years after it's driven off the lot. By purchasing a certified two- or three-year-old vehicle, you avoid that huge depreciation cost—yet you still have the advantage of lengthy warranty coverage. If you can get past your desire for a brand new car, it's a cost-saving alternative.

A final thought on saving depreciation: You can save the most by keeping your present car. The fact is, in almost all cases, it is cheaper to repair your current vehicle and keep it than it is to buy a new vehicle, no matter how costly the repair may be. The key here is depreciation expense. Your current vehicle is probably well along in its depreciation phase, while a new car is just about to start its decline. And if you talk nice to the bookseller, he or she might even refund your money on this book.

If you still want to get another vehicle, stick around. There are more money saving ideas to come.

Let's Talk Terms

A vehicle that is used in a daily rental fleet, then returned to be sold by a dealer is called a **program car**. Program cars are much less prevalent now than a few years ago, because manufacturers found they adversely affected new-car sales.

Money Saving Tip

Because most of the depreciation a vehicle will experience will take place in its first few years, purchasing a two- or three-year-old vehicle can save you a substantial amount.

The Least You Need to Know

➤ The two ownership cost factors most worth your attention are financing and depreciation.

➤ In the long run it's less expensive to pay cash for your vehicle than finance it, unless you have an unusual investment opportunity that could net you a bigger return than the interest costs on your loan.

➤ Most car buyers choose to finance their vehicles. To get the best financing deal you must shop a number of financing sources.

➤ Depreciation will most likely be the biggest ownership expense you'll experience over the first five years of ownership.

➤ You can save on depreciation by purchasing a vehicle with good resale value.

➤ To limit depreciation costs on a new-car purchase, choose a well-regarded model from a large manufacturer.

➤ Another alternative that can curtail depreciation costs is to purchase a two- or three-year-old vehicle instead of a new car. The highest percent of depreciation occurs in the first year; if you buy an older car, you can dodge the first couple years' depreciation.

Chapter 5

Take a Long Look at Yourself

In This Chapter

➤ Assessing your needs and desires

➤ Your current ride

➤ Dream vehicles

It is a rare person who chooses her or his vehicle for strictly practical reasons. Oh, I don't want to say it *never* happens. Sure it does. Occasionally it snows in Los Angeles, too. But buying a vehicle for sound, rational, dollars-and-sense reasons is certainly not the norm.

But if you're like most people, you want style and fun from this costly purchase—not just a drab, cost-effective machine to get you to work and back. You want something a bit more expressive of who you are and how you picture yourself—qualities you'll look at in this chapter.

What Do You Need from a Vehicle?

Let's take a look at your needs first, because they are often easier to determine than your wants. The fact is, everybody's needs are pretty similar. So the reason so many different types of vehicles are on the market is to address wants, not needs.

But let's not get ahead of ourselves. Right now we simply want to take a long look at your vehicle needs, the tasks the vehicle *must* perform to meet your utilitarian needs. Think about these needs for a minute and, if it makes you feel better, you can jot them down on a piece of paper.

They'll probably look something like this:

1. Commuting to and from work.

2. Shopping, running errands.

3. Transporting friends and family on social occasions. If you're single and don't use your vehicle for work (except to get there), that might well be the extent of your vehicle "needs." As you can see, these simple criteria leave your buying choices wide open. There isn't a four-wheel vehicle on the market that can't perform these rudimentary functions. You could buy a two-passenger Mazda Miata or an eight-passenger GMC Suburban.

   Of course, if you have a family and your vehicle will perform transportation duties, you need to determine how many people your vehicle needs to tote around. Count up the number of spouses and children you have. (Take your time; make sure you remember them all.) Assess how frisky you feel about adding to your family (by birth, adoption, or kidnapping) before your ownership period runs out. Add the passenger count to your list of needs. Roughly the same principle applies if you use your vehicle to transport clients or sales prospects.

4. Transportation for (you decide what). Now, if you use your vehicle in your occupation, or you have a hobby or other activity for which you haul a lot of stuff around, that should figure into your assessment. For instance, if you're in construction, it might be helpful to haul building materials in your vehicle, and if you carry expensive tools you'll want to be able to lock them up. The same goes for caterers, sculptors, woodcarvers, furniture purveyors, and dealers in fine antiques. So you can add:

   Hauling materials.

   Lockable storage for tools and equipment.

   Towing capability—how heavy is that boat or trailer? If you're a boating enthusiast or an equestrian or horsewoman, you might need to tow a boat or trailer. Add that, as well as hobby-related needs like gear-carrying, to your overall list.

5. Four-wheel drive (if you think it will do you any good). If your work or play takes you to destinations that can't be reached by conventional roads or must be reached by roads that are often snow-covered, you might need four-wheel drive. Of course, four-wheel drive won't make it everywhere. In fact, cynics will tell you it just allows you to get stuck deeper in that mud bog or snow bank—but if the world listened to cynics we wouldn't have automobiles at all. Tell them to shut up and add four-wheel drive.

All-righty, then. You have a short list of the functions your vehicle needs to fulfill. Even if it includes every item on the list, there are scores of vehicles that will fill the bill for you. Certainly this list will clear away some of the chaff in your search for the right vehicle, but more work remains before you can zoom in on the perfect vehicle.

What's Wrong (and Right) with Your Current Ride?

Now it's time to narrow the list down to exactly what you want your new vehicle to do for you. Probably unbeknownst to you, you have the perfect tool sitting right outside in the garage, driveway, or at the curb. That tool is your current vehicle. The concept is so simple that many people fail to take advantage of it, but a great way to start choosing your next vehicle is to assess your current one.

Pull out that piece of paper again and jot down the things you like about your current car, truck, or van. Do you like its size? Comfort? Handling? Performance? Cargo capacity? Fuel economy? Do you like the way it looks? Its color? Do you like the way the interior is finished? Do you like the sound system? How about the way the controls work? Is it easy to get in and out of? Is it easy to load with cargo? Do you like the fact that it's paid for? Or that the monthly payments on it are low? If you want, you can use the Current Vehicle Checklist in this chapter to evaluate your current car.

Running through a checklist like this simply brings out the positive attributes of your current vehicle. Generally, this list will be filled with pluses; odds are you did at least a subconscious assessment of your needs before you bought it.

Now that new-vehicle time is near, it's a perfect opportunity to learn from your previous experience and obtain a vehicle that reflects your needs and wants even better than the last. So take another look at your current vehicle, this time with an eye toward what you would change.

Current Vehicle Checklist

Check the ratings that apply, then total the checks in each column. The column with the highest number of checks indicates the overall rating for your car.

Attribute	Excellent	Good	Fair	Poor
Size				
Comfort				
Handling				
Acceleration				
Braking				
Transmission				
Cargo capacity				
Fuel economy				
Exterior styling				
Interior styling				
Sound system				
Color				
Ease of entry/egress				
Ease of loading/ unloading				
Towing capability				
Off-road/ snow capability				
Cost/payments				
Total checks:				

For instance, do you want a larger vehicle? More comfort? More maneuverability? Better fuel economy? Do you want more cargo space? More doors for easier entry? Do you want more style, image, or prestige? Do you want more equipment, like power windows, power mirrors, and power door locks? Would you like automatic transmission, or do you like the sportiness and control of changing gears yourself? Have you joined the world of compact discs or is your music library on cassettes? (If it's on 8-tracks, I'm afraid there's no hope for you.) Again, a short checklist like the Checklist of Improvements Wanted in this chapter is in order.

Checklist of Improvements Wanted

Circle your choice in each row.

Attribute	Description		
Size:	Bigger	Smaller	Same
Comfort:	More	Less	Same
Handling:	Sportier	Cushier	Same
Acceleration:	Faster	Slower	Same
Braking:	Antilock	Conventional	
Transmission:	Automatic	Manual	
Cargo capacity:	More	Less	Same
Fuel economy:	Higher	Lower	Same
Exterior styling:	Different	Same	
Interior styling:	Different	Same	
Color:	Different	Same	
Sound system:	CD	Cassette	Radio only
Ease of entry/exit:	More doors	Fewer doors	Same
Ease of loading/ unloading:	Trunk	Hatchback	Tailgate
Towing capability:	More	Less	Same
Off road/snow capability:	Four-wheel-drive	Two-wheel-drive	
Cost/payments:	More costly	Less costly	Same

Running through this brief checklist will help you get a handle on what you want from your next vehicle. Circle the answers that apply, and you'll have a thumbnail sketch of the kind of vehicle you should consider.

In fact, while you look at the relatively minor issues, don't forget to address the major issue—namely, do you want an entirely different type of vehicle than the one you have? Despite what the little voice in your head says, there's nothing wrong with that. Just because you drive a four-door sedan today doesn't mean you're destined to drive four doors for the rest of your life. As I mentioned earlier, most vehicles can perform most if not all the duties you want from your vehicle. There's no reason not to take advantage of this fact.

I'll bet you already have more than a grain of an idea about your next vehicle. In fact, it wouldn't surprise me if you already have a make and model in mind. Is that bad? Not at all. Certainly, like a spouse, some vehicles are better to fall in love with than others, but if you've developed a hankering for a certain kind of vehicle or a specific model, I won't try to dissuade you. I simply suggest that you perform your "due diligence"—do some research to determine if the vehicle in question is truly worth your love and affection.

What's Your Dream Vehicle?

I'm not here to tell you that all your dreams are going to come true. But there's no reason not to fantasize about your dream vehicle. At the very least, thinking about your dream vehicle will help you decide what attributes are important to you. For instance, if you've always dreamed of owning a Ferrari, it's a good bet that a compact four-door will leave you unfulfilled. If, on the other hand, you dream of motoring through pristine woods to an idyllic fishin' hole, then a sleek sports car won't be your cup of tea.

I'm not suggesting you mortgage your home and plunk down 200 grand for a new Ferrari. But if you have an affinity for Ferraris, take a good look at other sports and sporty models that are more within your affordability zone. If you dream of off-road adventures in a Land Rover, consider other four-by-fours that might be a bit less dear.

Finally, if you can get past the "I have to buy a new car" fetish, you might well find that your dream vehicle is affordable if you're willing to consider a previously owned model. These days, some used cars are an even better value because many manufacturers back them with long warranties. If you're looking for a solidly built four-door sedan, you might find that a two-year-old Lexus, BMW, or Mercedes-Benz is priced competitively with many vehicles from lesser brands. It will have similar warranty protection and it may actually hold its value better.

The Least You Need to Know

➤ A high percentage of vehicles on the market can perform the basic tasks; look at *your* needs to help you choose the right vehicle.

➤ Consider bedrock issues like the number of people you must transport with the vehicle and the body style that appeals to you.

➤ A close look at what you like and dislike about your current vehicle will help you make an informed choice about your new vehicle.

➤ You might find that you can actually afford your dream vehicle—if you buy it used.

Part 2
Stalking the Right Vehicle

Now you know where you fit on the automotive landscape. You've looked at yourself and determined your basic needs. Now is a good time to consider the safety of your vehicle of choice. This part looks at the sometimes conflicting philosophies of active and passive safety and lets you arrive at your own conclusion.

To make the car acquisition quest a rational process, you should also construct a shopping list based on important parameters like affordability. This part helps you determine how much vehicle you can afford and tells you why some cars are better to fall in love with than others.

Unless you are dead-set on a particular vehicle, the research phase of your hunt for new wheels is a crucial one. Part 2 is full of hints to make that research as pleasant and simple as possible.

UH-OH...

Chapter 6

Safety First?

In This Chapter

➤ Passive restraints

➤ Crash testing and crush zones

➤ Airbags and child safety seats

➤ Antilock brakes

➤ Driver responsibility

It used to be axiomatic in the auto industry that "Safety Doesn't Sell." General Motors tried to take the market by storm in the Fifties by offering the availability of safety belts in many of its models, but instead of greeting the innovation with enthusiasm, the market treated it with a collective yawn. Then optional equipment, seat belts were ordered by very few consumers, and the industry got the hint.

In the mid-1960s a young Ralph Nader made a name for himself by writing the highly controversial book *Unsafe at Any Speed*. The book attacked General Motors for the safety record of the Chevrolet Corvair, a model that had been on the market since the late 1950s. The brouhaha surrounding the book did gain Nader public attention and spawned the "safety lobby," but the public showed little interest in paying for auto safety.

It took government regulation in the late 1960s to make seat belts and headrests (to avoid whiplash) mandatory, but actual use of seat belts by the driving public was still disappointingly low. In the Seventies, the safety lobby took a run at getting the federal government to make airbags mandatory, as auto emissions standards had been several years before.

Bet You Didn't Know

Every automotive airbag contains an explosive device much like a shotgun shell that fills the bladder with gas when triggered by a front-mounted sensor.

Through the Seventies and into the Eighties, ever-tightening government regulations dragged the auto industry, kicking and screaming, into installing additional safety equipment, including the much-hated "seat belt interlock" that prevented the driver from starting the car until the safety belt had been fastened. (This led many drivers to leave the seat belt perpetually fastened—and tucked away between the backrest and the seat cushion.) In fact, despite the steady movement toward additional regulations by the government, in this period the public at large exhibited no particular enthusiasm for safety devices in general, and a serious antipathy for the seat belt interlock, in particular.

Meanwhile, the highway death toll continued to mount, and statistics continued to indicate to federal safety experts that much of the carnage could be reduced by the simple wearing of the seat-and-shoulder belts that were already mandatory equipment in all new cars. But the public didn't cooperate.

Given this intransigence by the public it was designed to serve, the National Highway Traffic Safety Administration issued regulations calling for "passive restraints." Essentially this was an effort to provide drivers and passengers protection they seemed unwilling to take the time or effort to provide for themselves. And the auto manufacturers were given several alternative methods of compliance—motorized seat belts, door-mounted belts that were in theory, if not in practice, designed to be left permanently fastened, and airbags.

These methods were tried, but soon it became apparent that airbags were the alternative of choice for most buyers. (If you've had to battle those silly door-mounted belts or been nearly decapitated by a misfiring motorized belt, you can see why.) Soon the press was filled with reports of lives saved by airbags. Those reports spawned TV commercials. Oddly enough, Lee Iacocca was a prime mover in the safety craze.

Which brings us to the Nineties, the (family) value decade. Never before have so many of us seemed so interested in health, fitness, and safety. As that great philosopher Huey Lewis once said, "It's hip to be square."

But is safety first? Not on most consumers' shopping lists. The top priority for most buyers is that old stand-by "value for the money." But safety is still important to many consumers, and that's why this chapter is dedicated to it.

Safety affects the choice of vehicle many consumers make. (Check the sales numbers on non-airbag-equipped vehicles versus their airbag-equipped competitors.) And it affects the resale value of the vehicle.

> **Money Saving Tip**
> If you're in the used car market, avoid vehicles equipped with motorized belts as if they had an infectious case of the measles. Resale value of such vehicles is extremely poor.

The Two Philosophies of Safety

Because safety is so important, let's look at the whole issue of safety for a moment. There are essentially two different philosophies regarding automotive safety that have currency—passive safety and active safety.

Safety by Design: The Passive Approach

The *passive-safety advocates* believe that individual drivers and passengers are too (pick one or more) lazy, stupid, busy, apathetic, or drunk to ensure their own safety in a motor vehicle. Of course, the key step that we all can and should take each time we get in a car or truck is to *fasten our safety belt*. This simple act can increase your chances of surviving a vehicle crash by as much as 10 times.

Sadly, however, a significant portion of the population fails to take this step. Even in states where seat belt use is mandatory—and that's *most* states, these days—as many as 40 percent of drivers and passengers don't use their seat belts. To me, this is a ridiculous disregard for one's own well-being, but it is an unfortunate fact.

In light of this, the passive-safety philosophy advocates safety devices that require no thought or effort. Further, the prime goal of passive-safety advocates is to make crashes survivable. Thus, they put emphasis on airbags, energy-absorbing steering columns, and auto chassis "crumple zones." If they could, the most fanatic passive safety-ites would have us driving slow, lumbering tanks that could emerge from a demolition derby with driver and passengers unscathed.

> **Let's Talk Terms**
> Devices that require little or no effort from driver or passenger are referred to as **passive safety devices**.

Passive-Safety Items

These pieces of safety equipment require no effort from the driver or passengers and are designed to help victims survive crashes.

Front airbags   Devices that inflate in a frontal impact, helping protect the front seat occupants from being injured on the steering wheel, dashboard, and windshield.

Side-mounted airbags   Devices mounted in the door pillars or seats that inflate in the event of a side impact, helping protect occupants from injury in common low-speed crashes involving the doors and side windows.

Knee airbags   Devices mounted under the dash board that inflate in the event of an impact, helping protect the occupants from knee and leg injury.

Crush zones   Portions of the vehicle's body and/or frame that are designed to collapse upon impact, absorbing the force of the crash. More rigid structures actually transmit force to the occupants, where it can do more harm.

Energy-absorbing steering columns   Steering columns designed to collapse in a frontal collision, reducing the driver's chance of being injured by the steering column.

Passive-safety advocates are staunch defenders of "crash testing." They believe that running vehicles into concrete walls at various speeds can teach a great deal about the consequences of auto accidents. They suggest that crashing more vehicles at higher rates of speed and in different manners will aid the cause of safety. Because of this, hundreds of vehicles are filmed in the act of being destroyed each year under the auspices of the Federal Department of Transportation.

Certainly we've learned a great deal from these efforts, and some of this knowledge has saved lives. On the other hand, critics suggest that much of this huge expense is wasted, because the concentration is on the wrong culprit. They would tell you passive-safety advocates are blaming the vehicle for injury and death when they should be blaming the driver. They argue that increasing the driver's ability to control the vehicle and keeping those who shouldn't drive off the road will have significantly greater benefits per dollar than trying to make all vehicles into "crashworthy" cocoons. This philosophy is *active safety*.

Active Safety Items

These pieces of safety equipment are designed to help drivers avoid crashes. Some may require effort and/or training to use properly.

Antilock brakes   A braking system that uses computer sensors to help prevent braking-induced skids. Such systems (also called ABS) prevent the wheels from locking during hard braking, allowing the driver to maintain steering control.

Safety belts   These are the most crucial pieces of safety equipment in your vehicle. When worn properly, seat belts keep driver and passengers in a position in which they are least likely to be injured in the event of a collision. Proper use of seat belts also positions occupants for the optimum benefits from airbags, if the vehicle is airbag equipped.

Traction control   A computerized system that helps prevent acceleration-caused slips and skids. Like ABS, traction control uses computer sensors to monitor wheelspin, limiting power if wheelspin is detected.

Rack-and-pinion steering   Generally regarded as the most direct and responsive steering system design, rack-and-pinion steering can help drivers avoid accidents by maintaining precise control of their vehicles.

Tires   Tires designed for wet weather or off-road traction can be especially helpful in maintaining vehicle control in adverse conditions.

All-wheel-drive   Not to be confused with four-wheel-drive, all-wheel-drive is a system in which all four wheels are always powered. This results in exceptional traction and a feeling of security when driving in inclement weather. Also referred to as full-time four-wheel-drive.

In contrast, those who advocate active safety stress the critical importance of crash avoidance. They will tell you that the best automobile accident is the one that doesn't happen, because driver skill and the capabilities of the vehicles prevented it from happening. They put their emphasis on better training, stricter licensing procedures, more stringent efforts to keep drunk and drug-impaired drivers off the roads, and equipment that improves vehicle handling and braking capabilities.

Let's Talk Terms
Active safety devices aid the driver in controlling her or his vehicle.

It's Your Decision

What, you may ask, do these philosophies have to do with you? The answer is, they can have a significant effect on the vehicle you choose and the equipment you select for that vehicle. If you can't be bothered with buckling your seat belt, have no real interest in improving your driving skills, have the means to pay for additional safety features, and are maybe not averse to having a drink or two before you slide behind the wheel, then the passive-safety philosophy is for you. Pore over the crash-test results from the National Highway Traffic Safety Administration. Peruse the analysis of crash test data presented each year in *Consumer Reports*. And pick a vehicle that you think will make a crash as survivable as possible.

If, on the other hand, you always buckle your seat belt and insist that your passengers do the same, always transport your child in a properly installed child-safety seat, keep your driving skills sharp, keep your vehicle well-maintained, understand how equipment that requires skill to use works, and never drive impaired by alcohol, drugs, or lack of sleep, then you are an active-safety proponent. You should pore over the reviews in the enthusiast press looking for vehicles that handle better than their competitors. After you choose such a vehicle, you should equip it with items that will increase its capability to maneuver and stop quickly. By doing this, you will have a vehicle that will give you the best opportunity to *avoid* an accident rather than survive it.

The Fallacy of Crash Testing

For nearly 20 years, the National Highway Traffic Safety Administration has crash-tested automobiles. A huge amount of valuable data has been learned from these procedures, and cars have been made safer because of it. I would never advocate doing away with these tests or failing to use the information that has come from them in vehicle design.

At the same time, I believe that choosing your vehicle on the basis of how it performs in a crash test does not make good sense. In the real world every crash is different, yet the crash tests in use by NHTSA simulate only one type of crash—a direct head-on collision—and there is debate among engineers and scientists on how well the test simulates *that*.

In today's NHTSA crash test, vehicles are towed into a concrete barrier at 35 miles per hour by ground-level cables. Inside the vehicle are high-tech test dummies, built to simulate human beings of various shapes and sizes—including adults, children, and pregnant women. The test dummies are instrumented for computers to record a wide variety of data and the crashes are filmed from several angles by high-speed cameras. This film is then reviewed frame-by-frame by engineers, who analyze the force of the impact and its consequences to the simulated human passengers. This is good science, and important information is obtained.

However, all current-year vehicles are required to pass this test. In each and every vehicle on the market, properly belted-in drivers and passengers should be able to survive a 35-mile-per-hour direct head-on collision with a vehicle of similar size and weight. That is a staggering achievement.

The problem is, few real-world accidents are direct head-on collisions with vehicles of similar size and weight. In fact, though various head-ons do lead the list of fatal crashes, direct head-ons between two similar-size vehicles might be among the *least* common of all auto accidents.

As you know, accidents come in all shapes and sizes, from a parking lot encounter with a concrete post to a loss of control that sends a car hurtling off a bridge. Vehicles hit each other at angles, from the side, and from the rear. They roll over. They strike objects, animals, and people. On my way to work today, I saw a minivan on its roof in the middle of the freeway and a small sedan buried deep in the rear-end of another sedan. Every one of these collisions could have serious consequences, leading to injury or death. But the NHTSA crash testing doesn't directly address them.

Bet You Didn't Know

During most crash testing the vehicle is not operating under its own power and its engine is not running.

Yes, some progress is being made. The Insurance Institute for Highway Safety, an insurance industry lobbying group, recently sponsored a test that attempted to simulate "offset crashes." In this particular test, 40 percent of the car's frontal area struck a "crushable" barrier at 40 miles per hour. The point of this test is to simulate real-world front-end crashes more accurately.

Bet You Didn't Know

The insurance industry pushed the government to adopt a five-mile-per-hour crash standard for auto bumpers, but then changed its mind when it discovered that the five-mile-per-hour bumpers were much more expensive to replace after a higher-speed collision.

Federal regulators have also just phased in a new side-impact standard (beginning in the 1997 model year). The test to determine compliance with the standard simulates a crash in which a car traveling at 15 miles per hour is rammed at a 90-degree angle by a car traveling at 30 miles per hour. Again, like the frontal crash, passing this test is a price of admission to the market; all cars must make the grade or their sale is illegal.

In reviewing crash-test data and real-world accident data, one thing becomes crystal clear: In a collision, mass wins. This means, all things being about equal, the larger, heavier vehicle provides better survivability to its occupants than a smaller, lighter vehicle. But could the driver of a smaller, lighter vehicle avoid a collision through better brakes and more maneuverability than the larger, heavier vehicle? That question remains unanswered for the time being.

The bottom line for you and your family on crash testing: Review the NHTSA, IIHS, and *Consumer Reports* data and analysis before you choose a vehicle, but don't rely on the vehicle to protect you and your family in a collision. I can't stress enough the importance of taking active steps like buckling your seat belt, using properly installed child-safety seats, and never driving when impaired.

Airbags: Are They a Panacea?

The NHTSA estimates that airbags have saved between 1,000 and 1,200 lives since they were introduced, and experts predict that the number could jump significantly as vehicles equipped with airbags become the norm. Further, airbags have saved thousands of others from serious injury, including the disfigurement that can occur when a driver or passenger goes through a windshield, and thousands more will be saved as airbags become more widespread. Airbags are a significant safety advance.

You should remember, however, that current airbag systems are not designed to *replace* seat belts but to be used in conjunction with them. A properly worn seat belt positions the driver and passenger so the airbag can work most effectively. You should also know that front airbags are only effective in preventing injury in frontal crashes. In collisions from the rear, side impacts, and rollovers, front airbags are essentially useless.

Even more disturbing are recent reports from the NHTSA indicating that more than 25 people, including several small children, have been killed by airbags. Many of these were infants, who were struck in the head while being transported in rear-facing child-safety seats. Of the adults killed, many were simply thought to have been sitting too close to the steering wheel that contained the airbag unit. Others were killed when the rapidly deploying airbag turned objects on the dashboard or the vehicle's own trim into shrapnel.

On a more positive note, several auto manufacturers have recently introduced airbag systems designed to help eliminate injury and death in side-impact crashes. Volvo led the pack, followed closely by Mercedes-Benz and BMW. General Motors and Ford should also be offering side-impact airbags on more-expensive models by the time this book goes to press. Korean manufacturer Kia has already introduced a "knee airbag," and others will soon follow suit.

The bottom line for you or your family on airbags: Buy a vehicle equipped with them for their intended use—as a supplement to seat belts—and make certain all passengers wear their seat belts properly at all times. Don't expect airbags to replace the protection provided by the use of seat belts. And by all means, if you are transporting a baby, use a properly installed infant carrier. Don't use a rear-facing child-safety seat in the front seat of a vehicle equipped with a passenger-side airbag, unless you have one of the relatively few vehicles in which the passenger airbag can be turned off—and make sure the airbag is indeed turned off.

Would I buy a new vehicle without dual airbags? No, but it's my opinion that religious use of seat belts will deliver more and better protection in more circumstances than any current airbag system.

Bet You Didn't Know

Airbags are designed to be used in conjunction with a seat belt, and they are essentially worthless in anything but a frontal crash.

Antilock Braking Systems

If a tree falls in an empty forest, does it make a sound? Of course it does. But if an accident doesn't happen, does it appear in driving safety statistics? No way. Which is why it is hard to assess with statistical accuracy the effectiveness of many active safety measures like antilock brakes.

One key piece of active safety equipment is an antilock brake system. Not really a new idea, antilock brakes were made more effective, and cheaper, by the application of computer power. Today's antilock brake systems (ABS) use electronic sensors to detect if one or more of a vehicle's wheels is beginning to lock (that is, stop rotating) and, when imminent lock-up is sensed, it ceases braking effort for a split-second to allow the wheel to continue to turn. This is felt through the brake pedal as a series of rapid pulses. The theory behind antilock brakes is simple: It's impossible to steer a vehicle experiencing wheel lock-up. (In layman's terms, this is a skid.) Only when the wheels are rotating do you have steering control.

Unfortunately, the real benefits of ABS (maintaining steering control under braking) have been undersold, while the less well-documented benefits (shorter stopping distances in real world conditions) have been oversold. Not only that, ABS is not like an airbag. To get the most benefit, drivers need to be trained in the proper techniques for ABS use.

Because of all this, antilock brakes have come under fire. An insurance industry study claimed that ABS failed to reduce the number of auto accidents and (very telling to the insurance industry) failed to reduce the cost of accidents. Studies by NHTSA were inconclusive. One found that ABS-equipped cars were more likely to be involved in single-vehicle "leaving-the-road" accidents, while another showed that ABS-equipped vehicles were less likely to be involved in frontal collisions on wet roads.

Expert analysis of the former results speculated that the "leaving-the-road" accidents were explainable by the fact that drivers with ABS-equipped vehicles felt "invulnerable" or "able to do anything." Expert analysis of the latter suggested that vehicles equipped with ABS were far less likely to go into a skid in the wet, so their drivers were better able to avoid accidents in those conditions.

As one who has road-tested thousands of ABS- and non–ABS-equipped vehicles over the years, I heartily recommend ABS as a valuable and possibly life-saving piece of equipment. However, to get the full benefit, it must be used properly.

Proper use consists of two simple procedures:

1. When you engage the brake, hold the pedal down firmly and don't relax your pressure even when the pedal begins to pulse.

2. Continue to steer your vehicle around potentially dangerous objects.

In simple terms: Stomp and Steer.

Sadly, though simple, this technique eludes many drivers who have been trained to pump the pedal under hard braking. With ABS this is the worst thing you can do, since it thoroughly confuses the computer that is attempting to pump the brakes for you. Additionally, studies have found that in panic situations many people simply quit steering all together. They simply jam on the brakes and hope.

My advice: Order a car with anti-lock brakes, make the salesperson demonstrate how to use them, and learn how to use them yourself.

Other Active Safety Items

Antilock brakes are a key piece of active safety equipment but there are others you should consider. One often overlooked "system" is the vehicle's tires and wheels. In my experience, no vehicle alteration is more cost-effective in providing better handling and braking performance than a tire/wheel upgrade. The base-level tires on many of today's vehicles, particularly less-expensive vehicles, are little more than "rim-protectors" that offer little to enhance the vehicle's handling and often work to the detriment of a well-designed suspension system. By choosing the optional tire-and-wheel package, you can usually achieve improved handling.

Traction control is another system that has safety benefits. It might be thought of as "reverse ABS" in that it uses similar sensors (or the same sensors) to detect the onset of *wheel-slip* (tire-spinning in layman's language) and corrects it with lightning-quick, computer-dispatched instructions to engine and brakes.

All-wheel drive is another active safety boon, particularly for those of you who live in inclement climates. (Note, I'm not referring to four-wheel drive here. Four-wheel drive also has its uses, but they are less directly safety related.) All-wheel drive means that all four wheels are always powered, as opposed to four-wheel drive (sometimes called part-time four-wheel drive) where the vehicle is most often in two-wheel drive and the driver must choose to power all four wheels. Today's sophisticated all-wheel-drive systems often use the computerized technology of ABS and traction control along with torque-sensing differentials to provide power to the wheels with the most traction while withholding power from the wheels most likely to slip.

Let's Talk Terms
A system in which all four vehicle wheels are powered at all times is called **all-wheel drive**, alternatively called **full-time four-wheel drive**.

I know that sounds like a boat-load of technical jargon. It simply means an all-wheel-drive vehicle is the most stable and reassuring vehicle to drive, particularly in adverse conditions like rain or snow.

The Bottom Line on Safety

Try as they might, the passive-safety forces have been unable to legislate safety on the highways. That's because accidents result from a complex interaction of driver error, inattention and impairment, difficult weather conditions, poor visibility, and vehicle shortcomings. (To learn to drive better, refer to the 10 Commandments of Safe Driving, listed in this section.) And while it might be technically feasible to design vehicles that will severely curtail fatalities even in high-speed collisions, from a practical standpoint, trying to eliminate fatalities and serious injuries through vehicle design alone is doomed to failure. Humans will seemingly always find ways to kill themselves and each other.

If you're planning to buy a new vehicle, choose a model that meets or exceeds all current safety standards and has driver, passenger, and possibly side-mounted airbags. (Note: Some side airbags are seat-mounted.) Equip that vehicle with antilock brakes, and, if you live in an area with frequent rain and/or snow, consider an all-wheel-drive system.

If you're planning to buy a used vehicle, your preference should be for an airbag- and ABS-equipped vehicle. However, I wouldn't hesitate to consider a non-airbag, non-ABS vehicle if it were well-maintained and met my other needs. I say this because all vehicles are equipped with the most important safety system: seat belts. I also feel the major cause of auto accidents and resulting injuries is the fault of drivers much more than their vehicles.

The 10 Commandments of Safe Driving

1. Fasten your seat belt properly every time you're in a moving vehicle.

2. Never drive under the influence of drugs or alcohol.

3. Never drive when over-tired.

4. Devote your attention to driving.

5. Always transport children who are too young to wear standard seat belts in properly installed, government-approved child-safety seats and carriers.

6. Drive at speeds appropriate for conditions. Being the fastest or the slowest vehicle on the road can be dangerous to you and others.

7. Signal lane changes and turns.

8. Be extremely careful in making left-hand turns.

9. Keep a proper interval between your vehicle and the one in front of it.

10. Learn to use antilock brakes properly.

Making yourself a safe driver at all times and working toward getting and keeping unsafe drivers off the road is, in my opinion, the clearest path to better auto safety for us all.

The Least You Need to Know

➤ There are two overriding philosophies regarding auto safety—passive safety, emphasizing crash survivability, and active safety, emphasizing crash avoidance.

➤ Crash testing of automobiles provides a wealth of valuable data, but choosing a vehicle strictly on the basis of its results in current crash tests doesn't make sense.

➤ Airbags are important passive safety equipment that should be used as a supplement to the key piece—the safety belt.

➤ Antilock brakes can prove very valuable as an active safety tool, but they require driver training to achieve the full benefit they offer.

➤ Active safety equipment like upgraded tires, traction control systems and all-wheel-drive can provide important safety advantages.

Chapter 7

Constructing Your Shopping List

In This Chapter

➤ Your affordability zone

➤ List-building criteria

➤ Personal preferences

➤ Falling in love

➤ Fall-back positions

Some people simply fall into a car purchase. They stroll into a dealership on a whim, fall in love with the red convertible by the window, and drive it home that afternoon. It's an American cliche.

As odd as it may sound, there's nothing wrong with this approach. In fact, some studies indicate that buyers who shop just one dealership and don't haggle about the price are among the most satisfied customers in the car business. Of course, my guess is they can afford to be satisfied.

In contrast, some consumers approach car buying as if it were a search for the Holy Grail. Unwilling to trust their instincts or even their taste, they gather mountains of information, consult guide after guide, cross-examine friend after friend, and meticulously plan each move from Vehicle Selection to Final Offer. Their goal is the One Perfect Deal on the One Perfect Vehicle, and in their quest they're likely to drive everyone crazy as they shift from vehicle to vehicle and deal to deal.

I've got news for them: There is no perfect deal and there is no perfect vehicle. But a lot of very good deals and very good vehicles are out there if you play your cards right; a lot of miserable deals and dreary vehicles are also out there if you play your cards wrong.

My suggestion when you go vehicle shopping is to use your brain and your gut, your heart and your head. You can cost yourself a lot of hard-earned cash if you choose strictly on an emotional basis. A $20,000 purchase is one hell of an impulse buy. On the other hand, it would be nice if the machine you end up with gives you at least a twinge of pride instead of being just the lump of metal, glass, and plastic that gets you to work and back. This chapter helps you develop a shopping list to help you strike the balance between pride and practicality in your next car purchase.

What I want you to do is have a short enough list of possibles, so that you can do the proper research without driving yourself to distraction. You want a list of high-quality possibilities, vehicles that are truly worth your attention. I'll tell you how to do that research in the next chapter, and show you the three crucial steps in the vehicle acquisition process.

Separating Wheat from Chaff

As I told you in Chapter 1, there are a lot of choices out there. About 250 car, minivan, truck, and sport utility vehicles under 41 different brands crowd the American marketplace. Each model comes in various *trim levels* and can be equipped with dozens of options to further complicate your choices.

Let's Talk Terms

Sub-models within a model line, usually differentiated by equipment differences and an alphabetic designation are referred to in the industry as **trim levels**. For example, if the brand is Doofus and the model is Goofus, the various trim levels might be the low-line Doofus Goofus DX, mid-level Doofus Goofus RA, and the top-of-the-line Doofus Goofus BLT-NO MAYO.

Certainly, you can't wade through all 250 models in your search for your next car. You don't have the time or the inclination.

However, I firmly believe you should consider at least two to four choices before settling on the vehicle you want to stalk, corner, and buy. The process often works better when you start with a large list and narrow it down, rather than when you start with a small list and add to it. There are several ways to approach this. Here are a few factors you can consider as you build the list of vehicles that you'll consider purchasing:

1. Affordability/price
2. Vehicle segment
3. Fuel economy
4. Performance
5. Image
6. Personal favorite(s)

Let's examine each factor in detail to see what your needs are.

Several Words on Affordability

In Chapter 12, when I talk about the importance of lining up your financing deal *before* you purchase a vehicle, I'll give you details on how to determine your price range. Right now, I'll just give you the basics. Your price range results from two factors: First, your cash on hand plus the *equity* (ownership value) of your current vehicle if you plan to sell or trade it in, and second, your net monthly income (your monthly paychecks minus your monthly expenses.)

If you're one of the few who are sitting on a pile of money and plan to pay cash for your vehicle, you don't have to worry much about number two. But to the rest of us, both are important. Number one is the money that will go to the down payment (traditionally at least 20 percent of the purchase price), and number two represents the money you can afford for your monthly finance payment. (If you currently have a car payment that will disappear when you purchase the new vehicle, be sure to remove that payment from your expense total before you calculate your monthly net income.)

Bet You Didn't Know

Some experts estimate that more than 50 percent of all Americans can't afford to buy a new car. This sends chills down the spines of many auto executives.

Your first affordability check is totaling your cash on hand and current vehicle equity. This should represent at least 20 percent of your projected new vehicle's purchase price. For example, if you have $5,000 in cash and vehicle equity, you should look at vehicles costing $25,000 or less. ($5,000 is 20 percent of $25,000.) If you want a higher-priced vehicle, you'll have to come up with more cash to satisfy the 20 percent down payment rule of thumb.

Some dealers and financial institutions will okay a loan with a down payment of less than 20 percent. Some will even offer 100 percent financing—no down payment at all. In most situations, however, I recommend putting 20 percent down. It limits your exposure to negative equity—owing more than the vehicle is worth at any given time (often referred to as "being upside-down")—and it could get you a significantly lower interest rate.

Money Saving Tip
Remember, you'll pay back significantly more than a dollar for every dollar you borrow, so putting down a substantial portion of the purchase price makes sense (and cents).

Chapter 12 will show you in detail how to calculate how much car you can afford. Just so you don't drive yourself nuts right now with the mathematical calculation, Table 7.1 shows the approximate affordability calculation for a number of interest rates and incomes. It will help you determine, roughly, how much you can afford to borrow for a car.

Table 7.1 How Much You Can Afford to Spend for a Car

Loan Rate (four-year)	Net Monthly Income (income less expenses)						
	$200	$400	$600	$700	$800	$900	$1000
7%	8,350	16,701	25,052	29,227	33,402	37,578	41,753
8%	8,193	16,386	24,580	28,676	32,773	36,870	40,966
9%	8,035	16,070	24,106	28,123	32,141	36,159	40,176
10%	7,886	15,772	23,659	27,602	31,545	35,488	39,432
11%	7,736	15,473	23,210	27,079	30,947	34,816	38,684
12%	7,595	15,191	22,787	26,585	30,383	34,181	37,979
13%	7,454	14,908	22,363	26,090	29,810	33,544	37,271
14%	7,317	14,635	21,953	25,612	29,271	32,930	36,589
15%	7,186	14,372	21,559	25,152	28,745	32,339	35,932

To determine your affordability level using Table 7.1:

1. Find the row representing the current car loan interest rate in your area.

2. Find the column that represents your net monthly income. To find your net monthly income, total your expenses and subtract them from your income.

3. The box where the row and column intersect is the maximum amount you should consider borrowing.

4. To that number, add your current cash and the equity in your current vehicle to determine the highest vehicle purchase price you should consider.

Okay, now you have a reasonably good handle on what you can afford to pay. Now it's time to look at various methods of constructing your shopping list.

Using Affordability as a Guide

One quick way to cut down your list of possible vehicles is to throw out all vehicles that exceed your affordability level. Let's assume that, after looking at your personal finances and the affordability chart in Table 7.1, you determine that you can't afford to buy a vehicle that costs more than $25,000. It would be prudent at this juncture to throw out all vehicles priced at more than $25,000. (Or consider leasing, which is covered in detail in Chapters 16 and 17.)

Sure, a dealer discount might lower the price from the manufacturer's suggested retail price—the so-called window sticker. But taxes and fees will drive that price right back up.

Do your brain a favor—limit your time and effort to vehicles you can afford. There are plenty of them. If you can't get that too-expensive dream vehicle out of your mind, then maybe you should decide that now is not the time to buy. Make a plan to build up your savings for a few months until you can afford the down payment and the monthly payments.

Bet You Didn't Know

State and local taxes and fees can add up to 10 percent to the purchase price of a new vehicle.

Choosing by Segment

An affordability check will wipe a large number of vehicles off your consideration list. If you're among the lucky ones who still have a number of vehicles on your list after putting them to the affordability test, one excellent way to shrink your list further is to set your sights on a particular segment. Like many people today, you might decide, "I want a sport utility vehicle," or "Our family really needs a minivan." By choosing an individual segment to concentrate your efforts on, you can go a long way towards a manageable shopping list, because very few segments have more than 20 competitors.

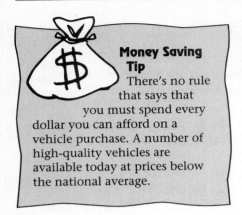

Money Saving Tip
There's no rule that says that you must spend every dollar you can afford on a vehicle purchase. A number of high-quality vehicles are available today at prices below the national average.

If you lock on a segment and couple that with an affordability check, you can often knock the list down to 10 models or fewer. That's still more than the optimum two to four models to examine in depth, but you're getting close.

The problem is, some buyers aren't certain what type of vehicle they want. When I was at *Motor Trend*, I received call after call from readers saying, "I'm looking at a Jeep Cherokee and a Honda Accord," or "I'm considering a Corvette, a Lexus LS400, and a Land Rover." Some might call that muddle-headed, but I don't. In both cases, the buyers were eyeballing very different vehicle types, but the vehicles were in the same general price range. They weren't natural substitutes for one another, but they weren't worlds apart either.

Further, nothing says you have to consider vehicles in the same price range. It's perfectly rational to choose between buying an expensive luxury car or buying a less-expensive vehicle and using the proceeds for another purchase or— hard to imagine in our spend-spend-spend society—keeping the money in savings.

Using Fuel Economy Numbers

Still another way to narrow your shopping list is to pick an arbitrary fuel economy number you'd like your new vehicle to achieve and toss out all vehicles that don't meet this standard. Of course, in the fuel crises of the Seventies and Eighties, this method was much more prevalent than it is today.

Although gasoline prices are rising somewhat as this book is being written, the increase seemingly has no effect on vehicle sales. Sport utilities and full-sized pickups—not noted for their fuel economy—continue to be among the most popular vehicles in the market. My guess is, unless fuel availability becomes a problem, fuel economy will not be a significant factor in the market for the next few years.

However, if for financial or environmental reasons you'd like to buy a vehicle based at least partly on its fuel efficiency, use that as one of your criteria.

Using Performance

Perhaps the opposite of fuel economy as a car-buying criterion, at least on the politically correct scale, is vehicle performance. For example, if brisk acceleration on a freeway on-ramp is on your wish list, you might eliminate all vehicles that fail to meet an acceleration standard—say, those that take longer than eight seconds to accelerate from zero to 60 miles per hour.

In similar fashion, if control in an emergency lane change is a priority, you might eliminate all vehicles that are slower than a certain miles-per-hour in a slalom. If brake performance is a priority, you might eliminate vehicles that cannot come to a stop from 60 miles per hour within a prescribed number of feet, say 160 feet.

You can find such performance numbers in auto-enthusiast magazines—*Motor Trend, Car and Driver, Road & Track, Automobile,* and *AutoWeek.* The next chapter gives you more details on using these magazines to come to a buying decision.

Is Image Everything?

If someone you admire, star or not, drives a certain vehicle, and you think it would be cool to emulate that person by driving the same vehicle, there's nothing wrong with that. Admit it or not, we all role-play a bit in the vehicle we choose. If you decide to buy a Mazda Miata because Tori Spelling drives one on *Beverly Hills 90210* or an AM General Hummer because Arnold Schwarzenegger has one, you're just a little more up-front about it than the rest of us.

Would I base my entire shopping list on the "cars of the stars?" No. But would I include a vehicle on my shopping list because I liked the way a star looked driving it? Sure. But I'd make sure to do my homework and not just fall for a pretty face.

Personal Preference

Examining all these list-building tools is a good exercise. If you truly don't know what you'd like, using one or more of these methods is a great way to go from being boggled by the hundreds of choices to having a good handle on what you'd like to look at. On the other hand, if you're like most consumers, I bet you already have a list in the back of your mind. It may not be well-structured. It may not be well-researched. And you might not know if you can afford the vehicles on it or not. But you probably have a list.

If you do, that's good, because you have a good jumping-off point to build the shopping list you'll use when you get serious. My advice is: Jot down your favorite vehicles. You might find that they're all from an individual segment, say, all sporty cars or all pickup trucks. You might also find that they all cost about the same, offer about the same level of performance, or even offer the same level of fuel economy. All this is good, because it will help you structure your choices.

Once you develop this list of personal "faves," apply all the other criteria that are important to you—affordability, performance, fuel economy, image—to the list. You will emerge with a useful list of vehicles.

What If Your Dream Car Is Beyond Your Means?

Before we go to the next chapter, however, you might be running into a common problem: You have a personal favorite on your list, but you just can't afford it. What do you do? The fact is, there are a few things you can do if your dream car just seems to cost too much:

➤ You can consider leasing it (see Chapters 16 and 17).

➤ You can delay your purchase until you save enough and increase your income enough to afford it (a Puritanical choice, I know, but a good one).

➤ You can buy the vehicle used instead of new.

If you don't think you're the type to drive a used car, just remember: Each of us—from the wealthiest oil sheik to the movie goddess to the guy with the world's worst clapped-out beater—drives a used car every day. And with that, I'll see you in the next chapter.

The Least You Need to Know

➤ To make a useable shopping list, you must determine your affordability zone by looking at your cash on hand, the equity you have in your current vehicle, and your monthly net income.

➤ Among the other criteria you can use in list-building are type of vehicle, fuel economy, performance, and image.

➤ One good way to construct a shopping list is to jot down the names of the vehicles you like.

➤ If you can't afford to buy your dream car, you can wait until you can afford it, lease it, or purchase it used.

Chapter 8

How to Shop for a Car

In This Chapter

➤ Shop wisely

➤ Newsstand shopping

➤ Auto shows

➤ Shopping the dealerships

➤ Look, don't leap

All right, folks, I think you're ready to shop for a new vehicle. But before you do, I want to give you one last warning: A vehicle purchase is one of the biggest purchases you'll ever make. A substantial percentage of your average monthly income will go toward your vehicle. In short, it's a big deal!

Despite this, many people still stumble through car buying and end up with a vehicle that may or may not suit their needs, and that they may or may not be able to afford. What I hope you'll do after reading this tome, and this chapter in particular, is approach car buying as a process. If you do, you'll most likely get what you want. If you don't, you'll most likely get what you deserve—which is heartache.

Except for those of us who go through life blessed with eternal good fortune, you must *prepare* for success to achieve it. And nowhere is that more true than in the acquisition of new wheels. Let's face it: The sharks are in the water, so you'd better be ready when you swim.

Don't Shop Till You Drop

Many of us prepare for new vehicle shopping like an Olympic boxer getting ready to face the reigning world's champion. We expect trouble; though we hope for the best, we expect the worst.

Others look at new car shopping like a trip to the dentist. Man, it's going to be painful! They just don't know how long the pain will last. Minimize discomfort, that's their motto.

Well, I'm not here to tell you that car shopping is always like a picnic in Jellystone Park. But if you approach the shopping experience as a rational process, it will not only be tolerable; it can be downright fun.

I know, you're scoffing. But wait a minute! New cars and trucks are a lot of fun. They're fun to drive. They look good. Hey, they even smell good. And if you play your cards right, you'll soon have a new car or truck of your own. Nothing wrong with that.

Want to know the key to making car buying enjoyable? It's very simple:

You control the process; you don't let the process control you.

In fact, that's so important, I think we should repeat it together:

The key to making car buying enjoyable is you control the process; you don't let the process control you.

The Car Selling Process

Let's look at what goes on inside a dealership, because that will reinforce my premise. First, don't think for a moment that what you experience inside a dealership happens by accident. It's part of a plan. Whatever you experience, good or bad, is happening for a reason, and the reason is, it's part of the car-selling process.

Now, there's nothing wrong with dealers having processes to sell their products. All good retailers have sales processes, and those processes are there to make it easier for you to buy. Expensive consultants roam the retail industry, telling merchants how high their shelves should be, what their signs should look like, and what slogans they should put on their shopping carts.

Things get a little hairier inside an auto dealership, however, because the prices are not clearly marked. Oh, each vehicle carries a very visible suggested retail price, but only the most naive among us pay that rate. Beyond the price issue, there are several other potential pitfalls. As this book unfolds you'll learn about all of them. My point here is just to reinforce in your mind that they are there, and that they are part of a grand scheme by the dealer—a grand scheme not to defraud you, but to relieve you of as much money as he can.

There's nothing wrong with this. The dealer's goal, like the goal of all businessmen, is to maximize his profits. Most dealers do this with honest effort, and part of this honest effort is contained in their sales procedure. Most often this procedure is a well-documented, well-researched, well-rehearsed process that takes place dozens of times each day.

My point here is not to cry foul and insist that all cars be offered by government-owned vendors who all charge the same price. My point is that to compete with the dealer and his sales process, you need an *acquisition process*. So listen up! I'm about to give it to you.

Bet You Didn't Know

Each year dealers pay sales and marketing consultants more than $5 million to set up sales processes within their dealerships.

The Auto-Acquisition Process

First let's discuss what a process is. The nitty-gritty: A process is a series of steps undertaken to arrive at a specific result. Okay, we know the result you'd like to achieve—you want to get a new car, van, or truck. But what are the steps you must take to get there?

Sadly, this is where most people come apart, because they don't divide the car-acquisition process into a series of steps. One day they decide they need a new car, and suddenly they've got one.

You know the scenario. Joe and Betty start thinking the old clunker is, well, getting old and clunky. Maybe it's getting a bit temperamental, maybe repair problems are beginning to occur, or maybe a fresher face has caught their eye. Whatever sets them off, the next thing you know they "drop in" at a dealership to "look around." If you had asked them before they walked into the dealership, they would have told you they had no plans whatsoever to buy a new car.

But then, once they were at the dealership, the new car looked so good compared to the car they drove in with. And the salesman said there was a sale on the model Betty/Joe were looking at. And, according to Betty and Joe, the monthly payments weren't bad at all. (No, not over seven years, they weren't!) The dealer gave Betty and Joe more money than they ever expected for their trade-in. And the dealer threw in undercoating and paint sealer for only $500 more. So Betty and Joe have a new car.

Did they get a good deal? It's pretty doubtful.

Are they happy? Could be they are.

But I figure you bought this book so you could be happy in the knowledge you got yourself a good deal on the right vehicle, not just because your daydreams told you so.

Bet You Didn't Know

According to recent statistics, the average new-vehicle buyer will visit fewer than three dealerships before acquiring a new vehicle.

What Betty and Joe did in the above example is dive into the deep end of the pool before they knew how to swim. Unfortunately for them, they didn't even *know* they couldn't swim, so instead of actually swimming, they took a bath. But, since they don't realize it, they might be as happy as clams. After all, they're about as smart as those zany little mollusks.

If you want to do better than Betty and Joe, I suggest you divide the process into three distinct steps:

1. Research

2. Shopping

3. Buying (or leasing)

Sure, it seems simple, but many people blur the lines between these three phases. Betty and Joe probably did no research at all, essentially skipped shopping, too, and charged right into buying. That might be exhilarating, but it sure can be costly.

If you want to save some money and get a vehicle that will truly serve your needs best, you need to take this three-step approach. Right now, of course, you're engaged in the first step—research. I commend you for buying this book—not because I wrote it, but because it shows that you can delay gratification until you're ready to make an informed, intelligent move. Take it from me, this trait will serve you well, because one attribute that can cost you a great deal of money in vehicle acquisition is impulsiveness—specifically, impulsiveness stemming from the worry that you won't get as good a deal tomorrow as you will today.

Let me allay your fears on that one. As I mentioned in Chapter 2, there are more than 40 brands of vehicles on the market. Even the smallest brand has hundreds of dealers (some have thousands), all competing for your business. Further, most factories are running well below their capacity, which means, in simple terms, they can make more of any model you want. Finally, in the overall sense, many experts think there are too many car companies to service the demand for vehicles, so the competition is absolutely cutthroat.

The salesperson who tells you, "This deal is only good for today," has a simple, very understandable goal. He wants to sell you a car *today*. He doesn't want you to walk out without buying or leasing a vehicle, because if you do, he can't be sure you'll ever come back. Statistically, he's probably right, so it's not surprising that he will try to tantalize you with an offer that can never be matched. Rest assured: It can, if not by the dealer who offered it, then by others who carry the same brand.

The point is, you should at no time in the process allow yourself to be rushed. Take the time you need to do your research. Take the time you need to do some good, comparative shopping; and take the time you need to solicit offers and conclude the buying process.

Research at the Newsstand

One great place to start your research is at the newsstand. That's where you'll find a vast array of auto and truck magazines and auto and truck buying guides. These present a terrific, low-cost way to do some vehicle research without any pressure from salespeople.

The major magazines in the automotive field are *Motor Trend, Car and Driver, Road & Track, Automobile,* and *AutoWeek.* Important titles for off-roaders are *FourWheeler* and *Four Wheel and Off-Road.* Each of these "books" has a somewhat different personality, flavor, and reason-for-being than others, but each can provide you with a hands-on report on the vehicle or vehicles you might be considering. At the newsstand, scan the cover blurbs and tables of contents for articles, road tests, and comparison tests that might be helpful.

Certainly single-vehicle tests that cover a car or truck you're interested in can be valuable. But you have to remember that most new vehicles these days are quite good, so when viewed in the absence of competitive products, the single-vehicle report will be positive as well.

Also, because these magazines derive the vast majority of their revenues from automotive advertising, the articles will rarely be very critical. This doesn't mean the reporter is lying

Money Saving Tip
You can purchase some invaluable research material at the newsstand in the form of magazines and buying guides for less than $10.

Let's Talk Terms
An article that compares two or more vehicles of the same type is a **comparison test**.

to protect the auto manufacturer; it simply means that, if he or she is going to present negatives, they have to be backed up with empirical data and that the negatives will be presented diplomatically. For example, instead of saying "The Schnitzel STX is one of the worst pieces of junk we've ever driven," the report would probably say, "We were somewhat less than impressed by the Schnitzel STX." The bottom line is, if a report on a vehicle seems negative, the vehicle is most likely one of the worst in its class.

One way to avoid having to read between the lines in the magazines is to obtain issues that contain "comparison tests." In a comparison or "shootout," several editor-writers drive and evaluate several vehicles in the same class, compare notes, and, very often, declare one of them the "winner."

Because the reporters drive the vehicles back-to-back, this information can prove particularly helpful to you in making a buying decision. But just because one model is declared the winner doesn't mean it's the only contender you should consider.

Very often several models will be grouped together toward the top of the list. This means in the course of the evaluations each model turned in very similar performances, and each is worthy of your consideration.

Another key item to remember: You must evaluate the evaluators. When it comes to getting information, you should keep in mind the automotive magazines are often referred to as "enthusiast books," because they cater to automotive fanatics. With their primary audience in mind, they always favor vehicles that offer performance and handling over those that don't. But if you're not a car enthusiast, you might find a vehicle that emphasizes performance and handling too expensive, too noisy, and too rough-riding for you, so keep that in mind. (The same holds true in the off-road magazines, but there the bias is toward off-road performance, sometimes at the expense of on-road comfort and driveability.)

And another thing, the writer-editors of the enthusiast magazines don't have to pay for the vehicles they drive and, human nature being what it is, they will often favor a more expensive vehicle over a less expensive one. (I mean, who wouldn't?) But I'm sure dollars-and-cents mean a whole lot to you, so pay attention to the "price-as-tested" within any magazine evaluation to determine if the vehicle is in your price ballpark.

Motor Trend, Car and Driver, and *Road & Track* also offer one more feature that can be very helpful in evaluating vehicles. It is called the "Road Test Review" or something similar, and it is a short summary of each vehicle the magazine has tested over the previous two years or so. The data centers around price and performance data gained from empirical testing, and it allows you to make quick comparison between vehicles in areas like acceleration, braking, and emergency maneuverability (see Table 8.1).

Table 8.1 Using Road Test Review Data

To compare:	Look at:
Acceleration	0–60, quarter mile acceleration times (lower=better)
Braking	60–0, 30–0 braking distances (shorter=better)
Emergency maneuverability	Slalom speed (faster=better)
Ultimate steady-state roadholding	Lateral acceleration "g's" (higher=better)

Of course, you should remember one important caveat when you examine this data. Most often the vehicles tested by the magazines are the highest performance examples of each model. This means that if equipment that enhances performance, like manual transmission or antilock brakes, is available, the tested models will include these items. You, however, might not be interested in driving a manual transmission-equipped vehicle, so accept that the acceleration time of a vehicle equipped with automatic will be slower than the manual version of the same car with the same engine. The good news is, if you compare "apples to apples"—models with similar-sized engines and the same type of transmissions—your comparisons will be valid.

A Guide to Buying Guides

One major failing of the enthusiast magazines is that the issue on the newsstand right now might contain no information about the model or models you're interested in. Again, because they are geared toward enthusiasts, most magazines devote little or no space to big sedans, station wagons, or minivans. That's not what turns on their readers.

But a solution to that also resides on the newsstand in the form of buying guides. Each November or December the "enthusiast" titles, along with *Popular Mechanics* magazine, publish a buying guide for cars. A couple of them also publish a buying guide for trucks, which, these days, includes sport utilities and minivans as well as traditional pickups. These relatively inexpensive guides can be a good jumping off point for your research, because they cover virtually every model on the market for that year.

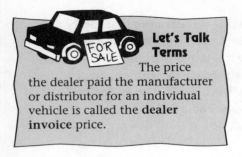

Let's Talk Terms
The price the dealer paid the manufacturer or distributor for an individual vehicle is called the **dealer invoice** price.

Each guide gives you a photo of each model, some brief technical data, and some information about the manufacturer suggested list price. (Generally the pricing is shown as a range from A for the base model to Z for the most fully equipped, highest-priced model.) In addition, the guides sum up the features of each vehicle and describe what's new for the current model year. Some buying guides also repeat one or more comparison tests that their parent magazines have published in the past year.

These guides can be very useful, but they do have a couple of shortcomings. Again, because they are published by companies that rely on automotive advertising, they are not very critical. Most of them simply lay out the technical data (some look at new features) and let you decide which vehicles are better than others. Not only that, the pricing data they provide is very sketchy. Most often it consists of only of Manufacturer Suggested List Prices.

A couple of other sources also publish buying guides, which provide significantly more information than the auto magazine guides. Plus, because these publishers don't rely on automotive manufacturer advertising, they often show a bit more candor about the comparative strengths and weaknesses of individual models.

These buying guides come from, respectively, *Consumer Guide*, *Pace*, and *Consumer Review*, and they contain more detailed product descriptions than the automotive magazines. Generally, their presentation is less artistic (they usually rely on black-and-white photos), but they offer more information about pricing, often adding so-called *dealer invoice* pricing to the MSRP data. Knowing what the dealer paid for a model gives you a negotiating leg up, so these guides can be valuable additions to your information arsenal.

Again, however, you must take the evaluations of the writer-editors with a grain of salt. Most often they don't do empirical testing of the vehicles at all, simply relying on seat-of-the-pants impressions backed up by other's test data.

The Report on Consumer Reports

Also on the newsstand is the *Consumer Reports Annual Auto Issue*, which contains a wealth of data for new car buyers. The issue includes short profiles of each model on the market, ratings of the new models, and predicted reliability and safety of each vehicle. There's a great deal to digest, and that's always been a criticism leveled at *Consumer Reports*—its reports aren't very consumer-friendly.

The enthusiast press also takes a few knocks at *Consumer Reports*, arguing that the publication is "anti-car" and treats automobiles as if they were refrigerators or toasters. But

Consumer Reports (along with J.D. Power and Associates) can take some credit for the improvement in the quality of cars and trucks that American consumers have seen over the last 20 years. Certainly, at $3.95, the *Consumer Reports Annual Auto Issue* is worth buying and using as an information resource, as long as you don't take everything in it as gospel.

The Intelligence on IntelliChoice

Finally, there is another set of publications worth looking at and, sadly, you won't find them on most newsstands or even in most bookstores. But they are worth a trip to the library to examine as you do your due diligence. (In fact, if you're particularly frugal, you can view all of the publications I've discussed in this chapter at most major libraries.)

Each year a Campbell, California-based company called IntelliChoice publishes its *Complete Car Cost Guide* and *Complete Small Truck Cost Guide*. These publications are the result of a significant amount of research, and their goal is to predict overall vehicle costs over time. (The typical ownership period IntelliChoice examines is five years.) To accomplish this, the organization looks at transaction prices and then predicts values for important cost factors such as depreciation, financing, insurance, state fees, maintenance, and repairs.

All of this makes good sense and results in an impressive presentation. The IntelliChoice approach is certainly a viable way to compare possible automotive purchases. However, IntelliChoice intentionally decides to leave unevaluated important factors like design, comfort, performance, and safety. Because of this, IntelliChoice is a very valuable tool, but not the only tool you should use as you assemble your short list of prospective vehicles.

Auto Shows—The Car Buyer's Friend

Leafing through the buying guides is a good way to get a lot of information in a short period of time. None of them is the definitive source of information, but each has its place as you begin to scope in on your next vehicle.

Once you take a dive into newsstand and/or library research, there's another great way to learn a great deal in a short span—attend an auto show. Unfortunately, in most major metro areas auto shows happen but once a year. If an auto show fits into your buying schedule, however, it's a simple way to view all the models in which you're interested in one place. And there's an added benefit—no sales pressure.

To make the most of an auto show, plan to spend at least a couple of hours. This gives you ample time to look at the vehicles and sit in them and get a feel for their interiors. Since you'll be spending a lot of time in this cocoon, it's worth taking the time to analyze which interiors you like best. Also, be sure to bring pencil and paper with you, so you can jot down important points and the MSRP of each model you're interested in. If you don't, the rich kaleidoscope of the auto show can quickly blur distinctions in your mind.

Bet You Didn't Know

Each year more than 25 million people attend auto shows in the United States.

An Auto Show Alternative

An auto show is the best place to see a wide variety of vehicles in a short span of time. But what do you do if there is no auto show in your area or you've missed this year's show?

A good alternative is to use several dealerships to create your own auto show. Perhaps the easiest way to do this is visit one of the auto malls that have sprung up in most areas of the country.

Though some auto malls are owned by one dealer, most are cooperative ventures in which several dealers get together at one location. Usually the dealers' showrooms are separate, but, because they are in close proximity, it will be easy for you to go from one dealer to another to eyeball various models from different manufacturers.

Let's Talk Terms
A collection of several dealership operations on one site is termed an **auto mall**.

Weekend newspapers and television ads are good sources of information on the location of auto malls. (In many cities across the country, it's more difficult to get away from the ads than it is to find the auto malls.) In the absence of a convenient auto mall, simply pick out nearby dealers that represent the brands you're interested in.

Shopping at the Dealership: Dos and Don'ts

Once you choose the auto mall and/or the individual dealerships to visit, treat the excursion like visiting an auto show. The key difference is, you must discipline yourself to refrain from any discussions with dealer sales personnel. It's important that you tell yourself you're not going to buy a vehicle the day you make your dealership visits—*no matter what.* When you're greeted by salespeople at the various dealerships, tell them you're "just looking" and you'll usually get the run of the place without interference. Don't be afraid to ask to look at particular models with the equipment and options you think you might want. But don't get into discussions of price. If you do, you may be led down the garden path to buying that day, before you've done your research.

Dos and Don'ts in the Dealership

Do:

❏ Tell the salespeople you're "just looking."

❏ Spend plenty of time with each vehicle.

❏ Sit in the front and rear seats.

❏ Check the trunk.

❏ Check under the hood.

❏ Take copious notes.

❏ Note suggested list prices and any additions.

Don't:

❏ Be afraid to ask to see a specific model.

❏ Engage in any price discussions with dealer personnel.

❏ Buy or lease a vehicle.

Allow yourself plenty of time in each dealership with each car. Get in the front and back seats. Look in the trunk to see how roomy it is and how easy or difficult it might be to load luggage into it. Look under the hood to see how easy or difficult it might be to check the oil and add fluids like windshield wiper solvent. Note the MSRP on each vehicle, so you can get a handle on what the relative prices are. And note any dealer additions to the MSRP. These additions will generally be found on a second sticker next to the required Monroney sticker. The additions might be called ADM (for *additional dealer markup*) or some other obscure acronym or term. What they mean is, the dealer is attempting to charge more than the suggested list price for the particular vehicle. (I'll discuss this at length in Chapter 15.)

At the end of the day, you will have a great deal of useful information. Most likely you will have eliminated some possible models from your shopping list. You may also have added a model or two. Plus, you'll have a better idea of the equipment you want and don't want and the relative suggested prices of each of the vehicles. You'll find this day will be more than worth the effort as you move forward to acquire your next vehicle.

The Least You Need to Know

➤ You must control the car-acquisition process; don't let the process control you.

➤ All dealers use a well-structured selling process.

➤ The acquisition process should be divided into three distinct phases: research, shopping, and buying/leasing.

➤ You can do a great deal of valuable, low-cost research at the newsstand and library.

➤ Auto shows are an excellent opportunity for hands-on experience with many vehicles in a short span of time.

➤ You can set up your own personal auto show by visiting several dealerships in the same day.

Part 3
Sighting Down Your Automotive Quarry

There are hundreds of vehicles on the market, and thousands of permutations of those vehicles. You can't choose them all. In fact, the best advice is to let the vehicle choose you. How? By shopping sensibly and getting the most out of the vehicle test drive. This part gives you plenty of suggestions on how to accomplish both without being a test driver.

Confused about options? Many people are, but there is a no-nonsense way to approach the whole option game, revealed (guess where?) in this part. Warranties are also a much-misunderstood species, so there will be some pithy advice on that subject as well.

And what should you do if you already own a vehicle? The conclusion of this part lays out your options and then helps you come to a rational, satisfying, and money-saving conclusion.

Letting Your Car Choose You

If you're as old as I am, I'm sure you've seen the following scene on TV:

A child enters an animal shelter. Dogs are barking; cats are meowing. At first the noise and clamor are overwhelming. But then the child sees a shy little dog in the corner of the cage, away from the others. Their eyes meet, and the child smiles and steps forward toward the dog, which responds by reaching out with its paw. A relationship is forged in that instant, a relationship that will last through this life and into the next one.

Sure, it's as corny as a Frank Capra movie. But that's just the kind of relationship I wish for you and your car. I want you to choose each other, and live happily ever after.

How do you get there from here?

Well, in Chapter 7, I gave you a few choice words on coming up with your shopping list, and in Chapter 8, I gave you some research and shopping hints, including the crucial concept of making the acquisition of a new vehicle a three-step process: research, shopping, then buying. Now it's time to get serious about step number two: shopping.

From Research to Shopping

When you concluded Chapter 7 you should have been ready to prepare a concise, coherent shopping list of vehicles that deserved your further attention. With any luck, this list consisted of four vehicles or less, and certainly it should have been no more than seven or eight.

Using the advice and information sources I cited in Chapter 8, you should have been able to knock some of those original names off your list. Looking at the enthusiast magazine and buying guide information probably led you to dump some of the vehicles on the original list. You might let one negative write-up go (the writer might just have been cranky that day) but if the combined opinions of several writers in several different publications are negative, it's reason enough to bump that vehicle from your list. Or you simply might have decided that the price, availability of features, or just the looks of one or more models wasn't to your liking.

An auto show visit might have helped you narrow your list still further. You might have really liked the Dweebman XG90 until you saw it at the auto show, but when you got a load of the standard yak-fur interior, you said no way—and the optional emu-skin leather seats were just as bad. Scratch that sucker!

Bet You Didn't Know

When you conclude the research phase of the acquisition process your shopping list should consist of no more than four different models.

Ditto for your auto mall auto show. The Ishimuri Waldo QT was high on your list until you checked out the trunk and found out that there wasn't enough room to stash your bowling ball and your golf clubs simultaneously. Or you thought the Schnellwagen

Uberlord might just be the ticket, but the quality of the paint finish wasn't to your liking when you saw it up close and personal. And that green! You wanted a green car, but not one that looks like a Seven-Up bottle.

Addition by Addition?

Running your list through a vigorous research phase is a good idea, but sometimes the process doesn't go as smoothly as you might expect. By doing research, your hope is to narrow your choices down to the inevitable one. However, as the research continues, your progress in shrinking the list might slow considerably.

Let's say you're looking at the Wheezmeister Weasel, a compact sedan, and you find a comparison test on compact sedans in one of the auto enthusiast magazines. In reading the conclusion of the test, it becomes obvious the editors didn't like the Weasel too much—it finished eighth in a field of seven—but did offer high praise to the Hotmobile Toledo. And in fact, that Toledo does look awfully appealing in the photos that accompanied the article. It's a no-brainer to drop the Weasel, but should you add the Toledo?

You bet you should.

As a matter of fact, similar things might happen to you several times in the course of your research. You might have come to the auto show with a secret hankering for the Squea-mish Rastaman, but parked on the turntable right next to it was a Squeamish Leadbelly that, to your eye, had better styling and a much lower list price. (Goodbye Rastaman, hello Leadbelly.)

And elimination might come for several reasons. Say, the Fernbull Oregano photo in the buyers guide was an eye-catcher and it got a positive review, but *Consumer Reports* and J.D. Power and Associates rated it below average. Unless you really love it, why take a chance?

Or, when you did your research you noted that two contenders—the Isobar HTZ and the Drooler 900—had nearly identical manufacturer-suggested list prices. But when you made your triumphal dealer research tour, you noted in your little black book that the Isobar was being offered with a special factory discount of 600 bucks, while the Drooler's list price was pumped up by floor mats, undercoating, and ADM to the tune of $1,500. If you like the Isobar about as much as you like the Drooler, you'd be justified in 86-ing the Drooler from your list.

At times it might not seem like you're getting anywhere—and if you start adding more models than you're deleting, you're not doing it right. But over the course of your research, you should be able to knock down your list until there are just a handful that you deem worthy of your serious consideration—no more than four, maybe just two or three.

Bet You Didn't Know

A key goal of your research is to limit your choices to a manageable number; so if you add a vehicle to your list, drop one as well. Now's the time to make these decisions.

When you accomplish this, my friend, you have graduated from the research phase. Now you are ready for some serious shopping.

Get ready, because you are about to visit some showrooms with shopping on your mind.

Making the Shopping Experience Work for You

All right, be prepared, because up to this point you've been splashing around in the wading pool. Now you're about to go swimming with the sharks.

And I use the term "sharks" advisedly. Just as there is nothing inherently evil about sharks—they're simply one of nature's many creatures—there is nothing inherently evil about automotive dealers and their salespeople. Extending the metaphor, though they're not evil, sharks can be dangerous, and so it is with dealer personnel. They can be dangerous to your pocketbook.

To swim with them and keep your pocketbook safe from harm, you simply have to know the ropes. You must proceed in a rational, reasoned manner, recognizing that you have all the weapons you need to fend off the dangerous ones. You just have to use them.

Money Saving Tip
When you enter a dealership during the shopping phase of the acquisition process, remember that's all you're there to do. Don't mix shopping and buying or you'll pay for it.

Your key weapon in the shopping phase is to remind one and all, including yourself, that you are shopping, not buying. If you want to use a phrase that will make sense to the dealer personnel, tell them you are a "serious shopper," or that you are "shopping seriously for a vehicle." You might add, "I'm planning to buy a vehicle in the next week." These two short phrases will get the attention of the salespeople you speak with, because it will tell them you're not a casual browser, a "looky-loo" who just came in to get out of the rain.

Getting the Info You Need

Armed with your two-, three-, or four-vehicle shopping list, you should pick a day or a weekend to visit at least two dealerships that carry each model you're interested in. Take a notebook and pencil to jot dot the important information, because if you don't write it down, it will soon become a jumble in your mind.

On this excursion, you will be talking to dealer salespeople and test driving several vehicles, so be certain you give yourself enough time. It will be difficult to accomplish what you need to at each dealership in less than an hour. That means if you have a four-vehicle list, your shopping trip will take you eight hours plus the driving time from one dealership to another. (Rather than making it "The Day in Dealer Hell" I would suggest dividing that schedule up over a weekend.)

"Just what do I need to accomplish on my shopping trip?" you may be asking. There are a number of things, all important to getting yourself the most satisfying vehicle and deal you can. Namely:

1. Determine which vehicle on your shopping list is your favorite, which are still contenders, and which should be crossed off.

2. Determine what equipment you would like on your new vehicle and your exterior and interior color preferences. (I'll discuss optional equipment at great length in the next chapter.)

3. Determine what, if any, special incentives like cash-back, dealer cash, manufacturer-sponsored leasing, or discount financing, are being offered on the vehicles in which you're still interested.

4. Using number three, determine the approximate purchase prices (not just sticker prices) of the vehicles in which you still have an interest.

5. Determine which dealer or salesperson you feel comfortable doing business with.

In the simplest terms, you will be shopping for the vehicle, the price, and the dealer. Before it's over, you might change your mind on all three, but shopping is an important information-gathering phase of the vehicle acquisition process. If you do it correctly, you'll be well on your way to getting the right deal on the right car.

Shopping at the Dealership

Now it's time for your first serious shopping trip to a dealership. Remember the paramount fact: Shopping is an information-gathering phase. Buying will come later, certainly not today.

Bet You Didn't Know

In most dealerships the salesperson who greets you isn't chosen at random. Instead, they use a rotation system, taking turns serving customers as they enter. In industry lingo, a new customer is referred to as an "up."

As you enter the dealership, you will undoubtedly be "greeted" by a salesperson. My suggestion is that early in the conversation you tell the salesperson these salient facts:

1. You are a serious shopper who plans to buy a vehicle within a week or less.

2. You currently have two, three, or four models (whichever is accurate) on your shopping list, and you are gathering information to narrow it down to one.

3. Under no circumstances do you intend to buy today, but you do intend to buy from the dealership and salesperson that gives you the best deal and with whom you feel most comfortable. (This last is a not-so-subtle hint that you expect respectful, helpful treatment.)

4. You would like to first look at and then test drive the model you are interested in, equipped with the features and options you are considering. Be as specific here as you can.

While the salesperson walks you over to the model in question, she or he will probably ask you a couple of questions about yourself—what you do for a living, where you live, and so on. It's not just small talk. The salesperson is trying to "qualify" you, that is, determine how expensive a vehicle you can afford and what kind of vehicle you might like. Sometimes I think it would be less painful if you just handed the salesperson a card with your occupation, address, and net worth on it, but this "qualification" ritual has been going on for decades. In any case, since you already eliminated from consideration any vehicle you couldn't afford, you will pass this time-honored rite without difficulty.

The vehicle the salesperson leads you to can be a very telling clue about both the salesperson and the dealership. If she or he immediately shows you a model very similar to what you asked to see, right down to the optional equipment and maybe even the color, you potentially have a good salesperson to deal with. At least the salesperson is listening to you.

If, on the other hand, the salesperson leads you to another model or a version of the model you're interested in equipped very differently from what you asked to see, be wary. This is the sign of a salesman who wants to sell you more car than you want, and you don't want to be sold. In fact, throughout the process that's a good thing to keep in mind: You want to buy, but you don't want to be sold.

Money Saving Tip
One way to make sure you don't enter a deal impulsively is to leave your checkbook and credit cards at home during your shopping expedition.

Giving It the Once-Over

The cliché about a showroom visit is that most of the time is spent kicking tires. Well, kick a tire if you must, but there are a number of other things of more importance you should look at. The Vehicle Inspection Worksheet later in this section helps you rate a vehicle in a number of categories. Make copies of the Worksheet and use it for each vehicle you examine. The detailed list of categories includes:

1. **Overall appearance**   Does the vehicle look good to you? Is it something you would be proud to own? Do the tires and wheels fill the wheel wells or are there unsightly gaps?

2. **Exterior finish, paint quality, panel, and trim fits**   Take a closer look at the exterior of the vehicle. Is the paint smooth or rippled with "orange peel"? Do the exterior panels fit together well or are there gaps and irregularities? Do the badges and trim fit properly or are they crooked or sloppy?

3. **Underhood**   Does the engine compartment look tidy? Are the important pieces like the oil fill cap, washer fluid reservoir, and dipstick easy to locate? Is there an underhood light?

4. **Trunk or cargo area**   How spacious is the area? How easy is it to load luggage or other cargo into it? Does the trunk lid open down toward the bumper or is the opening several inches above the bumper line, requiring you to lift things higher? Does the cargo area have a cargo net, helpful for small packages? Is there a light? Do the wheel wells intrude on interior cargo space, making it harder or impossible to load wide objects such as a bicycle?

5. **Interior overall appearance**   Do you like the appearance of the interior? Does the upholstery fabric match or coordinate with the dashboard and trim or are there obvious mismatches? Are the fits between the panels neat and tidy?

6. **Driver's seat comfort and adjustability.** Is the driver's seat comfortable? Does your position in it offer good visibility? Do the seat and backrest adjust to accommodate many driving positions? After putting on the seat belt, is it comfortable? Is the upper seat belt anchor adjustable?

7. **Dashboard legibility**   After positioning yourself comfortably in the driver's seat, do you have good sightlines to the instruments like the speedometer, tachometer, and fuel gauge?

8. **Controls**   From your position in the driver's seat, are the controls for the heater, ventilation, and air conditioning easy to see and reach? Are the controls easy to understand and use? Are the windshield wiper controls easy to use? Do the wipers feature an intermittent mode? Adjustable speeds? Is the cruise control easy to understand and use? Are the sound system controls easy to understand and use?

9. **Steering wheel**   Does the steering wheel feel good in your hands? Is the steering column adjustable for rake (does it tilt)? Does the steering column telescope? Is the horn button(s) in a good, easy-to-find-position? Are other controls—sound system, cruise control—on the steering wheel/steering column? Are they easy to use? Can you see the instrument panel with the wheel adjusted to where you like it?

10. **Front passenger seat comfort and adjustability**   Position yourself in the passenger seat. Does it feel comfortable? Does it adjust to accommodate a number of positions and body types? Is the seat belt comfortable? Does the upper seat belt anchor adjust?

11. **Special touches**   In the interior are there purpose-designed items like cupholders? Compact disc and cassette storage? Eyeglass compartment? Garage door opener compartment? Built-in garage door opener? Compass?

12. **Sound system**   In addition to AM-FM radio does it offer cassette capability? Compact disc? Single-play or multi-disc magazine? Is the magazine in the trunk or accessible within the vehicle? Does the unit offer special features like "random play" and "repeat" in addition to more standard features like "next" and "previous"? Are the controls understandable and easy to use? (I suggest taking a cassette and a CD that you know and playing them on the vehicle's unit to check the sound quality and ease of use.)

13. **Rear seat comfort**   Is the rear seat comfortable? Will it accommodate one, two, or three passengers? Are the seat belts comfortable? Do the seat belts stow well or are they messy? Does the rear seat offer a fold-down arm rest? Do the rear seats split and/or fold down to increase the cargo area?

Vehicle Inspection Worksheet			
	Excellent	Average	Poor
Overall appearance			
Exterior finish			
Underhood			
Cargo area			
Overall interior			
Driver's seat			
Dashboard controls			
Steering wheel			
Passenger seat			
Special touches			
Sound system			
Rear seat(s)			

I know this is a lot to check, but I ask you, would you rather check it now or discover that your new vehicle is missing an important feature and/or sadly lacking in quality *after* you've paid thousands of dollars for it?

And you should also note: You can do all these things *before* a test drive in the showroom or on the dealer's lot. Your goal is to go beyond overall impressions to specific likes and dislikes. You're looking at pluses and minuses, looking for the vehicle that delivers the most pluses and the fewest minuses.

Taking the Test Drive

Maybe I'll be labeled a heretic for saying it, but for new cars, the test drive is much less important than it used to be. In fact, I'm convinced that a large proportion of the driving population could choose a vehicle without ever going on a test drive, *if*—and it's a big if—they perform the steps I just outlined above.

That said, I still believe the test drive can be very valuable in choosing the right vehicle for you. Remember to concentrate on the driving experience. Don't let yourself be distracted by other things—like the salesperson gabbing in your ear or the neat folding cupholder in the console. One key to a successful test drive is taking it alone or with a trusted friend/significant other instead of with the salesperson. Some dealerships might balk at sending you down the street unaccompanied in their brand-new, unpaid-for wheels, but by all means *ask*. If the dealership won't let you…well, that tells you something right there.

If you performed the multi-step walkaround outlined in the preceding section, you can concentrate on the driving experience in the test drive. If you haven't, drive the car for several minutes, then find a convenient spot to park where you can look the vehicle over from top to bottom. (When I was road-testing cars for *Motor Trend*'s Car of the Year and Import Car of the Year competitions, I would drive the vehicle for 45 minutes; stop and do a 15-minute walkaround note-taking session, and then drive the car for another 30 minutes or so, correcting and updating my notes at the conclusion of the drive.) I'm not suggesting you spend an hour-and-a-half on each test drive, but don't make it a quick spin around the block either.

As I said, during the test drive, you want to concentrate on the driving dynamics. And you want to check these dynamics in several types of driving, including stop-and-go city streets and highway-freeway-interstate. Following are some areas you should analyze. Make copies of the Test Drive Worksheet from this section, and use the worksheet to evaluate each car in the following categories:

1. **Ride comfort**   Is the ride soft, harsh, or somewhere in the middle? Does the vehicle develop unusual ride characteristics like bucking, weaving, or hobby-horsing? Does it develop vibrations over unusual surfaces? Are the seats comfortable and supportive when driving?

2. **Quiet**   Is it quiet in the cockpit? Is there an objectionable amount of wind noise, tire noise, engine noise, or exhaust noise? Is the turn signal noise obnoxious?

3. **Acceleration**   Does the vehicle accelerate smoothly and strongly as you push the accelerator pedal? Does the vehicle seem powerful or weak? Are there "dead spots" when you begin to accelerate or as you accelerate?

4. **Braking**   Does the vehicle slow smoothly as the brakes are applied? Does the braking action seem *progressive*, that is, more braking the harder you push the brake pedal? Are there objectionable vibrations through the brake pedal? Is the car's steering affected by braking?

5. **Handling**   Does the vehicle seem easy to maneuver? Is the steering too light, too heavy, or just right? Does the vehicle respond quickly to turns of the wheel? Does it respond too quickly (it feels jumpy) or too slowly (it feels lethargic)? Is the vehicle easy to park?

Test Drive Worksheet			
	Excellent	**Average**	**Poor**
Ride comfort			
Quiet			
Acceleration			
Braking			
Handling			

If you examine these areas and answer these questions, you will have an excellent test drive, a test drive that will convince you whether the vehicle is a keeper or not worthy of further consideration.

Discussing Price, Availability

Now, for every vehicle that is still worth talking about, you need to determine what, if any, special incentives like cash-back, dealer cash, manufacturer-sponsored leasing, or discount financing, are being offered. You should ask your salespeople these questions and watch their eyes light up. (This will tell them you're nearly ready to buy.) Again, assure them you're not going to buy today, but you will buy soon and you need this information to firm up your decision.

If they are worth their salt, the dealer personnel won't just tell you about the special deals and financing available (though they will probably not divulge much about cash-to-dealer incentives), they'll also try to swing you into making a deal right then and there. Their usual gambit will be to cite a discount off the sticker price, likely adding that the offer is good for "today only."

The discount from the suggested list price may well sound good (it may well *be* good, since the salesperson and the dealership still have many other profit cards to play) but resist temptation and file away the offer. You're not going to use it now, but you might use it later—as a negotiating tool.

If the salesperson wants to know if you're going to finance the vehicle or pay cash, tell her or him you're going to pay cash and want to know the "cash price." Perhaps there will be some hemming-and-hawing but they should provide you with a figure. Write it down in your little black book. Ask the salesperson for his or her card, say thank you and walk out the door.

Repeat this process at the other dealerships until you've seen at least two dealers who carry the vehicles that remain on your "possible" list.

Then go home, relax, look over your notes and give yourself some time to get perspective on what you've learned.

You've had a busy day. But it will pay dividends, as you'll see in the next chapter when we discuss options and warranties on the way to choosing your target vehicle.

The Least You Need to Know

➤ As you move from research to shopping you'll narrow your list of "possibles" still further.

➤ In your research you will eliminate some vehicles, but you might add others.

➤ In the showroom you must proceed in a rational, reasoned manner.

➤ When you visit the dealership you want to determine what vehicle and what equipment you want.

➤ A thorough inspection at the dealership will go a long way toward helping you choose the right vehicle for your needs.

➤ On the test drive concentrate on the driving experience.

➤ If you're interested in a model, don't be afraid to ask for the "cash price" of that vehicle.

➤ All right, Pilgrim, you're ready. And don't worry; we're all counting on you.

Options and Warranties

In the late Teens and early Twenties, Henry Ford made enough money to buy his own third-world country by telling customers, "You can have any color as long as it's black." (You didn't think you could go through a whole book on car-buying without hearing that old saw, did you?)

But even as Ford's KISS (Keep-It-Simple-Stupid) philosophy of basic transportation was making him one of the richest men in the world, it was going out of style. While Ford was pounding out flivver after flivver, each one just the same, General Motors captured industry leadership by offering buyers choice.

Not only did GM offer its customers the choice of several nameplates—Chevrolet, Oakland (soon to become Pontiac), Oldsmobile, Buick, and Cadillac—it also offered buyers their choice of equipment on each model. No, the idea didn't originate with General Motors. The fact is, factory-installed options were part of the auto industry before the assembly line. But the money men at General Motors were quick to discover that factory options were serious cash generators. Chrysler, Nash, Hudson, Packard, and Studebaker were quick to catch on, and soon even Ford Motor Company began to offer optional equipment.

The reason options have proven to be a gold mine is very simple. Options are additional sales and additional profit opportunities—and more for you to consider, as you'll learn in this chapter

Let's Talk Terms

Equipment or features that are not part of **standard equipment** but are available to customers willing to pay for them are **optional equipment**, commonly called **options**.

Why the Car Business Is Option-Happy

It all goes back to what I told you in Chapter 1—the car business is an incredibly competitive, dog-eat-dog business. Even though cars, trucks, sport utilities, and vans cost thousands of dollars, the profit margin on an individual vehicle isn't very large because of the pressure of competition. If you examine base prices of similar vehicles from different manufacturers, those base prices are generally lumped very close together. Not only that, the profit margins are razor thin.

Offering optional equipment, however, allows both the manufacturer and the dealer a second shot at boosting their profits. The industry has found that many consumers will pile on the extra equipment, sometimes boosting the purchase price past the base price by one-third or more.

Options work beautifully for the manufacturers, because, as they see it, the easiest person to sell is the person who is already a customer. So if you have a hot prospect ready to sign the sales contract, why not try to boost the bottom line with everything from power mirrors to floor mats, a more-powerful engine to back-seat reading lights?

Bet You Didn't Know

Some options—like CD players and sound systems—are warranted by their manufacturers, not the auto manufacturer. This can sometimes complicate service of these items.

Adding to options' desirability—from the car companies' point of view—is the fact that both the factory margin and dealer margin on optional items is fatter than it is on the vehicle itself.

This means that both factory and dealer live to sell you optional equipment. In fact, many dealers will sell the car at cost and rely on options and the *back end*—financing, insurance, and add-ons—for the profit that keeps them in business.

You can bet dealers love it when you ask for a car that's "fully loaded."

There are three categories of options:

1. **Factory-installed**   Equipment added to the vehicle when it is built and generally available through all dealers of that make.

2. **Dealer-installed**   Equipment added to the vehicle at the dealer's facility or by an associated vendor; these options may or may not be offered by all dealers of the same make.

3. **Port-installed**   Equipment added to an import vehicle by the port facility after it arrives from an overseas factory; generally available through all dealers of that make.

The trend today is away from individual options and toward *equipment packages*, several items packaged together. (Another oft-used term for the same concept is *preferred equipment group*.)

In the hey-day of the domestic industry it used to be common for customers to order individual options from a laundry list as long as a basketball player's arm. You could go down the list checking off boxes for automatic transmission, power brakes, power steering, power windows, whitewall tires, push-button radio, and scores of other nifty items. If you ordered a car this way, it would arrive from the factory at the dealer's showroom in four to six weeks virtually custom-made to your requirements.

As import manufacturers entered the North American market, they quickly discovered they couldn't do business that way. Their overseas factories were simply too far from American showrooms to make this viable. At the same time, they desperately wanted to get in on the profit opportunities offered by options.

So they did a very smart thing—they began to group popular options in special equipment packages or separate *trim levels*. This way they could build vehicles with the equipment customers wanted, yet not force their customers to wait for a vehicle to be built across the ocean and then be delivered by ship.

In addition, the importers supplemented this strategy by offering optional equipment to be added in U.S. port facilities once the completed vehicle arrived (*port-installed*) and optional equipment to be added in the dealer's own facility (*dealer-installed*).

Though it grew from necessity, the packaging of options into groups and trim levels also had the benefit of improving quality. Rather than custom-building each individual car, truck or van, the overseas factories could build long series of nearly identical vehicles, which, in turn, led to fewer mistakes on the assembly line.

Bet You Didn't Know

Honda has been one of the last bastions for what was once a common option—dealer-installed air conditioning. These days, factory-installed air conditioning is predominant in the U.S., though it's not as popular elsewhere.

It also made ordering at the dealership easier and more foolproof. Using the checkbox system, many vehicles arrived at dealer's facilities lacking equipment that had been ordered, or equipped with items that had not been ordered. Packaging groups of options eliminated that problem.

Finally, packaging groups of options made them easier to promote and easier to sell. So there's no secret why the domestic manufacturers have rushed to adopt option packaging.

One added fillip the American manufacturers have added to the strategy are so-called *value-priced* or *one-price* models. These models are not only equipped with an array of popular options, but at a Manufacturer's Suggested List Price so low and so compelling that it is designed to eliminate dickering. (I'll give you more information about value pricing in Chapter 15.)

Are Options for You?

If you don't mind living a monk-like existence and driving the automotive equivalent of a bread-and-water diet, you can save yourself a great deal of money by saying no to options. The so-called base models, referred to as *strippers* in the industry because they are stripped of most equipment, are the lowest-priced versions of each model on the market. Often they are hard to find because the factories don't make many and the dealers don't stock many, but, if you can find one and you can live without luxuries, you can save yourself some money.

How much? Here's a typical example. In a recent model year, the Chevrolet Cavalier base four-door sedan had a Manufacturer's Suggested List Price of $10,700, while the Cavalier LS, a higher trim level, had an MSRP of $12,900. That's $2,200 or about 20 percent more for the LS version.

However, the LS version offered useful items like four-speed automatic transmission, air conditioning, AM/FM radio, tachometer, remote trunk release, and several other features. In comparison, the base Cavalier was equipped with five-speed manual transmission and didn't have air conditioning. Lest you think the base model was a total penalty box, note it did come equipped with a host of standard features including anti-lock brakes, dual airbags, and power steering.

What this illustrates is intelligent option packaging. By lumping two options that are in high demand—automatic transmission and air conditioning—into a package, Chevrolet assured itself and its dealers that a high percentage of Cavalier buyers would choose the higher-level version and pay about 20 percent more in the bargain.

This is not to pick on Chevrolet. Most manufacturers, particularly those in the very price-sensitive lower and middle ranges of the market, use the same strategy. I simply want you to understand what the strategy is.

Matching the Options to Your Model

Most of us want our vehicles to be equipped with at least some optional equipment. It makes our day-to-day life with the vehicle more pleasant and convenient. Your goal, however, should be to make cost-effective option and equipment package decisions.

Just as the auto manufacturers have an option strategy, you should have an option strategy as well. The strategy I suggest is matching the options to the model you buy.

In other words, the key to getting value for your option dollar is purchasing options and/or packages that are appropriate for your new vehicle and passing on those that are inappropriate.

Let's assume you're in the market for a small, fuel-efficient, subcompact car to use primarily for commuting. A base model might have an MSRP of around $10,000. Option Package 1, which costs $2,500, adds automatic transmission, air conditioning, and power steering. Option Package 2, which costs $1,750, adds power windows, power door locks, cruise control, and tilt steering wheel. Option Package 3, which costs $3,000, adds glass moon-roof, multi-disc CD player, and leather seats.

You can buy the base car or add one or more of the option packages. What makes the most sense?

> **Money Saving Tip**
> One of the few segments in which buyers prefer manual transmission to automatic is the sports car segment. Corvette buyers will routinely pay 5 to 10 percent more for a manual-equipped used vehicle.

I'm sure you can come up with the answer yourself if you simply analyze what equipment is appropriate. Here's how my thinking would go:

The base car, at $10,000, might be just fine for commuting. With manual transmission and no air conditioning, it will probably be the most fuel-efficient version. But if I were going to commute in this vehicle every day, I would sure like to have the convenience of automatic transmission, the comfort of air conditioning, and the added ease of power steering. Yes, the added $2,500 adds 25 percent to the price of the vehicle, but I'm pretty confident that it will help significantly at resale time. (For more information on improving resale value, see Chapter 11.)

Continuing with the example, it certainly would be convenient to have power windows and locks, cruise control and tilt wheel, but I definitely would not choose those items instead of automatic and air conditioning. If I add them in addition to Option Package 1, suddenly the price of my little economy car is up to $14,250, some 42 percent more than the base model. That's a bit steep, and I doubt that those items, though convenient, will add much to my resale value for this type of car.

Option Package 3 also is filled with good stuff, but they are totally inappropriate for an economy car. The person buying a used economy car is looking for cheap transportation. Period. He or she doesn't need a moon-roof, leather seats, or a CD changer. You'll never get your money out of them at resale time.

The Strategy in Action

I'm sure you can see where we're going here. Choosing the right options is not just a matter of deciding what you want, but also what the next buyer of your vehicle will want. When it comes to options that can add to a vehicle's appeal at resale time, you have to get into the mind of the next buyer.

Money Saving Tip
Be careful about getting too wild and expressive with your choice of options and colors. That bright yellow car with the burgundy leather interior might look terrific to you, but it might be nearly impossible to trade in without taking a huge loss. Remember, most car buyers are conservative in their choice of colors.

First, you must decide if the individual option or package will give you good value for your money, and then determine if you can get at least a portion of your money back at resale time. If the option won't contribute to the vehicle's resale value, it doesn't mean that you shouldn't buy the option. But if you do, you must be prepared to eat the cost.

As the vehicles you're considering get more expensive, higher and higher levels of equipment become appropriate and cost-effective. For example, you'll never get the next buyer to pay extra for leather seats in an economy car; you might get the next buyer to pick up part of the cost in a family car; and you might have a hard time reselling a luxury car without them. The same holds true for CD players. If you're about to buy a sports car, a high percentage of sports car buyers still prefer manual transmission, so if you're thinking about an automatic you should realize that it may cost you at resale time.

Options That (Almost Always) Make Sense

There are a handful of options that almost always make sense and can prove beneficial at resale or trade-in time. In fact, because so many buyers find they make sense, manufacturers are making them standard equipment on more and more models. They are:

Automatic transmission Except for sports cars—a breed that is rapidly dying—automatic transmission has become a virtual necessity for the motoring public these days. Automatic transmission makes day-in, day-out driving much easier—especially in heavy traffic situations. It is more durable and requires less maintenance than a manual transmission, and it carries fewer penalties in terms of lower fuel economy and poorer acceleration than it used to.

Unless you're absolutely dying to shift it yourself or you are buying a true-blue sports car, I heartily suggest purchasing automatic transmission. Most often, you don't have a choice about what automatic you get, but you should know that electronically controlled four- and five-speed automatics are better than the older conventional three-speed.

Power steering/power brakes These twins used to be found only on zooty luxury cars. In fact it was a badge of honor to see "PS, PB" in a car's classified ad. Now it's very difficult to find vehicles that aren't equipped with power steering and power brakes, but if you're considering a model that doesn't offer them standard, step up to the option price.

Air conditioning In other areas of the world, air conditioning isn't favored in nearly the proportion it is here in the United States. For those who live in the southern tier, air conditioning is a virtual necessity, but even in the northern areas of the country it is installed in a high percentage of new vehicles.

Options That Can Add Value

In addition to the above-mentioned "sure shots" there are other options that have the potential to hold at least some of their value when it comes to resale time. Among them are:

Antilock brakes   First antilock brakes were over-hyped, then they got an unfair bad rap. My opinion is that antilock brakes can add significantly to the safety of your vehicle—*if* you know how to operate them properly. As optional equipment, they rarely cost more than $1,000 on an MSRP basis (meaning you should pay less), and I would opt for them when available. In some instances they will hold some of their value; in others, economy cars, for instance, they won't add much, if anything, to resale value.

Power door locks   This is not only a convenience item, but, in high-crime areas it can be a safety and security feature. When equipped with a remote keyless entry, power locks allow you to unlock your door quickly, without fumbling for keys, and also illuminate the vehicle's interior lights so you can see a potential bogeyman. Many cars now also come with panic buttons that will sound an alarm and flash lights to ward off potentially dangerous situations. Women and wimpy guys like me particularly like this feature.

Cruise control   A virtual necessity for long trips on interstate highways, today's cruise controls are very sophisticated and largely troublefree. They are appropriate for any vehicle beyond the economy class.

CD player   Until the next technology comes along—and who knows when that might be?—compact discs are where it's at, musically speaking. While it doesn't make much sense to install a $5,000 system in a $10,000 car, it's been done. Today's trend is toward in-dash single-play and magazine-type units, and away from trunk-mounted magazines.

Alloy wheels/optional tires   No package as dramatically improves the looks and handling of a vehicle as alloy wheels and upgraded tires.

All-wheel-drive/four-wheel-drive   Except on very select models, all-wheel-drive won't get you any added resale value on cars, and in fact, it may actually damage resale. On sport utility vehicles, however, all-wheel-drive or four-wheel-drive are virtual necessities. (To read more about all-wheel-drive and four-wheel-drive, see Chapter 6.)

Theft-deterrent system   I remember when we used to call these burglar alarms. Today, they are much more sophisticated and do hold some of their value at resale time.

Options Whose Value Wilts

Of course, there are a few options that might be great to have, but generally don't hold their value worth beans. Among these ho-hummers are...

➤ Sunroof/moon-roof.

➤ Traction control.

➤ Heavy-duty battery.

➤ Heavy-duty cooling system.

➤ Heavy-duty suspension (unless on a tow vehicle).

➤ Auto-dimming headlamps, which turn on and off without touching a switch.

➤ Headlamp wipers.

➤ Steering wheel-mounted sound system controls.

Are Bigger Engines Better?

Yes.

All right, that was the former editor of *Motor Trend* speaking. Frankly, I believe you are usually best served by choosing a more powerful optional engine when the choice is available. And I say this not just because I like performance—I do—but because adding the more powerful engine usually results in a more pleasant vehicle for the average driver.

Of course, the obvious benefit of more power is better acceleration. This gives you more peace of mind when merging into expressway traffic or passing on a rural two-lane road. But a more powerful engine usually offers better driveability as well. At highway cruising speeds, most optional engines will generally turn fewer revolutions per minute, which means they will feel "less busy" and often quieter.

In addition, most four-cylinder engines vibrate much more, both at idle and in normal cruising, than do six- and eight-cylinder engines. The penalty for a larger engine is usually reduced fuel economy, but computer engine controls have radically increased the fuel efficiency of larger engines.

Generally, more powerful engines add to resale value. Of course, the sudden onset of another fuel crisis could change things dramatically. But, despite concerns over the environment, many consumers seem to like the all-around benefits of optional engines.

Pluses and Minuses of Optional Engines
Pluses...
✔ Better acceleration
✔ Smoother operation
✔ Quieter operation
✔ Better driveability
✔ Increased resale value
Minuses...
✔ Reduced fuel economy
✔ Higher initial cost
✔ Higher maintenance cost (potentially)

Words on Warranties

Time was, the standard automotive warranty was 12 months or 12,000 miles, whichever came first. This meant that after a year, no matter what, you were on your own.

Today, things have changed, as longer warranties have become a price of admission for the manufacturers and a competitive tool.

Relatively long warranties are a price of admission in the new-vehicle market, because consumers are very warranty-conscious. In fact, an oft-cited reason for buying a new car instead of a used one is the peace of mind offered by the manufacturer warranty. Many interpret the length of the warranty as a statement by the manufacturer on how confident it is in the vehicle. A warranty of 4 years/50,000 miles seems to many to express more confidence in a vehicle's quality and reliability than a 2-year/24,000-mile warranty.

Of course, virtually all manufacturers offer at least three different types of warranties: overall, powertrain, and corrosion-protection (sometimes referred to as "rust-through.")

The overall warranty covers just about everything on the vehicle other than the powertrain (which has its own warranty), the tires (warranted by the tire manufacturer), and the sound system (warranted by the sound system manufacturer). The powertrain warranty covers the vehicle's driveline—basically the engine, transmission, and related systems. The corrosion-protection warranty covers rust holes in the body.

As this is being written, the norm in overall warranties is 3 years/36,000 miles, while many luxury car manufacturers offer 4 years/50,000 miles. Three years/36,000 miles also is the standard for powertrain warranties, but in this area the terms vary widely. From luxury manufacturers, terms as long as 6 years/70,000 miles are not uncommon, and Volkswagen is attempting to make some marketing hay with a 10-year/100,000-mile offer. The rust-through warranties are less likely to be tied to a mileage figure, and most of them run five years or more—long enough for you to trade the vehicle in or resell it.

All this said, the natural question is: Are warranties important? Yes, because if you get a bad vehicle or a vehicle with a major problem in an expensive system like the engine or transmission, they can save you thousands of dollars.

Are longer warranties better than shorter warranties? Certainly. They protect your wallet longer. Are vehicles with longer warranties better than vehicles with shorter warranties? Not necessarily. In fact, a case could be made that the reverse is true. (Manufacturers of poorer quality cars often feel that they have to offer a longer warranty to soothe reliability fears in the public at large.)

Should you buy a vehicle because of the warranty? In most cases, no, but if two vehicles are even in your mind and one has a long warranty and the other has a short one, it might act as a tie-breaker.

Do all manufacturers respond to warranty claims by consumers in the same helpful, nurturing manner? Emphatically, no. That's why simply looking at warranty terms can be misleading. Since there's no definitive, publicly available survey on warranty administration, your best bet is to ask everyone you know about their experiences with the warranty procedures of the various car companies.

Money Saving Tip
Don't think that warranty protection only applies to new cars. These days a number of auto manufacturers are offering warranties on used vehicles sold through their affiliated dealers. Often these used vehicles go through a "certification" program to assure that they are in top mechanical condition.

Where Do We Go from Here?

With this chapter's presentation on Options and Warranties swimming in your head, plus the information you gleaned from last chapter's shopping expedition, you should be very close to choosing your next vehicle. And not just the model but the optional equipment you want as well.

You're almost ready to begin the buying phase—but just a minute; don't you already own a car?

We'll talk about that important issue in the next chapter.

The Least You Need to Know

➤ Options represent a second profit opportunity for dealers and manufacturers.

➤ The profit margin on options is higher than the margin on the vehicle itself.

➤ Today's trend is toward option packages and away from individual options.

➤ You should match the options to the vehicle.

➤ Automatic transmission, power steering, power brakes, and air conditioning are options that virtually always make sense.

➤ Other options are worth considering but may not add to resale value.

➤ More powerful optional engines can enhance the driving experience and aid resale.

➤ You should take a close look at warranty terms, but don't base your buying decision on warranties.

Chapter 11

Hey, Don't You Already Own a Car?

In This Chapter

➤ Common mistakes when you're selling

➤ Determining and maximizing value

➤ The importance of mileage

➤ Appearance counts

➤ Honesty pays

All right, by the time you finished the previous chapter, you should have been well on your way to deciding what your next vehicle will be. At the very least, your search should be narrowed down to just a couple possibilities. But before you charge ahead into the buying phase of your quest, you must address one very important issue right now. If you wait till later it could cost you thousands of dollars.

What is that issue? Your current vehicle, that's what. Of all the potholes that the average car buyer falls into on her or his way to a good deal on new wheels, the disposition of your current vehicle is likely the deepest and most costly. The funny thing is, many car buyers don't realize they've hit the pothole. They don't feel the lurch or hear the bang. But this pothole can rip the oilpan right out of your good deal. You'll never even notice the hundred-dollar bills streaming from your wallet like dirty crankcase oil.

It's Not the Dealer's Fault

I know, many of you might be saying it's those shifty car dealers. Well, you're right that the dealer is often the beneficiary when it comes to the disposition of your current vehicle, but I submit to you—it's not the dealer's fault.

The business of selling cars is the rightful descendent of the horse-trading industry. It rewards the shrewdest, most persistent hagglers, and it doesn't suffer fools easily. You have to remember that the *real* value of each and every vehicle, just like the value of every horse in the horse-and-buggy days, changes daily.

Every minute, new vehicles come on the market from factories across the USA and around the world, and from the hundreds of thousands of individuals who are selling their vehicles on any given day. Since none of these vehicles carries a fixed price, a dealer has to be a shrewd operator to survive. One key to that survival is being able to quickly evaluate the value of any vehicle, whether it's going out the door as a sale or coming in the door as a trade-in.

Just remember this simple fact: When you trade in a car, you're selling something. And if you sell something without knowing what it's worth, it's *your* fault, not the fault of the person buying it from you.

Horse-Trading in Action

Let's look at a typical new-car transaction, and I'll show you what I'm talking about. Mandrake Funkelhazy has his heart set on a brand-spanking-new Snerdmann 4000RF family sedan. He's checked a buying guide and learned that the car, equipped as he would like it, carries a manufacturer's suggested list price of $26,000.

Arriving at the Snerdmann dealership, Mandrake uses his rusty negotiation skills in a battle of wits with the salesperson and gets him to come down 5 percent off the suggested price, which would mean a cash price of $24,700. To Mandrake this doesn't seem bad at all. In fact, he's secretly a little proud of himself that he's persuaded the salesman to come down so much. In Mandrake's mind, his negotiation prowess has earned him a quick $1,300.

Bet You Didn't Know

More than 40 million new- and used-vehicle transactions occur each year, and each and every one of them is unique.

Not so fast, Mandrake. What comes next trips up poor Funklehazy. Like most of us, he can't afford to pay cash for his car, so he must finance it. After agreeing on the cash price, he lets the salesman in on this little secret (which was no secret to anyone in the dealership the second Mandrake strolled in), and the salesperson says, "No problem; we can finance you right here. What do you want to use as a down payment?"

Also like most of us, Mandrake is not over-burdened with ready cash, but he does have a car, a Potash Beekeeper that he made the final payment on just two months before. Poor Mandrake's problem is that he has no real idea what the old beater is worth. He hasn't worried about finding out, either, because he's going to trade it in as a down payment on his Snerdmann.

Learning that Mandrake has a trade-in (something that also comes as no surprise), the salesperson asks the dealership's used-car manager to look over the vehicle. The used-car manager eyeballs it, scratches himself, and says, "Look, there's not much demand for these old Beekeepers anymore, but I'll give you $8,000 for it."

With nothing to base his judgment on other than the weather that day and the ball scores he heard on his way to the dealership, Mandrake decides that $8,000 is a good price for his old Potash. He suddenly has an $8,000 down payment, which, in turn, means his loan will be for $16,700. A few computer keystrokes later and the salesperson quotes Mandrake a monthly payment of $440 for a four-year loan.

"Gosh, that's more than I want to pay," Mandrake wheezes, and the salesperson comes back with $375 a month for five years. Mandrake's mind flashes quickly to his rudimentary monthly budget and says, "Okay." The salesperson and Mandrake shake hands and the deal is done. Half an hour later, Mandrake drives into the sunset in his shiny new Snerdmann 4000RF.

Where's Waldo?

Maybe it all sounds reasonable to you. Why shouldn't it? You don't have any more information than Mandrake did. But when you read what comes next, tracking down Mandrake's mistakes is as easy as finding Waldo.

There are really two Waldos here: First, the money Mandrake got (or *didn't* get) for his used car, and second, his loan terms. Mandrake tripped over number one because he had it in his mind that he was "trading in" rather than "selling his car." When you trade in your car, you *are* selling it. If you expect

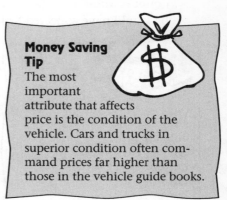

Money Saving Tip
The most important attribute that affects price is the condition of the vehicle. Cars and trucks in superior condition often command prices far higher than those in the vehicle guide books.

to sell something, you better have a good idea of what it's worth. Price it too high and it will never sell; price it too low and you cheat yourself out of the money you should get for it. But because Mandrake was "trading in," he didn't bother getting a good idea of his car's worth before he entered into negotiations to sell it. Bad plan.

In Mandrake's case, the dealership gave him $8,000 for a vehicle that had a wholesale value of $9,000. The next morning, the dealer could take that tired old Potash Beekeeper to the local auto auction and receive $9,000 for it, less a slight charge from the auction house. And in many areas where there are public vehicle auctions, Mandrake could have done the same thing.

But wait—as they say on TV—there's more. Mandrake's old Potash was in average condition for its age, so the dealer might decide to wash it, wax it, and put it out on his used car lot. In fact, he probably will, because the car's retail value is about $10,800.

So, where's Waldo #1? Mandrake let $1,000 fall in the pothole when he accepted the dealer's offer of $8,000 when his car was actually worth $9,000 wholesale. Because he was trading the car in, Mandrake should have expected to receive the wholesale value of the car. No more, but certainly no less.

He let another potential $1,800 fall in the pothole when he decided to trade his car in rather than sell it himself. I say "potential" because Mandrake wasn't likely to receive the $10,800 "full retail" price in a private sale. Private sale buyers are bargain hunters who take a chance on buying a car from an individual rather than a dealer, who presumably will be there tomorrow to back up the car if something goes wrong. Plus, Mandrake would have had some selling expenses—a want ad and maybe some signs from the office supply store.

But let's be conservative and say Mandrake could have sold his Potash for a net of $10,000 after paying for his want ad and signs. Had he done this, he would be $2,000 ahead of where he ended up. Sure, selling the car himself would have been a hassle, but I doubt it would have taken more than four hours of his time. And for four hours of work, he would have collected $2,000. How often do you make $500 an hour?

Let's Talk Terms

The price a dealer pays to acquire a vehicle, new or used, is called the **wholesale price**. The price a consumer pays a dealer to acquire a vehicle is called the **retail price**.

When you look at the complete deal, Mandrake didn't do himself any favors. In essence, he gave the dealer $2,000 simply because he didn't know the territory.

As for Waldo #2—the loan terms Mandrake accepted—I'll get into that in great detail in the next chapter. Suffice it to say that Mandrake didn't know that the current car loan rate in his market was right around 10 percent. So when he agreed to the loan terms of $375/month for five years, he didn't realize that the 12.5 percent interest rate on the loan was 2.5 percentage points higher than the going market rate. That's 25 percent higher.

Over the course of the loan this difference will cost Mandrake $20 per month or a total of $1,200. By making two mistakes that many car buyers make, Mandrake cost himself at least $3,200.

What Can You Do About It?

In the next chapter, I'll give you a thorough process for avoiding the financing pothole. Right now I want to show you a couple of methods that will allow you to avoid the car-disposition pothole. The first thing you need to do is get a good handle on your current vehicle's worth. That seems like a no-brainer, but many people, especially those who are planning to trade in their current vehicle, don't even bother to take this very basic step.

It might seem like a hassle, but if you fail to make the effort you can be sure it will cost you in the long run. The fact is, getting a ballpark estimate of your current vehicle's value is considerably less challenging than making a good soufflé. (Or at least I guess it is; I've never made a good soufflé.)

How to Determine Your Car's Value

I have, however, determined many cars' value in the course of buying and selling used vehicles. One important thing to remember is that every used car is unique. While you can buy virtually identical new cars from dealer after dealer, once they reach buyers' hands, they shift from being a commodity item to a one-of-a-kind whose worth depends on things like mileage, maintenance, and even climate.

What this means, as you try to determine the worth of your vehicle, is that you never arrive at the exact value until you actually sell it. You don't have to establish the value with scientific specificity—you just want to get as close as you can. That being said, what should you do? One easy solution is to buy one of the used car price guides on sale at many large newsstands and bookstores. You can look up the model and year, and right next to it you'll find two prices—the wholesale price and the retail. How difficult is that?

Not very. But, sadly, the information you get by doing this, while far better than nothing, could well be inaccurate to a significant degree. To make your best deal, you need to determine the value of your car, in the words of Van Halen, right here, right now. The problem with vehicle price guides is that they are neither right here, nor right now.

There are three reasons the price you see in the guide books might not be the appropriate price for your vehicle:

Lemon
Some dealers use price-guide discrepancies to the buyer's detriment, showing one customer a book with a low-dollar evaluation when assessing a trade-in, and showing a new buyer a high-dollar evaluation when selling that vehicle. Make sure you come armed with your own information if you're going to sell your used car to a dealer.

➤ The guide books are national or, at best, regional in scope. They can't take into account the special conditions in your local market—where you will sell your vehicle.

➤ The guide books suffer a time lag from the time the data was gathered until the publications hit the newsstands and bookstores. Since prices are volatile, this can make a big difference.

➤ There are wide discrepancies between the various guides. (On my desk are two guides from different publishers I obtained at about the same time. One quotes the retail price of a 1991 Ford Taurus LX as $9,200, while the other lists it at $8,050—a difference of more than 14 percent.)

Several publishers are trying to address the time lag problem by delivering the information over the telephone, via fax, and posting it on on-line computer services. This is helpful, but it still doesn't address regional issues, and it certainly doesn't address the overall accuracy or inaccuracy of these services.

What's a Mother to Do?

Given the "Kentucky windage" in most price guides, what's the best course of action? If you're really ambitious, here's one procedure:

1. Drive the car you're planning to sell to several dealerships in your area.

2. At each dealership, ask to see the used-car manager.

3. Tell the used-car manager you'd like to sell your car, and ask him if he'd like to make an offer on it.

4. If he does make an offer, note the figure.

5. Then, if you're in the mood for sparring, tell him you think his offer is low; you think your car is worth (pick a reasonable figure, but at least 10 percent) more.

6. Note his response, thank him for his time, and be on your way.

After you while away an afternoon in this simple, devil-may-care manner, you should have a very good idea what your vehicle is worth—on a wholesale basis. Likely, too, you'll be amazed by how close the prices you were offered by the dealers are. (Hey, they're businessmen.)

Use the Newspapers

Another good gambit, one that I favor because it involves much less personal interaction, is whipping out the Saturday or Sunday classified section and looking up the prices of vehicles of the same year, make, and model as your current ride. If there are just two or three, that's not much of a sample, and it won't do you a heck of a lot of good. (Of course, the person looking to buy a car like yours in that area won't have much information to go on either.)

If you live in a large urban area, though, over a couple of weeks you should be able to get a good grip on the going price for your vehicle. Remember that the prices you see in the classifieds are *asking* prices—prices the owners are seeking, not necessarily getting—so lower the figure by at least 10 percent to get an estimate of the current *selling* price. And if you're certain you're going to trade in your vehicle with a dealer rather than sell it yourself, taking another 10 to 15 percent off the price will get you to the approximate wholesale figure.

Money Saving Tip
In most of the country there are publications devoted to vehicle advertising. These can be cost-effective places to advertise a vehicle you have for sale and to gauge the local market price for your vehicle, or a used car or truck you're considering.

Do Some Experimentation

Over the years I've heard many people complain that the vehicle they had for sale "just wasn't selling." Nine times out of ten when I heard the asking price, I could immediately see why. Most often, their asking price was at least 10 and often 25 percent more than the current market value. When they lowered the price, the phone started ringing.

You can use this to your advantage, especially if you're in no hurry to sell your vehicle. This is what you should do:

1. Find a local newspaper or other publication in which you can run an ad for a small amount of money or even for free.

2. Choose an asking price for your vehicle based on your research in used car price guides, newspaper classified sections, and dealer visits. If anything, the price you choose should be on the high side. Remember, you can always drop your price, but it's darn hard to raise it.

Money Saving Tip
The publications that accept your ads for free might ask for a portion of the proceeds from the sale of your vehicle, so be certain you understand the terms and can live with them.

3. Place an ad that says something like this:

   1994 Potash Beekeeper, red, A/C, auto trans, new tires, excellent cond. (Your Asking Price) (Your phone number).

4. Wait for the phone calls to stream in.

If the phone calls do stream in, you probably priced the vehicle about right. When you get a solid offer from a buyer who will pay in cash or a certified or cashier's check, take it. There's no chance you'll get as much from a dealer. If the phone calls don't stream in, drop the price 10 to 20 percent and try again. Repeat the process until you get some phone calls. I'm confident you *will* sell that car. It's just a matter of the price.

> **Bet You Didn't Know**
>
> When selling a car, always insist on cash, a certified check, or a cashier's check. Further, call the financial institution where the check originated to verify its authenticity. Unfortunately, there are many criminals who counterfeit checks. A prospective buyer may ask to leave a deposit, promising to return later with the balance. Make sure this deposit is significant and make it clear that if the deal falls through, the deposit is not refundable. Buyers who make a deposit are asking you to take your car or truck off the market. If they renege, you deserve some compensation.

How Important Is Mileage?

Mileage is far less important than the overall condition of the vehicle. But mileage is still an important factor for vehicles less than five years old. (After five model years, mileage becomes a non-issue. When a car hits its fifth birthday, the maintenance the car has received becomes more important. Buyers of these vehicles are usually just looking for transportation.)

In evaluating mileage, the key factor to remember is that 15,000 miles per year is considered about average. Therefore, a two-year-old vehicle with 30,000 miles is considered average. A three-year-old vehicle with 45,000 miles and a four-year-old vehicle with 60,000 miles are also considered average. If your vehicle has more miles on it than these averages you might have to accept somewhat less for it, particularly if it is not in pristine condition.

How much less? Perhaps 2 to 5 percent less than the price of an average-mileage version for every 10,000 miles over the average mileage figure for that model year.

On the other side of the coin, low mileage might add to value, but only if it comes in conjunction with a vehicle that is in tip-top condition. The bottom line is this: Mileage is important, but the condition of the car is much more important.

Should You Sell It Yourself or Trade It In?

If your priority is to get rid of your old car and acquire a new vehicle for the absolute lowest expenditure of money, your choice is clear: Sell your old car yourself to a private party. If you use the advice in this chapter on pricing and selling it, you're certain to get more than a dealer will give you. That only makes sense: The dealer will only give you the wholesale price for the vehicle as a trade-in, but if you sell it yourself you will get something close to the higher retail price.

If, however, you don't have the time or inclination to sell the car yourself, you are a trade-in candidate. There's nothing wrong with that, but you will pay, and pay dearly, for the convenience of the trade-in. Further, by trading in, you open yourself up to a confusing double-transaction at the dealership— trading in your old vehicle *and* buying the new one.

A compromise between selling your current vehicle yourself and trading it in is selling the car to a different dealer or selling it through an auction. This is reasonable because it does separate the trade-in transaction from the new-vehicle purchase. If you do this, though, you must resign yourself to getting the wholesale price for your vehicle, not the higher retail price.

> **Money Saving Tip**
> Beware of a dealer who offers you much more for your trade-in than you know it's worth. There is only one source for this inflated "trade-in allowance"—the dealer is planning on taking a higher profit margin on the new vehicle than he would in a no-trade-in transaction.

Getting the Most Money for Your Used Car

Most people aren't mechanics, or very discerning test drivers, but practically everyone can tell if a car looks clean, shiny, and well-maintained. Whether you sell the vehicle yourself or trade it in, concentrate on your vehicle's appearance. Never would I recommend doing anything unethical like rolling the mileage back or lying about the vehicle's condition. But I do recommend making your vehicle look as good as you can. Spend an hour or two washing and polishing the exterior, and thoroughly clean the interior. Further, don't think the used-car experts at the dealership, who will assess your trade-in, are immune to this gambit. They respond to good-looking cars just like the rest of us.

What if your vehicle has mechanical problems? You can take two steps in this situation:

1. Have the problem fixed before you sell the car and "merchandise" that fact by telling prospective buyers, "I just had the fuel injectors replaced."

2. Simply tell prospective buyers truthfully what the problem is, what you think it will cost to fix, and that you have adjusted the price accordingly.

You'll be amazed at the success you can have with option number two. Very often prospective buyers have a brother-in-law, uncle, or good friend who is "a great mechanic," and they will convince themselves they can get the job done for less money than your estimate. In this instance, a problem honestly admitted and accompanied by a price adjustment becomes a selling point rather than a hindrance.

Of course, if you're trading in, the used-car manager knows darn well he can get the problem or problems fixed cheaper than you can. He buys service and parts wholesale; you buy them retail. Again, a problem accompanied by an honest explanation and a drop in your asking price can actually be an advantage.

I never recommend trying to hide a problem and foist it off on the new buyer. Number one, you'll have to live with the negative karma for the rest of your life. Number two, you don't want to be stalked by a violent, vindictive, used-car owner.

The Least You Need to Know

➤ Do research in local papers and other publications, or with local dealers, to gauge the value of your car.

➤ A vehicle's mileage is not nearly as important as the vehicle's condition.

➤ If you want to minimize your net dollar outlay when you replace an older vehicle with a new one, sell your current vehicle to a private party.

➤ To maximize the value of your current vehicle concentrate your efforts on appearance inside and out.

Part 4
Setting the Stage for the Right Deal

To build a good house you first need to lay a firm foundation. The same is true with building a good automotive deal. Part 4 gives you several key steps to getting your vehicle acquisition deal off on the right foot.

You'll learn why cash is king in the dealership and why it's best to line up your car loan before you even walk in the doors of a dealership. A key item to remember: The lowest monthly payment doesn't mean you're getting the best deal. This part will tell you why.

This part also tells you the best days, weeks, and months of the year to go vehicle shopping. Many have described dealerships as the last vestiges of the Arabian bazaar. In these chapters you'll see why manufacturers and dealers do what they do, who the salespeople are, and, most importantly, how you can best deal with it all.

Finance First

As I mentioned in Chapter 4, the simplest transaction is a cash transaction. You learn the price and pay it in cash—no hidden charges, no flim-flam, no prevarication. But, as I also told you, the vast majority of us finance our vehicle purchases instead of buying with cash.

Hey, I wish I had 20 or 30 grand to plunk down on the barrelhead when I buy a car, but I don't. Odds are, you don't either. So listen up, this is the important part—because we don't have the money in the bank to make a cash purchase, buying a car is actually a *multi-transaction* process.

Sure, we all know we're buying a vehicle. But we're also buying financing. (Plus, as you learned in the previous chapter, if you currently have a vehicle, you're also selling a vehicle—another (hopefully) separate step on the stairway to new car heaven.) Frankly, this is where many people get all caught up in their underwear. And that's why this chapter helps you work through the financial side of the process.

Will That Be Cash or Credit?

It happens every day. Budding car buyers stride confidently into the dealership armed with good information about the vehicle they want to buy. They know the trim level and options they want. Many of them are even equipped with a close approximation of what the dealer paid for the vehicle, the *dealer invoice price*. For all intents and purposes, they are loaded for bear. After all, when you go to Sears to buy a refrigerator, do you have any idea what Sears paid for the doggone thing?

Money-Saving Tip

An increase of one percentage point in the annualized percentage rate (APR) will cost you about $500 over the course of a four-year loan on a vehicle that costs around $20,000. If most people would shop for financing as diligently as they shop for a car, they could save serious amounts of cash.

Yet, even though these consumers have the information to address transaction #1, Buying the Car, they have next to no information on transaction #2, Buying the Financing, and only vague ideas about #3, Disposing of Their Current Car. Because of this they can leave a lot of money with the dealer, and they might not even know it happened.

How can you avoid this tale of woe? The first thing to remember is Cash Is King in a dealership. You've heard the expression, "Cash talks; bull walks"? It was probably coined by a car dealer. Dealers love people with money. People with money can afford to buy cars, and they don't waste dealers' time.

I know it's hard to get tearful over the hard times of auto dealers, but each day, in dealership after dealership after dealership, a potential customer will walk in, monopolize several hours of a salesman's time, drag in the sales manager for another hour of hot debate over a $50 set of floor mats, and, finally, stand ready to sign the sales contract only to discover, after a credit check, he can't afford to buy the vehicle. Up in smoke! All for naught! Holy wasted effort, Batman!

That's why dealers love cash customers. They're only human. (Yes, folks, dealers are human!) They like the path of least resistance, just like you and me. So, as I said, Cash Is King.

But you said most of us finance, you may be saying. Yes, but there is a method by which you can be a finance customer and still get the advantages of being a cash customer.

Furthermore, this method separates the acquisition of a new car into the two steps of buying a car and buying financing. What is this magic method?

Line up your financing *before* you go to buy.

Don't Stumble, Shop

Many buyers stumble through the entire vehicle-buying process. Fact is, thousands of people enter car dealerships each day, seriously shopping for a car, with little or no idea what they can afford to pay.

Wouldn't it be nice to enter a dealership, not only confident that you know what you can pay, but also knowing that a financial institution has preapproved a loan for that amount?

With something like that in your hip pocket, you can negotiate with the salesperson just as if you had cash. If you let it be known you have cash and/or pre-approved financing, you'll immediately get the salesperson's attention and respect; and, if you play your cards right, you'll get better deals in both transactions: buying the car and buying the financing.

There's no magic formula for this. All you have to do is shop for your financing from the several sources who offer loans before you enter the dealership. In most instances, you can do much of your shopping over the telephone.

> **Money Saving Tip**
> Dealers love people with cash, but they also like to add to their profits by selling financing. When negotiating your deal, hold out the possibility of financing your purchase through the dealer if that's a real option for you. It may help you negotiate a better purchase price.

How to Shop for a Car Loan

The first step in learning how to shop for an auto loan is finding out where to look. As I mentioned in Chapter 4, there are seven sources of auto financing:

1. Finance companies
2. Dealers
3. Banks
4. Credit unions
5. Home equity loans (usually from banks or savings and loan institutions)
6. Borrowing against insurance, investments, and/or retirement funds
7. Borrowing from family and/or friends

You know you're going to visit a car dealer, so in shopping for a car loan, my advice is to go to the dealer last. If you talk with a dealer about financing before you sound out any other loan sources, you could succumb to the pressure to buy a car. Instead, investigate several other sources on the list first.

But even before you do that, take a close look at your own finances. (Write everything down.) First, examine your assets, your cash on hand, and the stuff you own. How much money do you have in the bank that you can devote to a vehicle purchase? If you currently own a vehicle, how much is it worth? If you still owe money on your current vehicle, do you owe more than it's worth? Or do you have some equity in it? Do you have stock or other investments that you might sell to add to your vehicle fund? This will give you a good idea of how much cash you can gather together for a down payment.

Second, examine your liabilities, the debts you have, and the cash expenditures you must make each month. How much money do you spend every month on food? Clothing? Your rent or house payment? Medical bills? Prescription drugs? Car, home, life, and medical insurance? Child care? Entertainment? Charity? Laundry and dry cleaning? Home repair and maintenance? Hobbies? Parking? Taxes? Utilities? Gas, oil, and vehicle maintenance? Current car payments? Boat and/or recreational vehicle payments? Revolving charge account payments?

It's best to put together a comprehensive list, so if you think you're forgetting a category or two, look in your checkbook register and your credit card statements, and add the necessary expense categories.

Once you put your list of monthly expenses together and add up the items, compare that total to your monthly income. If you have a current car payment that will replaced by the payment on the new vehicle, make sure you don't count it when you total your monthly expenses. This will give you a good idea of how big a monthly payment you can handle comfortably.

As you shop for a loan by telephone, have this information at hand. The loan agent will be impressed by your preparedness, and that could help you secure a loan.

Checking Your Affordability Quotient

In assessing what's affordable given your current financial situation, there are a couple rules of thumb to go by. Of course, you made a rough calculation of this in Chapter 7, Table 7.1. First, to obtain a standard auto loan, you usually must have at least 10 percent of the vehicle's purchase price in cash or equity in your current vehicle for a down payment. Further, many experts recommend putting down no less than 20 percent of the purchase price in cash, trade-in, or a combination of the two. If you don't, you risk financial hardship should you decide to sell the car before the finance period ends.

Simple math tells you that 20 percent of the purchase price of a $20,000 vehicle is $4,000. Remember, too, that purchase price, includes sales tax, state fees, and perhaps some other charges; it is not just the sales price you negotiate with the dealer. This all-inclusive price is often known as the "out-the-door" price.

In addition to the down payment, the other side of vehicle affordability is the monthly payment. These days, the trend is to lower the monthly payments on increasingly expensive vehicles by lengthening the loan term. It used to be that most auto loans were 24- or 36-month contracts. These days, 60-month (five-year) and even 72-month (six-year) loans are not uncommon.

They're not uncommon, but they're not advisable either. As you'll see later in this chapter, the shorter the loan term, the more money you save, all other things being equal. Plus, longer-term loans often leave you vulnerable to being *upside down*—owing more money than your vehicle would be worth if you sold it—for a longer period of time.

While not something you want to go out of your way to experience, this only matters if you want to sell your vehicle before the end of the loan term. In that case, you'll have to come up with additional cash to pay off the current loan before you can originate a new loan. Instead of being an asset you can use as part of a down payment, your vehicle and loan structure is a liability.

I strongly suggest that you consider a loan term of more than four years *only* if you are very confident you will keep the vehicle at least the length of the loan. In fact, in all cases, a good basic rule is to plan to keep your vehicle at least as long as the loan term.

Given all this, you should do several things when you shop for financing:

1. Ask the institution for its annualized percentage rate (APR) for car loans.

2. Tell your financial institution you would like to obtain a car loan of no more than four years and you believe you have the cash and/or equity in your current car to make a 20 percent down payment. (If you have a current vehicle, the loan agent can help you evaluate its worth.)

3. Tell the financial institution how large a payment you think you can comfortably make each month.

With this data in hand, the loan officer at the financial institution can tell you precisely how large a loan you will be able to qualify for, which tells you how expensive a car you can afford. Very often, he or she can also fill out the loan-application papers for you over the phone and speed you on to a rapid loan approval. With your loan approved, you can negotiate with dealers as if you had cash—a big advantage.

The Scenario in Action

Let's say that Lucy Iffleschneider has a little more than $1,000 in the bank, about $3,000 in equity in her current car, and can afford to pay no more than $410 per month in car payments. She calls one of her local loan institutions and finds that their car loan rate is 10 percent APR. After the loan officer attacks the spreadsheet for a few minutes, she or he tells Lucy she can afford to pay slightly more than $20,000 for a vehicle, if she wants to put 20 percent down and pay over a four-year period.

The simple math shows why. Twenty percent of $20,000 is $4,000, neatly matching what Lucy has in cash and ownership equity. At 10 percent APR, a four-year loan on $16,000, which is the amount financed, will cost $405 per month.

Money Saving Tip

To avoid the hazards of being upside down, plan to put at least 20 percent of the purchase price down as your initial payment and accept a loan term of no longer than four years (48 months).

Lucy may have her eyes on a $25,000 vehicle, but those numbers won't pencil. She doesn't have the required $5,000 down payment, and the $507 a month payment is too much for her.

After several other calls, she finds a second loan source offering car loans at 8 percent APR. She might think that lower interest rate will put that $25,000 vehicle in her driveway, but it turns out, even with the lower interest rate, she'll have to scrape up more money for both the down payment and the monthly payment to afford a $21,500 vehicle—a lot less than that $25,000 luxo-boat. (In this instance, the 20 percent down payment is $4,300 and the monthly payment is $420.)

Money Saving Tip

Simply because you walk into the dealership with a preapproved loan doesn't mean you shouldn't investigate the dealer's financing terms. Quite the opposite—tell the dealer about your preapproved deal and see if he can beat it.

Lucy may not be able to purchase her dream vehicle, but she did save some money by shopping two loan sources. Over the course of a four-year loan on a $20,000 vehicle, the difference between an 8 percent APR and a 10 percent APR will save her $730.

Further, when she enters a dealership to negotiate her deal, she can bargain as if she has $20,000 in the bank. Seeing that she has done her homework and is ready to buy, most dealers will be serious about giving her the best price they can. They realize that if they don't she'll be out the door.

The Usual Suspects

With the "why" of getting a loan preapproved before entering the dealership out of the way, let's take a detailed look at the various sources of financing. Most Americans finance their vehicles using one of the first four alternatives on our list (finance companies, dealers, banks, and credit unions). Let's look at the advantages and disadvantages of each:

Finance companies earn their profits by making borrowing easy and convenient. Essentially, they are like any retailer, except the product they sell is money. They buy money wholesale, then mark it up and sell it at retail. Very often, they are less conservative than banks and other financial institutions, which means if your credit is a bit shaky they may be more willing to lend you money than a bank. But, generally, you will pay for this with a higher interest rate. (I'll discuss the implications of this later in this chapter.) In fact, finance companies are among the most expensive sources of auto financing.

Many consumers obtain financing from the dealer who sells them the vehicle. But few realize that these loans may come from any one of three sources:

1. The dealership may fund and carry the loan itself.

2. The dealership may arrange for a loan using bank funds and acting as the middleman.

3. The dealership may arrange for a loan through one of the auto manufacturers' so-called *captive* finance companies.

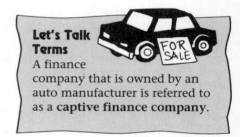

Let's Talk Terms
A finance company that is owned by an auto manufacturer is referred to as a **captive finance company**.

This all might be transparent to the vehicle buyer, but each source of funds has different implications.

These days it is rare for dealers to fund their own loans. Since the car business is so capital-intensive, few dealers want to tie up their cash in loans to customers. In addition, most would rather let somebody else chase down late payments and repossess vehicles. However, if a dealer does offer its own loans, it might be a relatively inexpensive source of money, because the margin on the loan—the difference between the borrowing rate and the lending rate—isn't split between two businesses. On the other hand, some dealers specialize in financing consumers with iffy credit ratings, and those interest rates will be significantly above the prevailing market rate.

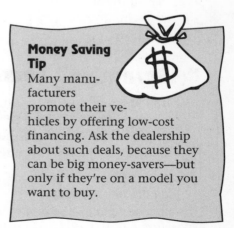

Money Saving Tip
Many manufacturers promote their vehicles by offering low-cost financing. Ask the dealership about such deals, because they can be big money-savers—but only if they're on a model you want to buy.

If the dealer is simply acting as a middleman for a bank, the implications are obvious. You can expect to pay slightly more for these funds than you would if you borrowed them directly from the bank, because the dealer is likely to add a bit to the interest rate for his trouble in setting up the loan.

Finally, if the dealer is acting as a middleman for a captive finance company, the implications are both positive and negative. Certainly, as a middleman, the dealer will try to get a slice of the financing dollar, which could push the interest rate up. But captive finance companies are in the business of financing vehicle purchases, and their goal is to keep their interest rates competitive so that the manufacturer with which they're affiliated can sell more vehicles.

Because there are three sources of dealer financing, each with different positives and negatives, ask the dealer where the financing is coming from. Then negotiate and make your decision accordingly.

Borrowing from a bank isn't too difficult to comprehend. In theoretical terms, the bank obtains funds from its depositors, offering to pay them interest on the deposits, and then lends money to what it hopes are creditworthy consumers, requiring them to pay back the funds with interest. The difference between the interest the bank pays on its deposits and the interest it is paid by its borrowers is its margin. Subtract from the margin administrative expenses, bad debt losses, and other costs, and you arrive at the bank's profit.

Of course, banks compete against one another, which means they will pay similar interest rates to depositors and charge similar interest rates to borrowers. Because of the intensely competitive nature of banking, banks can be a relatively low-cost source for car loans.

In some ways credit unions function like banks, but the key difference is the depositors "own" the credit union and operate it for mutual benefit. Individuals who are not members of the credit union can't obtain loans. But if you belong to a credit union through your employer, union, or fraternal organization, you will find it a good source for a low-cost loan.

"Alternative" Loan Sources

The first four sources of auto financing—finance companies, dealers, banks, and credit unions—are widely known and widely used. But the other three sources on the list have the potential to save you money versus these traditional sources. They go largely underutilized today, because relatively few people think to tap into them.

One "alternative" method of auto financing gaining popularity these days is the home equity line of credit. There's a simple reason for this surge in the use of home equity loans for car buying—the interest you pay on these loans is tax deductible. (Once upon a time all interest on consumer debt was tax deductible, but the Feds have tightened the screws in light of the budget deficit.) Depending on your tax bracket, you could save a considerable amount over the course of the loan. For example, if you're in the 31 percent income tax bracket and the home equity loan you use to purchase your vehicle has a 10 percent interest rate, when all is said and done, you'll pay an effective interest rate of around 7 percent. Over the course of a four-year loan on $20,000, this will save you about $1,350.

Using a home equity loan also has its downsides. If you haven't already established a home equity line, you might be required to pay for a property appraisal and a title search to assure the lender that you have the equity in your home to borrow against. You might also have to pay an origination fee and lender points (which, essentially, is cash due at the beginning of the loan). Pay close attention to these fees and charges because they could wipe out any savings you might realize because of the tax deductible nature of the interest you will pay.

> **Money Saving Tip**
>
> Some so-called experts warn against the use of home equity loans because a financial reversal could threaten the equity you have in your home. That is a potential threat, but the key issue is this: Don't take on any loan—car, home equity, or business—that you are not confident you can repay. If you repay a home equity loan you use to buy a car, it is usually a low-cost source of funds.

Another potential pitfall is the fact that some home equity loans carry variable interest rates. Standard auto loans are fixed-rate loans. You and the financial institution agree on an interest rate, and that's the rate you pay over the life of the loan. In contrast, variable rates fluctuate based on a key interest rate indicator within bounds specified by the loan contract. Because the rates vary, your monthly payments could vary widely as well. This can play havoc with your monthly budget.

Finally, acquiring a home equity loan means you're using the ownership you have in your home as collateral guaranteeing the loan. This has serious implications if you fail to pay off the loan. Look at it this way: If for one reason or another you can't pay off a standard car loan, the financial institution simply repossesses your vehicle. It's not pleasant, but it is simple. In essence, the vehicle itself was the collateral. But if you can't pay off a home equity loan, your home is, in theory at least, at risk. The lender can put a lien on it, and, depending on the money you owe and your equity in the house, seize it. This is an extremely rare occurrence, but it is something to keep in mind when you borrow against your home to finance your new vehicle.

Tapping Unorthodox Sources

The two other loan alternatives I suggested earlier, borrowing against insurance, investments, or retirement accounts and borrowing from friends and relatives, are the most unusual sources of car finance capital, yet they might prove to be among the least expensive of all seven I've mentioned.

You might be surprised to learn that you can borrow large sums at attractive interest rates on insurance, securities (stock) you hold, or even your 401(k). Check with your insurance agent and your insurance policies to find out if this is possible in your case. Your agent should be able to fill you in on the interest rate you will pay and the repayment requirements.

If you'd like to borrow on securities, your stockbroker is your best source of information. And the best source of information on loans against 401(k) retirement plans is the human resources department of the company where you originated your 401(k). In both these cases you are essentially borrowing from yourself, so the interest rate will be relatively low.

Finally, we have the ultimate low-interest source of auto loans—friends and relatives. You might not have the requisite cash to buy your next new car, but you might know someone who does. Furthermore, their assets might be languishing in a regular passbook savings account that's earning them minimal interest. Often, you can pay them back at double the passbook rate and still be way ahead of where you'd be if you took out a conventional car loan.

No, borrowing from friends and relatives isn't a source everyone should try to tap in on. But where appropriate, it can be a win-win situation. My only bit of advice, should you opt to go this route—please pay your friends and relatives back in a timely manner. The relationships you could lose will be your own.

Bet You Didn't Know

Co-signing a car loan is an age-old ritual that actually has a simple premise: The signer of the car loan bears the initial liability to repay the loan, but if he or she fails to do that, the financial institution can seek payment from the co-signer. Think of the co-signer as a relief pitcher, ready to go into the game if the starting pitcher (the signer of the loan) runs out of gas.

The Financing Bottom Line

Shop, shop, shop for your auto financing. Consider all the above-listed sources (which, by the way, are listed in descending order from those that are generally most expensive to those that are generally least expensive). Make phone calls to several financing sources before you go on your buying mission and note their terms. Be certain that you're comparing apples to apples with comparisons of APRs over the same loan length. Then get a loan preapproved from the low-cost institution you feel comfortable with.

When it comes time to talk with the dealership about financing, you want to examine two key areas: The interest rate you will be charged, which should be expressed in the standard "annualized percentage rate" (APR) and the length of the loan term.

Use Table 12.1 to calculate how much your monthly payment will be based on the APR, the total borrowed, and the length of the loan. Find the APR in the far left column of Table 12.1. Move right to the column for the term of the loan. Take the amount where the APR row and the loan length column intersect, and multiply the value by how many thousands of dollars you're borrowing. For example, multiply the amount by 12 if you're borrowing $12,000. The result will be the total monthly payment for the loan.

Table 12.1 Loan Payment Table

Annual Rate	Payment per $1,000 (Multiply payment amount in the appropriate column by $1000s borrowed to arrive at total monthly payment.)			
	Two years	*Three years*	*Four years*	*Five years*
7%	44.77	30.88	23.95	19.80
8%	45.23	31.34	24.41	20.28
9%	45.68	31.80	24.89	20.76
10%	46.14	32.27	25.36	21.25
11%	46.61	32.74	25.85	21.74
12%	47.07	33.21	26.33	22.24
13%	47.54	33.69	26.83	22.75
14%	48.01	34.18	27.33	23.27

In these days of very expensive vehicles, there is constant pressure to lower the monthly payment. In fact, many buyers key in on the monthly payment to the exclusion of everything else. But you must keep in mind that getting the lowest monthly payment doesn't mean you're getting the best deal. In fact, in most cases, quite the opposite is true.

Remember, there are two ways to achieve a lower monthly payment:

1. Obtain a lower interest rate.

2. Agree to a longer loan term.

You should attempt to achieve number one, and be very wary of those who would lead you into agreeing to number two. Getting a lower interest rate will save you money in the long run. Getting a longer-term loan will cost you money in the long run.

The Least You Need to Know

➤ When you finance, acquiring a vehicle becomes a three-transaction process: Buying the vehicle, buying the financing, and selling your current car.

➤ You can get many of the benefits of having cash by getting a loan preapproved before you enter the dealership. Shop, shop, shop for the best car loan terms.

➤ Determine how much you can afford to pay for a new vehicle by determining your cash on hand, your equity in your current vehicle, and your monthly budget of income and out-go.

➤ Tapping unorthodox sources of financing, like borrowing against current assets or borrowing from friends and relatives, could save you money.

The Best of Times, The Worst of Times

In This Chapter

➤ Timing's importance

➤ Conventional wisdom versus revisionist thinking

➤ Best week, best days, best hours

➤ Incentive time

I'm not sure who was the first person to say, "Timing is everything," but when it comes to the car market he or she had it right. Because the car and truck market is always in a state of flux and competitive pressures are intense, forging your deal at the correct moment has the potential to put you hundreds of dollars ahead.

The major difficulty lies in determining the right time to strike. Years ago, before the car market became riddled with cash-back offers, factory-to-dealer incentives, and cut-rate financing, it was much easier to determine the best time to buy a new car. These days, there are so many factors at work, many of them in conflict, it's much harder to point to specific days on the calendar as "hunting season." Nevertheless, this chapter provides some suggestions on timing.

The Best Months to Buy a New Car

The conventional thinking is that the mid-winter months, particularly January and February, are the best months to buy a new vehicle. In most of the country, the weather during these two months is the worst it will be all year. Since bad weather keeps customers from visiting new-car showrooms, and many buyers don't want to subject their brand-new vehicles to harsh winter weather right out of the box, dealerships are relatively empty.

Best Months to Buy

Conventional Thinking...	Revisionist Thinking...
January	April
February	May
August	June
September	October
	December

And, if the inclement weather weren't enough, a high percentage of consumers also find themselves "tapped out" after their holiday buying spree in December. Every day the mail brings another round of credit card bills, reminding consumers about the money they don't have. All this dreariness and gloom doesn't exactly put consumers in a car-buying mood.

In the dealerships during the depths of winter, the salespeople get tired of talking to each other, weary of the constant games of solitaire, and begin to ache for a real, bona fide customer to walk in the door. When that customer appears, so the conventional thinking goes, she or he is greeted with open arms and treated to the deal of a lifetime.

Almost equally good, again according to the conventional wisdom, are the waning days of summer, August and into September, before the next model year's vehicles begin to arrive. These two months have become so synonymous with bargain shopping that many manufacturers and dealer groups sponsor special "Bargain Clearance Days" promotions during this period. The new models are coming, and dealers want to clear out the old to make way for the new. Spectacular deals are the natural benefit for those smart enough to hold off until late summer, or so the theory goes.

Revisionist Thinking

While there is something to be said for both theories—that mid-winter and the end-of-summer are the two prime buying seasons—let me offer both support for those theories and some contrarian views.

Although the mid-winter doldrums hit the car business nearly every year and there are good deals to be had in this period, they are far from guaranteed. For one thing, nothing says *you'll* be free from the post-holiday bills that snow under so many others, and if you're cash-poor, you're not in a good position to bargain. You're likely to make a lower down payment and finance more of your purchase—and buying is more expensive that way.

Further, there is no guarantee that the dealer will offer you a better deal than you would receive at other times of the year. To get yourself a favorable deal in the depths of winter, you must leverage the fact that you are one of the few buyers in the market at the moment and you're in no hurry to buy. If you don't, the dealership might well try to make this month's rent off you and your deal alone, since there might not be many other deals. At the very least, you're likely to be double- or triple-teamed by the dealership's most crafty salesmen. Why not? They have time on their hands, and you're the only customer they've seen in weeks!

There are other negatives about mid-winter as well. It's a bad time to sell your current vehicle or even trade it in. Private buyers are considerably less eager to brave winter weather, and, just as new-car buyers are cash-poor, so are used-car shoppers. Lacking customer traffic, dealers aren't very eager to load up on used-car inventory either.

Finally, while some manufacturers crank up their incentives during the middle of winter, many of them prefer to fish when the fish are biting and save their cash-back and special financing offers for spring. Weak sales through the middle of winter is an annual rite, and most manufacturers prepare for it by slimming production in December. With fewer vehicles in the pipeline, there's little pressure to put on a sale.

So while mid-winter might be a good time to buy, it takes more to get a good deal than just strolling into a dealership in January or February.

Late Summer Bargains?

August and September do have some appeal as new-car shopping months. Most manufacturers want to get rid of current model-year vehicles. If a large number of them are still clogging dealers' showrooms when the new model year's vehicles arrive, it will have a very chilling effect on sales of the new models. Because of this, factory incentives run rampant in August and September on all but the most popular models.

Late summer is also a decent time to sell your current vehicle. By then most people have recovered from their overspending at Christmas (if they're ever going to), and the weather is conducive to shopping. In addition, many car owners who are wondering whether their old heap will make it through another winter decide to buy a newer car. Traffic in dealer showrooms is good, which helps used car sales. That, in turn, boosts the value of your trade-in.

Balancing all this, however, is the fact that if you buy a new, current-model-year vehicle in September, in less than a month it will be one year old.

Why? Because the auto industry works on a 12-month cycle called a *model year* that traditionally begins every October 1 and ends every September 30. Further, every vehicle on the market has an assigned model year that's part and parcel of its legal identification. In fact, the vehicle model year is recognized by both federal and state law.

> ### Bet You Didn't Know
>
> The traditional model year begins October 1, but the federal government allows auto manufacturers some leeway in model-year designation. If a vehicle goes on sale any time after January 1 of a particular year, it can be designated as the following year's model. For instance, a new vehicle that hits the market on January 2, 1997, can be designated a 1998 vehicle.

What this means is, every August and September, thousands of bargain shoppers may outsmart themselves.

How Bargain Hunters Fall into the Depreciation Trap

Let's say Betty Bluenose is a bargain hunter. There's nothing she likes more than saving a few bucks. Betty is in the market for a new car and decides that she wants a Pickney Walrus 110. Ever the shrewd shopper, she waits until after Labor Day to launch her buying expedition.

Betty does some homework and discovers two important facts:

1. The Manufacturer's Suggested Retail Price for the Pickney Walrus 110, equipped as she would like it, is $29,000 plus a $600 *destination charge.* (Which is essentially a charge the manufacturers make because they're manufacturers and you're not.)

2. And, to help clear out this year's inventory, Pickney Motor Manufacturing is offering its dealers $2,000 in cash for every Walrus 110 they sell during the months of

August and September. (This last bit of info she gleans from *Automotive News*, a weekly industry newspaper available in many libraries.)

Bet You Didn't Know

Every car manufacturer charges its dealers a *destination charge* on each vehicle, but it has little to do with getting the vehicle to its destination, and it does not vary by the distance from the factory to the dealer. It's a charge of $300 to $800 that the dealer then passes on to the car buyer. A great system, isn't it?

She charges into her local Pickney dealership, wielding this information like a saber, and gets the salesperson to slash $2,000 from the price of the vehicle. That's nearly a 7 percent price cut. (Of course, she leaves the dealer with his full profit margin, because, in essence, the dealer is selling the vehicle at its suggested retail price.)

What Betty doesn't realize is that in less than four weeks, her current-model-year Walrus with the MSRP of $29,600, for which she paid $27,600, will be worth just $23,000 at retail and a lowly $20,000 wholesale. And, fair or not, Clem Puttybrain's Pickney Walrus 110, which he has been driving since the previous November, 10 months before Betty bought hers, will be worth almost the identical amount.

Because the model year changed, Betty's Walrus 110 has depreciated $4,600 in the period of less than four weeks, while Clem's car, which might have cost $1,000 more than Betty's identical car, depreciated $5,600 over 10 months. Betty's monthly depreciation is $4,600; Clem's is $560. So who's the bargain shopper now, I ask you?

If Betty is forced to sell her new vehicle quickly, say two months after she bought it, she will take a bigger loss on a per-month basis than Clem would if he were to encounter the same circumstances. If she holds the vehicle for several years, she will make up her early loss and outperform Clem. Unlike Betty, Clem had the opportunity of driving a current model year vehicle for 10 months instead of just a few weeks.

The real winner in this scenario might be Lena, who waited until October 15 to buy her Walrus 110. Her vehicle is the same model year as Clem's and Betty's, and it had 5,000 miles of demonstrator use on it, but she paid just $23,000—$4,600 less than bargain-shopper Betty and $5,600 less than early buyer Clem.

The Best Week to Buy a Car

Three units of time are important in the car business: The model year, the calendar year, and each month. These are the "reporting periods," the various time frames in which vehicle sales are tabulated and reported to manufacturers' home offices and to the press. Because of the intensely competitive nature of the business, there is always pressure to turn in a good report. Car companies practically go to war to earn "bestseller" titles for the model year and calendar year, and the monthly figures are highly scrutinized as well.

On the dealer front, the monthly sales reports are even more important. Many manufacturers operate on what is referred to in the industry as a "turn-and-earn" basis. This means that the dealers must sell vehicles in the current month ("turn them over") to earn the privilege of getting hot-selling, high-demand vehicles the following month. In practice, if a dealer is close to reaching a threshold of unit sales that will gain him more high-demand, high-profit vehicles in the following month, it could be in his best interest to sell you a vehicle below his cost.

Bet You Didn't Know

Experts estimate that Ford spends millions in extra marketing and incentive dollars each year to maintain the Taurus's position as the best-selling car in America.

Of course, don't hold your breath waiting for this to happen, but if it will ever happen, it will be in the last week of a month, maybe even the last day of the last week of the month. Getting a deal like this is akin to winning Lotto and about as rare, but even if you don't hit the Big Spin, the last week in the month is still a good buying week. Dealerships and individual salesmen are all eager to turn in good monthly sales figures. In many dealerships the salesperson who sells the most vehicles each month gets a cash bonus, so if your salesperson is vying for the monthly title she or he might work extra hard for you.

Money Saving Tip
The last few days in the life of an incentive like cash-back or discount financing are excellent days to purchase a vehicle.

Again I must warn you, though, it takes more to get a good deal than just waltzing into a dealership during the last week of the month. You have to do your homework, and *use* the knowledge you gain. Given a consumer who has done the research and is prepared to bargain negotiating in the first week of the month, and another consumer with little knowledge and negotiating skills buying in the last week in the month, I can guarantee you the first consumer will get a better deal.

The Best Days to Buy a Car

As just mentioned, the best day of the week to buy a car might well be the last day of the month. Whether it falls on a Monday, Thursday, or Saturday doesn't really matter. Extrapolating from that, the best day of the year to buy a car might be December 31. Not only is it the last day of a month, it's the last day of the year. Some buyers swear by it. You might have better things to do that day.

There's little doubt that the best days to shop for a new vehicle are the quiet days—Tuesday, Wednesday, and Thursday in most locales. You'll get more attention from the salesperson on the less-hectic days, unlike the busy weekends when the salesman is looking past you half the time, trying to scope out a real "buyer." On the other hand, busy weekends can be a good time to use the dealership as an auto show. If you say you're "just looking" the salespeople will generally leave you alone.

Bet You Didn't Know

Often dealers' best salespeople don't work on the quiet days of the week. They want to be around on the weekends, when most of the action hits.

In my opinion the best day to buy a vehicle is the day you feel well-rested, alert, and prepared to make a deal. If you are distracted by large crowds or if you are distracted by distracted salespeople, pick a quiet day to make your deal. The important thing is to give yourself the opportunity to make your decisions in a calm, rational manner. For some that occurs on the weekends, for others in the relative calm of a weekday night.

The Best Hours of the Day to Buy

In many ways, I just have to say ditto to what I just suggested. Certainly, there is something to the belief that dealers might be more likely to give you a better deal toward closing time, simply because they don't want you to walk out the door never to return. If you're talking about the last hour of the week or the last hour of the month, there might be that much more impetus to "close" your sale with a better-than-average deal.

Bet You Didn't Know

Experts say that caffeine can actually increase your alertness and mental acuity. So, when that dealer salesperson offers you a cola or a coffee, consider taking the offer.

Appealing as this may sound, if you're not alert or prepared as the dealership reaches closing time, this gambit won't work for you; it will work against you. Instead of putting the pressure on the dealership and the salesperson, you might feel pressure yourself. And when you feel pressure to make a deal, odds are the deal you make isn't going to be a very good one.

Let's face it, you're an amateur negotiator going up against negotiating pros. You need to be at your best to hold your own. So if you feel sharper and more energized in the morning, try to make your deal then. If you're a night person, head for the Midnight Madness sale. The key is keeping your wits about you. If at any time you feel too tired or too confused to make a decision, then don't. Trust me, there will be cars for sale tomorrow. And the next day. And the next.

The All-Time Best Hour of the Best Day of the Best Month to Buy a Car

I hinted at it earlier in this chapter, but now I'll finish the thought. The best hour of the best day of the best week of the best month to buy a car is when the manufacturer has an incentive you can use on the vehicle you have decided to buy. In the past several years the car business has become incentive riddled. These manufacturer-subsidized "sales" take various forms: Special lease offers, discount financing, factory-to-dealer cash back, factory-to-customer cash, even extended maintenance and warranty coverage. Car companies have found that when they turn the incentive faucet on, sales follow. When they turn the incentive faucet off, sales dry up.

Money Saving Tip
Don't get too concerned if you miss a manufacturer-sponsored incentive. If it worked once, the manufacturer will undoubtedly run it, or something similar, again.

Since most companies don't want their vehicles to be on sale 52 weeks a year (if they are it isn't much of a "sale," is it?), they will strategically apply incentives and then remove them throughout the year. Your mission, should you decide to accept it, is to acquire your new vehicle in the midst of an incentive period that makes sense in your individual circumstances on the model you want to buy.

Certainly, the key is that the special offer work for you. For example, a special lease offer, no matter how attractive, won't do you any good if you've resolved to buy your next vehicle. And a discount financing offer for a two-year loan is meaningless to you if you feel a four-year loan is much better in your present circumstances.

Remember, the manufacturers put on these "sales events" for two reasons. The obvious one is selling more vehicles under the terms of the sale. But the other reason is to create an impression that now is the time to buy, an impression that generates sales at more profitable terms to the manufacturer and dealer.

How Do You Find These Incentives?

Some of these special offers are hard to miss. Manufacturers and dealer groups spew the information on special leases, cash back, and discount financing over the airwaves and in newspapers with such frequency that it's hard for anyone but a Montana recluse to avoid it.

On the other hand, factory-to-dealer offers are largely invisible unless you know where to look. One good place to look is the industry trade publication *Automotive News*, available at many libraries and on some larger newsstands. Its "Incentive Watch" column lists current manufacturer incentive programs, including factory-to-dealer cash offers.

Another source of incentive information is *CarDeals*, a newsletter published by the non-profit Center for the Study of Services, a Washington, D.C.-based organization. Information on purchasing the newsletter can be obtained by calling 800-475-7283.

If you are a member of the American Automobile Association (a.k.a AAA or Triple A) or one of its affiliated auto clubs, you can also obtain incentive information for its pricing and buying service. Call your local auto club branch for more information.

Automotive Consumer Services, an Irvine, California, firm, markets pricing reports and other information at 800-790-9992. IntelliChoice, a Campbell, California-based information service, offers incentive information and the industry's most detailed examination of factory-subsidized leases. Its toll-free number is 800-227-2665.

For you online addicts out there, IntelliChoice has a site on the World Wide Web. A service called AutoVantage is available on CompuServe, America Online, and Prodigy, and it provides a wide range of pricing and buying services. Edmunds Publications also tracks incentives and offers this information on the Internet at www.edmunds.com.

Money Saving Tip
Many car-buying and price services track incentives with up-to-the-minute accuracy. Listings for them appear in Chapters 15 and 19.

Taking Advantage of the Incentive

With knowledge of the incentive offer in hand, you can approach dealers from a position of strength. If, for example, the incentive is $2,000 in factory-to-dealer cash, you know that the dealer has $2,000 more to work with in addition to his normal gross margin on the vehicle. Some or all of that money should become part of the discount you receive on the price of the vehicle. And, since you know how long the offer will last, you know how much time you have to negotiate a positive deal for yourself.

As always, the best procedure is to refrain from acting impulsively. Don't put any pressure on yourself to buy, and don't let the dealer pressure you either. Just remember, any incentive offer out there is very likely to be repeated at a later date. In fact, the new terms might well be more appealing than the old.

To sum up, the best day to buy a car is the day you feel prepared and comfortable about the transaction you're going to make.

The Least You Need to Know

➤ Timing your purchase is important in getting the best deal you can.

➤ The conventional wisdom is that the mid-winter and the end of summer are the two best times to buy.

➤ Other good times to buy are in the spring, when many incentive programs are in force, and the fall, when there are bargains on last year's models and the current year's models will be "new" for the longest period of time.

➤ The last week in the month is the best week to buy.

➤ The best days to shop are the quiet days—Tuesday, Wednesday, and Thursday.

➤ The best day to buy a car is the day you feel alert and prepared to negotiate a deal.

➤ The best time of day to buy a car: ditto above.

➤ The all-time best hour of the best day of the best month to buy a car is the hour you feel alert and prepared to make a deal, and there is a current incentive on the model you want to buy that makes sense in your circumstances.

Chapter 14

The Arabian Bazaar: Dealers and Dealerships

In this chapter, let's take a brief look at the auto business from the retail side, because for you as an aspiring car buyer, that's where the action is. Industry estimates show that there are fewer than 25,000 new-car dealers in the United States, and that figure is dropping (down from 40,000 in 1955) as dealers consolidate and offer more lines of vehicles through fewer stores. Some place the figure as low as 22,000, but to simplify the calculations, let's say there are 25,000.

All this means that in a typical year, 25,000 U.S. dealers will sell new vehicles to about 10 to 11 million individual buyers. That works out to about 400 new-vehicle sales per dealer per year. In other words, 1.1 new-vehicle sales per day.

Now imagine for a minute the typical dealership, the building it's housed in, the vast amount of real estate around it, and the people it employs. Consider for a moment the advertising it does on television and the ads it runs in the newspapers. All this supported by 1.1 vehicle sales a day.

Don't shed any tears for car dealers. The fact is, some of them are among the richest people I've ever met. However, the point is being a car dealer is not an easy business, and, of more interest to you, you are a very important person to the car dealer. She or he needs his 1.1 sales each day and today *you could be the 1*.

What Dealers Try to Do

If you're a businessperson and you know you're only going to sell one thing today, what would you do? Well, I know what I'd do—I'd do everything I could to maximize my profit on that one sale. Dealers, being perfectly rational businesspeople, do exactly that. Virtually all of their efforts are devoted to racking up the biggest profits they can on each individual sale.

As I mentioned in Chapter 12, they institute sales systems, after-sales systems, and service systems that are designed to wring as much money out of each transaction as they possibly can. And there's nothing morally reprehensible about this. They're just trying to make a buck like everyone else. So if they offer you $25 floor mats for $100, a $60 wax job for $300, or a $400 extended warranty for $750, don't be offended. Just say no.

The Dealer-Manufacturer Marriage

Many consumers look at a Dodge dealer as part of Chrysler Corporation, a Chevy dealer as part of General Motors, and a Ford dealer as part of Ford Motor Company. But that's not the case at all. Each dealer is an independent businessperson who holds the rights to sell one or more car lines in a particular area.

While the ideal is that the manufacturer and the dealer operate in perfect harmony, whistling show tunes while walking hand-in-hand through the verdant meadow of customer satisfaction, the reality is that the manufacturer and the dealer are often in conflict. Sources of conflict arise on many different issues. Among them:

➤ Manufacturers want to sell as many vehicles as they can, and one way to sell a lot of vehicles is to have a lot of retail outlets for those vehicles. What this means for the individual dealer, though, is more competition, something she or he needs like a second nose.

Bet You Didn't Know

Most dealers look at nearby dealers who sell the same brand or brands of cars and trucks as their primary competitors, not dealers who sell competitive brands of vehicles.

➤ Manufacturers can never seem to build enough of the hot-selling models, but always have plenty of the slow-selling vehicles. To "encourage" dealers to try to move the slugs, many manufacturers allocate each dealer's supply of hot-sellers based on sales of the rest of the line. No matter how equitably this is done, many dealers have problems with it.

➤ Manufacturers have instituted lengthy warranties on virtually all of their new vehicles, but, in an effort to limit their warranty costs, they are often a bit stingy about paying dealers for warranty work on customer cars. This means that good dealers often have to pay for warranty claims work with their own funds, while, at the same time, unscrupulous dealers charge the manufacturers for warranty work that isn't performed.

The bottom line is that even when manufacturers talk the talk of customer satisfaction, many dealers don't walk the walk. Conversely, some dealers do a much better job of satisfying their customers than you expect, given what they get from their factories in terms of product quality, training, and support. It's a jungle out there.

Shopping for a Dealer

In addition to shopping for a vehicle, you must also shop for a dealer from which to buy that vehicle. Both choices are very important. J.D. Power and Associates' magic formula that determines the company's famous Customer Satisfaction Index gauges both areas to be nearly equal in weight.

What this means is, if you pick the wrong vehicle, you're screwed, and if you pick the wrong dealer, you're also screwed. But how do you shop for a dealer?

It's not easy because there are no published guides to good dealers. There are, however, some good places to start. One gambit is choosing a model from a brand known for the satisfaction its dealers provide. The stellar example of that is General Motors' Saturn Corporation, which has become a perpetual leader in what is known as "sales satisfaction"—the customer's experience in buying the vehicle and taking delivery. These days Saturn is more well-known for the quality of the buying experience than for the quality of its vehicles.

The Japanese luxury brands—Lexus and Infiniti—are also heralded for having good, accommodating dealers. These brands regularly score significantly better than average in J.D. Power and Associates and *Consumer Reports* studies on dealers, as illustrated in Table 14.1.

Table 14.1   J.D. Power and Associates 1995 Sales Satisfaction Index—Top 10 Brand Names in Sales Satisfaction

Brand Name	Sales Satisfaction Index	Brand Name	Sales Satisfaction Index
Saturn	160	Mercedes-Benz	147
Infiniti	150	Audi	145
Cadillac	149	Lincoln	141
Lexus	149	BMW	140
Volvo	148	Jaguar	140

What these brands (Saturn, Lexus, and Infiniti) share is the fact that they were started from scratch within the last decade or so. The architects of each of these brands' dealer organizations were able to pick and choose individual dealers, unlike brands that have been in existence longer and are basically "stuck with" the dealers they've got.

These new brands also have significantly fewer dealers than older brands. For example, Saturn is covering the United States with around 350 dealers, while Chevrolet has about 4,000. This means dealers bump heads less often, competition between dealers is some-what decreased, which in turn allows them to afford to satisfy their customers better.

Money Saving Tip
Individual state franchise laws make it very difficult and very costly for a manufacturer to "fire" a dealer. However, you can and should "fire" a dealer by walking away if you're uncomfortable with the deal being offered or the dealer's attitude toward you.

Of the older brands with traditional, large dealer networks, Buick, Oldsmobile, Cadillac, Lincoln, and Mercury are noted for satisfying their customers better than the norm. Some would also suggest, with more than a grain of truth, that the relatively older customers of these brands are easier to satisfy and not as put off by stupid dealer tricks as are younger buyers.

Among the European imports, Mercedes-Benz, Saab, Volvo, and BMW are most often cited as being among the best. In this instance, the late-Eighties success of the Japanese luxury brands lit a fire under the European importers and their dealers that caused rapid improvements.

Interestingly, lumped down at the bottom of the least-customer-friendly dealers are those of some of the highest quality vehicles available, including Toyota, Honda, Nissan, and Mazda. Of course, these manufacturers would tell you that their customers are the pickiest out there, and there is some truth to that. It should also be noted that many of these dealerships had their heyday in the era of the so-called Voluntary Restraint Agreement (the agreement that limited imports of Japanese cars), when many of them were tacking thousands of dollars in pure profit to the sticker prices.

Relying on Personal Referral

I can't tell you how often I've been asked to recommend a good dealer of this brand or that brand over the years, and frankly I'm reluctant to give much advice to friends and acquaintances about individual dealers, because things can and do change very fast within a dealership. As volatile as the car business is, salespeople, sales managers, and even dealer principals can be gone overnight. But if you have a friend, relative, or acquaintance who enjoyed a good relationship with a dealer, you should certainly take that into account in your search for the right dealer.

I would not, however, take the referral at face value. Several times over the years dealers have told me they just love personal referrals—because referral customers can be the most profitable customers they will see all year. At first glance this sounds backwards, but when you consider how dealers' minds work, it really makes sense.

Say a good friend tells Lonnie Melmeister, "If you're going to buy a car, you should go see Larry Whitebelt over at Potash of Nebbishtowne. He'll take care of you." He'll take care of you all right. Lonnie, looking for any way to avoid a negative confrontation with a dealer, trots over to Potash of Nebbishtowne, asks to speak to Larry Whitebelt, and Larry couldn't be nicer. He's pleasant, well-spoken, and well-dressed, and Lonnie likes him.

The only trouble is, Lonnie has walked in with his guard down. He's expecting to be taken care of, so he hasn't researched the vehicle he wants to buy, he didn't shop for financing before he walked into the dealership, and he has no idea what his trade-in is worth. So Larry Whitebelt makes him feel as good as gold while he relieves him of every loose piece of gold he has, except for the fillings in his back molars.

Lemon
Many car salesmen use "bird dogs," individuals who steer business their way by giving personal referrals. Most often these "bird dogs" get a piece of the action if the person they referred buys a vehicle.

The lesson to be learned here is not to *ignore* referrals. Indeed, you should listen to them closely and speak to those salespeople and dealers who have been genuinely recommended. But then put them to the test. By the time you complete this section of the book, you will know how to gauge the worth of your trade-in vehicle, you'll know how to shop for financing, and you'll know how to find what the dealer paid for the vehicle you want to buy. When you've done your homework in all these areas, hold the dealer's offer up to all these standards. That way, you can see whether the personal referral was a good one, or just a misguided or even slightly dishonest attempt to help. Of course, it's pretty clear what to do if someone tells you they had a bad dealer experience: Take your business elsewhere; there are plenty of dealers who will treat you with honesty and respect.

The Dealer and His Salespeople

There are essentially two types of salespeople working in dealerships today. The first type is the career salesperson. He (and it usually is a he) has been selling cars for most of his adult life. He's almost undoubtedly worked in several dealerships during his career. In fact, he frequently moves from dealership to dealership depending on what brands are selling best and who's offering the best compensation. Most often he works on commission, and he likes it that way because he really knows how to "move the iron." He laughs at today's emphasis on "customer satisfaction" because he has been providing satisfaction, in his own way, of course, one customer at a time for a long, long time.

The second type is the more common type. He or she (and there are more and more *she's* in this line of work today) is not really a car salesperson at all. At least that's not the way they see themselves, because a month ago, before they got the pink slip or moved in from Idaho, they were doing something else. And if they get their way and the breaks go right, they'll be doing something else again soon. They really don't know much about cars or much about the car business, but this is what they're doing for now, and they're making the best of it.

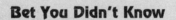

Bet You Didn't Know

Retaining good salespeople is one of every dealer's most difficult problems, because salespeople, by definition, are always looking for a better deal.

The common thread between these two vastly disparate types of car salespeople is the fact that they don't know a whole lot about the vehicles they're selling. In the case of the veteran car salesperson, he thinks too much product knowledge is a waste of time that could be better spent making cold calls or following up leads. In the case of the novice car salesperson, she or he hasn't had the time or the training to learn much about the products. And when it comes to competing products of other brands, they generally know even less. They might be prepared to list a few ways the vehicle they represent is better than its competitors, but that's likely the extent of it. What this means is: Basing your vehicle-buying decisions on their advice is absolute folly.

Why don't dealers do a better job training their employees? It's not so much they don't want to as much as it's extremely difficult to keep up with a workforce that is constantly turning over. Manufacturers offer terrific training these days, but it's frustrating to spend several hundred dollars to send a sales manager on a product knowledge trip, only to have that sales manager quit to work at a competitive dealership the week he gets back. In addition, many dealers started their careers as salespeople, and they figure they got along without much product knowledge. Why waste their salespeople's precious time?

How Are Salespeople Paid?

In an effort to boost their level of customer satisfaction, some dealerships have moved away from straight-commission compensation systems, but even in these dealerships, a substantial portion of the salesperson's pay is based on number of vehicles sold and/or dealership profitability. While the transaction in the dealership is not exactly "you versus the salesperson," it often comes down to something close to it. There's only so much potential profit available on each individual vehicle, and if you as a buyer cut that margin, it means there will be less for the dealership employees and dealer to divvy up.

Bet You Didn't Know

Most salespeople are more expert on the dealer's compensation system than they are on the vehicles they're selling.

Many dealers also use weekly, monthly, and yearly bonus systems and contests to reward salespeople for selling the most vehicles in a given period, with scores of variations on that theme. Dealers and manufacturers use "spiffs"—on-the-spot cash bonuses for selling a particular model, most often a slow-seller. Many compensation schemes motivate salespeople to sell vehicles the dealer wants sold instead of vehicles customers want to buy, resulting in negative effects on customer satisfaction. So if you walk in looking for a blue mid-size sedan and, after hearing your request, the salesperson tries to steer you toward a tiny red convertible, you can bet that some type of spiff is at work.

Down at the nitty-gritty level, the salesperson has a simple goal: As he or she very rightly should, the salesperson wants to make the most profitable deal for the dealership possible. You, in contrast, don't begrudge the dealership and the salesperson a reasonable profit but you would like to be one of the decision-makers on what that profit is.

What Salespeople Like to Hear

As I mentioned in Chapter 12, a salesperson's worst nightmare is spending hours with a potential buyer, walking them through model selection, color selection, equipment selection, trade-in assessment and financing, only to have the deal blow up in her or his face at the last minute.

The reason the salesperson hates when this happens—and it happens a lot—is that it costs him or her money. Most of a salesperson's pay depends on sales, so wasting time on a potential buyer who doesn't buy, for whatever reasons, is a major downer.

This is one reason salespeople ask you so many personal questions so soon after you meet. They are sizing you up, *qualifying* you, in the industry parlance, in an attempt to determine if you can actually afford the vehicle you purport to be interested in.

Since, after reading this far, you won't waste your time looking at vehicles you can't afford, you'll zip through this questioning with no problem. In fact, when the questioning starts you can shortstop the little dance by saying, "I don't want to waste your time or my time. I've checked my finances, and I know what I can afford." This alone will set you apart from the looky-loos, and the salesperson will respect you for it.

After you do your shopping, research competitive financing, and either sell your current car or get a good idea of its value as a trade-in, there's something else that will be music to a salesperson's ears. Tell them, "I'm a qualified buyer, and I'm ready to buy a car today if I get the right deal." Of course, you must actually be ready to buy that day, but if you are, this short statement will immediately get the salesperson's attention.

The Least You Need to Know

➤ The average car dealer sells 1.1 vehicles per day, so dealers try to maximize their profit on every sale.

➤ Some manufacturers promise more in customer satisfaction than their dealers deliver. Shop for a vehicle from a brand known for high levels of customer satisfaction.

➤ Take personal referrals on good dealers and salespeople with a grain of salt.

➤ Dealers motivate their salespeople with money and bonuses, so beware if a salesperson tries to steer you toward a particular model.

Part 5
Getting the Best Deal You Can

Part 5 takes the mystery out of vehicle pricing. You'll learn the difference between the Manufacturer's Suggested Retail Price and the dealer invoice price. Part 5 also helps you determine whether leasing or buying is best for you in your current financial situation. It also reveals the pitfalls inherent in leasing. This part will also help you brush up on your dickering techniques and prepare a negotiating plan. If you don't want to negotiate for yourself, this will outline your alternatives.

You must make certain that the deal you made survives your encounters with the dealership sales manager and finance and insurance manager. If you're not careful, add-on purchases like alarm systems and extended warranties can run up your costs considerably. And there are some add-on costs that you may not be able to avoid, no matter how hard you try. Part 5 also covers the right way to take delivery of your new vehicle. Many people drive off the dealer's lot with cars and trucks that are riddled with flaws. And if you get yourself a lemon through no fault of your own, this section will point out remedies.

Chapter 15

There's the Price, and Then There's the Price

In This Chapter

➤ The purchase price versus the suggested retail price

➤ Paying "over sticker"

➤ Dealer invoice prices and value pricing

➤ Your transaction goals

Nothing in the automobile-buying experience is more fraught with anxiety than the tap-dance over the final price. Auto prices are as ethereal as an angel's sigh, as easy to catch hold of as a dragonfly's wing. Yet nobody wants to get "taken" and pay more for their vehicle than the last person. And unfortunately, the auto industry's traditional method of doing business breeds mistrust like a swamp breeds mosquitoes.

If something sounds too good to be true, it usually is, and nowhere is that more true than in the automobile industry. Yes, some people get much better deals than others, and reading this book gives you a leg up on most "civilians". But incredible, unbelievable "steals" on new cars and trucks just don't happen. The car market is too competitive and too sophisticated for that.

Yes, you can save hundreds, even thousands of dollars on the purchase of a new vehicle if you know what you're doing. This chapter gives you some help in getting the best price.

Demystifying the Manufacturer's Suggested Retail Price

One of the biggest causes of confusion in the automobile business is the Manufacturer's Suggested Retail Price. The MSRP, displayed by law on the window sticker of every new vehicle sold in America, is the price the manufacturer *suggests* the dealer charge. Since the dealer is an independent businessman, the manufacturer has no way to enforce this price. Indeed, Federal anti-trust laws would make any attempt to do this illegal.

Because of this, the MSRP is not an actual price in the accepted sense. When you go to the drugstore to buy a tube of toothpaste, you pay the price listed. You don't think of paying anything else. But when it comes to cars the conventional wisdom is, "Nobody but idiots pay the sticker price."

Some 40 years after the Monroney label (the infamous window sticker) was instituted, it's hard to believe it was brought into being for consumer protection. That's because over the years it has caused so much confusion, hand-wringing, and obfuscation that one is hard-pressed to see the consumer benefit. For example, wouldn't it be better if each dealer simply posted its "cash price," rather than some largely fictitious manufacturer-inspired stab at it? That's the way retailers price virtually every other item we buy.

Let's Talk Terms

The Manufacturer's Suggested Retail Price is neither a real price (since relatively few buyers pay it) nor even a realistic suggestion of the retail price (since the manufacturers expect a negotiated price between dealer and consumer.) It's a largely fictitious number that serves as the starting point for negotiation.

Unfortunately, things aren't that simple in the automobile business. These days the manufacturers know that relatively few buyers will pay their "suggested" price, yet they must walk a tightrope in establishing their suggested list prices. They can't afford for them to be too high, because, though few consumers actually pay the sticker price, they do use sticker prices for comparison purposes. And they can't afford to go too low, because they want to give their dealers some maneuvering room to offer the customer a discount while still making their needed profit.

Who Pays the List Price and Why

Several groups of people pay the list price for their automobiles:

1. Those who are so wealthy and so busy they don't have time to dicker.

2. Those who are so unsophisticated that they think that's their only option.

3. Those who just can't face the confrontation of negotiating with a salesperson.

4. Those who, after a great deal of research, find value in vehicles that command their sticker prices or even more.

If you're currently reading this book, it's doubtful that you fall into category number one, and if you began reading as a member of category number two, I'm sure you're well past that by now. Only you and your therapist know if you're a category number three member, and if you are, Saturn Corporation seems to have been created just for you. So let's concentrate on category number four.

People in Category four recognize the realities of capitalism. They understand the law of supply and demand, and they don't fight it—they know dealers are trying to make an honest buck. So when they begin to price-shop a high-demand vehicle and find that the dealer wants sticker price or even more, they simply realize that they are shopping for a vehicle that is much in demand and whose supply is short.

Some examples: As this is being written, sport utility vehicles are all the rage. Factories can't seem to build enough of them. This has kept the prices of many sport utilities—Ford Explorer and Chevrolet Tahoe, for example—near, at, and in some cases above the "sticker" price. A few years ago, the Mazda Miata sports car was the object of the same sort of high-demand, short-supply situation.

Some dealers boost the vehicle's price simply by adding another sticker next to the Monroney label that displays the MSRP. Often the price addition is labeled something obscure, like ADM (for additional dealer markup) or MVA (market value adjustment). Another dealer ploy is to fill the vehicle with low-value, high-profit items like floor mats, pin striping, and cheap alarm systems, and then charge high prices for these add-ons, which are not included on the sticker.

Sadly, the Monroney label influences many dealers to take these somewhat devious routes to extra profit. In the absence of a Federally mandated sticker, it's my opinion that most of them would simply set their prices at market levels, the same way everything else is priced.

On the vast majority of vehicles, the price you aim for should be somewhat less than the sticker price. But if you run into several dealers who are asking a price higher than the MSRP for a particular vehicle, just remember they are not trying to rip you off; they are just doing their job, which, as you know, is trying to maximize the profit on their 1.1 sale each day.

Dealer Holdbacks and How They Affect You

If you thought the whirlwind revolving around Manufacturer's Suggested Retail Prices was confused and convoluted, wait until you hear about *dealer holdback*. You may be better off not knowing, but I'll tell you anyway. For each vehicle dealers buy from most manufacturers, a small percentage of the price is refunded to them when the vehicle is sold. This money is "held back" by the factory, then refunded later, most often quarterly. What it amounts to is a small, built-in discount on the price of every vehicle.

Currently, the holdback offered by the domestic manufacturers—General Motors, Ford, and Chrysler—is 3 percent of the MSRP. Holdback for other makes is usually less, right around 2 percent.

While this doesn't seem like a large amount, in total, it can run into serious money. For example, let's take Potash of Nebbishtowne, our average dealership, which sells 400 vehicles a year. Being incredibly average, each vehicle has an MSRP of $20,000. Since Potash is a domestic brand, the holdback is 3 percent, which translates to $600 on each vehicle. Certainly $600 is an amount you'd probably rather have in your pocket. On top of that, when you multiply that $600 by the 400 vehicles Potash of Nebbishtowne sells per annum, you've got yourself $240,000. A quarter of a million bucks is a nice, round figure in anybody's book.

Let's Talk Terms

The dollar amount refunded to the dealer by the manufacturer after a vehicle is sold is referred to as **holdback**.

This means a dealership could sell you a vehicle at what appears to be its cost and still make a gross profit of between 2 and 3 percent. This is something you should keep in mind when negotiating with the dealer. Don't, however, expect the dealer or the salesperson to sell you the vehicle at the invoice price just because they stand to make some money in holdback. If most dealers had to rely strictly on holdback for the revenue to keep their businesses going, they'd quickly go broke.

Dealer Invoice: What Does It Mean to You?

With just a little effort you can determine within a few dollars what the dealer paid for the vehicle you are about to buy. When you stop and think about it, that's one heck of a weapon for your price-negotiation arsenal.

Let's Talk Terms

The amount the dealer paid for a vehicle, before holdback, special reductions and incentives, is known as the **dealer invoice price**.

In the car business, a number of publications and services can provide you with "dealer invoice" pricing. This information is available for the vast majority of vehicles on the American market and the even wider variety of options and option packages that accompany those vehicles. Using this information you can determine, often to the penny, the amount the dealer paid for the vehicle you want to buy.

Certainly, knowing what the dealer paid gives you some idea of what the dealer might accept as a sales price. If nothing else, it may define the lowest level the dealer can go and still make a gross profit on the sale. But the sad fact is that knowing the dealer invoice price might not get you much closer to the price you should pay than knowing the Manufacturer's Suggested Retail Price. There are several reasons for this:

1. In a vehicle market filled with incentives, especially manufacturer-to-dealer cash, a dealer may be able to sell a vehicle at a below-invoice price and still make a substantial profit.

2. In a market where dealers must sell some less-desirable vehicles to get an allocation of more-desirable ones, it could be in a dealer's best interest to sell some of the slow movers at a loss—made up for by the arrival of more profitable vehicles.

3. In a market where some less-desirable units languish on dealers' lots for months, it may make sense to a dealer to sell the less-desirable units below invoice cost rather than continuing to pay interest (so-called *flooring charges*) on them.

4. In specific instances such as the turn of a model year or the replacement of a model by an all-new version, clearing out the old models at prices below cost may be an effective strategy for the dealer.

When all is said and done, knowing the dealer invoice price can be an extremely helpful bargaining tool. It is worth seeking out. But the market is so volatile, it's impossible to determine the proper dealer mark-up over the invoice price and, thus, the proper price you should pay. That mark-up (or in some cases, markdown) can change every day with the supply and demand of vehicles. In fact, knowing what the dealer paid for the vehicle might just make the whole transaction a bit more frustrating.

My advice: Use the dealer invoice price as a guideline, but shop widely and bargain seriously to get the best sales price.

How to Obtain Dealer Invoice Pricing

These days there are many sources of new-car dealer invoice pricing information. Several newsstand publications, including those from Edmunds, Pace Publications, and Consumer Guide, offer such information. Some feature detailed, item-by-item invoice costs for options and accessories as well as vehicle pricing. One thing to remember though, sometimes the pricing information is incomplete, so be certain that the guide has information about models you're interested in before you buy, and check the cover date to find the most current guide possible. Manufacturers may change their prices several times during the model year, so beware of older price guides.

To address the timeliness issue, several services now offer dealer invoice pricing information by mail or by fax. This information is updated daily as price changes take place. Several of these services try to track incentive programs as well. From most services, you can order information by telephone using a toll-free 800 number (see Table 15.1). Among the sources are Consumer Research Bureau, Automotive Consumer Services, Consumer Reports, Consumer Guide, Fighting Chance, and IntelliChoice. Reports range in price from a low of about $7 to a high of $19.95. Some services charge extra for fax or overnight delivery. A call to them will get their latest rates.

For those of you who have entered the online Age, dealer invoice pricing is available on CompuServe (Go AUTOMOBILES) and America Online (KEYWORD:CARS). Edmund's operates an Internet version of its price service at http://www.edmunds.com. And you can contact Kelly Blue Book at http://www.kbb.com.

In addition to the dealer invoice pricing, some services will supply you with prices that are variously described as the "fair" or "target" prices, the prices you should be looking to match. Take these with a large grain of salt; it's very unlikely they will reflect the market conditions in your area on the day you'll be shopping. Just remember, the dealer invoice prices are signposts to help you reach the deal you want; they won't make the deal for you.

Table 15.1 Sources of Dealer Invoice Pricing

Organization	Telephone Number
Consumer Research Bureau	800-392-1735
Automotive Consumer Services	800-453-7623
Consumer Reports	800-933-5555
Consumer Guide	708-329-5458
Fighting Chance	800-288-1134
IntelliChoice	800-227-2665

What Is Value Pricing?

Saturn Corporation has turned the automotive world on its ear in many ways, but in no way more than its pricing policy. Variously referred to as a one-price, no-haggle, no-hassle, or value-price method of operation, Saturn dealerships use the concept "the price you see is the price you pay." Rather than force its customers into a price dance with the salesperson, instead the vast majority of Saturn buyers pay something very close to, if not spot-on, the sticker price.

Of course, Saturn can't enforce this pricing policy. That would be a violation of anti-trust laws. But, because Saturn has relatively few dealers and because Saturn has convinced its dealers that this sales method is in the best interests of the entire group, this informal policy has become the de facto standard for Saturn. And Saturn buyers seem to love it. Their praise has vaulted Saturn to the top of J.D. Power and Associate's Sales Satisfaction Index chart, the industry's most recognized measure of customer satisfaction with the sales process. (I wonder if these buyers would be as happy if they knew that Saturn dealers garner average gross profits per vehicle that are among the industry's highest, rivaling those of top luxury brands.)

In any case, the success of the Saturn no-haggle, no-hassle pricing policy has spawned many imitators. In most of the imitations, the manufacturers have intentionally cut the spread between their suggested retail prices and dealer invoice prices in an attempt to keep the actual sales prices or, in industry parlance, *transaction* prices pretty much at suggested retail. Because their potential gross profit margin is trimmed, dealers have less room to negotiate and therefore end up selling more of their vehicles at or near sticker price. This purports to aid customer satisfaction, since customers don't have to engage in distasteful negotiations with the dealer.

As I see it, if you absolutely hate to bargain, look for one-price models or for dealers that offer no-haggle pricing. To find these models and/or dealers look for the buzzwords. They include phrases like "no-hassle," "value-priced," "no-haggle," and "prices clearly marked on each vehicle."

Buying at a "one-price" dealership or buying a value-priced model does, by and large, guarantee that other consumers who buy at the same time as you don't get a better deal. But as you know by now, there are other variables—financing and trade-in value among them—that can alter the overall effectiveness of your deal. Don't think that just walking into a one-price dealership will assure that you get a good deal.

Bet You Didn't Know

The one-price policy has become a more effective tool in selling used cars than new cars and has been adopted by Circuit City's CarMax used car superstore chain.

How Much Profit Does the Dealer Expect?

It always amuses me when I look in car buying guides and see the target sales price, the price the guidebook suggests the buyer aim at, described as the "fair price." My point is, who's to say what's fair? You? Me? Smokey the Bear? The Easter Bunny? Is there a Fairness Hotline somewhere? And fair to whom? The buyer? The seller? Or both?

I know I can't sit here at my word processor and tell you a certain percentage markup from the dealer invoice price or markdown from the MSRP is "fair." I can't even tell you what percentage is appropriate or even average. And of course, if you or I had the "average" it wouldn't do us any good, because the vehicle you or I want to buy won't be "average" and the deal you or I make won't be "average" either.

Money Saving Tip
The dealer markup over invoice cost on most high-volume vehicles is less than 10 percent.

The fact is, many dealerships don't make as much money per new-vehicle sale as they do per used vehicle. After all, hundreds of competitors are selling exactly the same product on street corners across this wonderful land of ours.

On this score, I suggest that you spend more of your effort shopping several dealers and seriously negotiating on price after you've gathered as much background knowledge as you can, and spend less worrying about how much gross profit over the invoice cost the dealer "should" get.

The Least You Need to Know

➤ The operative word in Manufacturer's Suggested Retail Price is "suggested." Most buyers don't pay MSRP.

➤ For hot models, you can pay more than the MSRP and still get a good deal.

➤ For a reasonable fee, numerous services now will tell you exactly what the dealer paid for the vehicle you're about to buy, via mail or fax.

➤ Value-priced (cars with a set price like Saturns) vehicles aren't necessarily your best value.

Chapter 16

TO LEASE OR TO BUY, THAT IS THE QUESTION, WHETHER IT BE NOBLER IN THE TRADE ROOM TO OPT FOR A TRADE IN...

Should You Buy or Lease?

In This Chapter

➤ Why leasing is growing

➤ Leasing's advantages

➤ Key advantage of buying

➤ When it's better to lease

➤ Leasing pitfalls

There is no single answer to the question, "Should I lease or buy my next car?", just as there is no simple answer to the question, "Should I wear a white sweater while eating Spaghetti Bolognese?" Making the right decision is a matter of your personal desires, values, financial status, and your ability to avoid making a mess of things.

Auto leasing has been around for decades, and once offered small business owners significant tax advantages over buying. Those days are long gone, but leasing has caught fire in the last few years for several reasons. Auto manufacturers find that leasing is a good way to put their vehicles on sale without appearing to cut their prices. Many dealers like leasing because consumers unfamiliar with its many nuances can be easy prey for "home run" deals. And many consumers believe that leasing offers them the chance to drive more car for their money.

For all these reasons, industry experts estimate that next year leasing will represent between 20 and 25 percent of the new-car market. Among the luxury brands it's often as high as 75 percent. If you're in the used-car market and don't believe leasing is for you, you may want to think again. Leasing isn't a big part of the used-car market yet, but several finance sources now offer used-car leasing.

Certainly with its growing acceptance in the marketplace, leasing must offer the consumer some advantages. It does, although you must remember that hula hoops, pet rocks, and mood rings have also enjoyed wide consumer acceptance over the years. Like chili pepper, leasing is neither good nor bad; it simply depends on how you react to it. This chapter takes a look at leasing and at specific situations when you may want to consider or avoid it.

Ahh...The Advantages of Leasing Your Next Car

Why are people leasing in unprecedented numbers? It's mostly a reaction to the rapidly escalating prices of new cars. To buy a car you either need a briefcase full of cash or a trade-in worth at least 10 percent of the new vehicle's purchase price. On the other hand, you only need a minimal amount of cash to initiate a lease.

Let's say you have no money in the bank and no trade-in vehicle, but you do have reasonably good credit. You can walk into your local dealer, sign a lease on the dotted line and drive out with a luxurious, leather-lined Lithemobile 200LX with very little difficulty.

Money Saving Tip

At the end of the lease, you may think you only have two options: Returning the car, or paying the purchase option price and keeping the car. But there is a third option: Offer a cash price lower than the purchase price. It might just be accepted.

If, on the other hand, you try to buy that Lithemobile 200LX (or even the less luxuriously equipped Lithemobile 100DX, powered by gerbils on a treadmill) without a substantial down payment, you may have a very difficult time.

In addition to the low down payment (or no down payment at all), leasing almost always offers a lower monthly payment than purchasing the vehicle over the same period of time. This stands to reason, since when you lease a car you only acquire its use for a period of time far shorter than the total life of the vehicle. Since many car buyers concentrate on the monthly payment, the low-payment aspect has heightened its popularity considerably.

Another advantage of leasing: You can structure the lease term to match your trading cycle. If you normally purchase a new car every two years, you might be better off with a two-year lease. (You might also ask yourself why you need a new car so often when the typical car is now under warranty for at least three years—if the manufacturer thinks it's good for at least three years, why don't you?)

Leasing also works to the advantage of those who don't know what to do with their current vehicle when it's time for a new one. You don't have to weigh the advantages of trading it in at a dealership versus selling it yourself, and you don't have to go through the hassles of selling it: Running want ads and meeting with prospective buyers. You don't even have to decide when to do all this. It's spelled out in the lease contract.

The Key Purchase Advantage

There are two ways to look at the leasing experience. Some might think the advantages mentioned in the previous section are worth the extra overall cost that usually accompanies leasing. Others simply aren't willing to pay the price for leasing's advantages.

Compared to the numerous advantages of leasing, there is only one key advantage to purchasing your next vehicle, but it's a big one: As you make payments, you build equity in a real asset. For many people this one advantage of buying far outweighs all the advantages of leasing.

Leasing is only renting over a specified period of time. Buying a vehicle, even using a loan, grants you ownership. And ownership, as they say, has its privileges—the ability to hold and use the asset for as long as you like or sell it, at your discretion.

When you buy a vehicle, you take a risk on its future worth and, most often, you gain a reward for taking that risk. In a lease, the financial institution takes the risk on the future value of the vehicle, and, most often, it gains the reward.

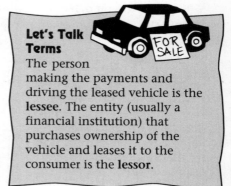

Let's Talk Terms
The person making the payments and driving the leased vehicle is the **lessee**. The entity (usually a financial institution) that purchases ownership of the vehicle and leases it to the consumer is the **lessor**.

Though new cars are far from the greatest investments in the world, because they depreciate so rapidly, acquiring equity by buying them is usually a better financial deal than leasing them. In pure dollars-and-cents terms, you are most often better off buying a car than leasing it if you can.

When It's Better to Lease than Buy

That being said, there are a few instances when it is still better to lease your new vehicle rather than buy it. Here are some of those special circumstances:

➤ You simply can't afford to purchase your dream vehicle but you're confident you can make the lease payments through the end of the lease term.

➤ You feel the quality and dependability of the vehicle is questionable but you'd still love to have it. Leasing allows you to try it out for a couple of years. If you love it at the end of the term you can buy it; if you hate it, just drop it off and say good-bye.

➤ You would like to have a bright, shiny new vehicle every two or three years. (It's okay to admit you're shallow.)

➤ The manufacturer is making a lease offer that's so financially compelling that you can't afford to pass it up. Many manufacturers now put models on sale, not by lowering the price, but by offering special lease deals.

➤ You can't stand the hassle and the bargaining involved in selling your old car and buying a new one.

Dodging Potential Bullets

We're all aware that auto acquisition is always filled with potential booby traps. But because leasing is so new to so many people, it has brought with it some brand new pitfalls. The first among the potential pitfalls is the *acquisition fee*. This, essentially, is a payment you make to be allowed to make more payments. Many consumers look at this as the equivalent of a down payment, but there's one key difference—A down payment delivers equity to the buyer; an acquisition fee simply delivers cash to the dealer or finance company.

Let's Talk Terms

The **acquisition fee** is charged to the lessee to initiate a lease. A **disposition fee** is charged to the lessee to dispose of the vehicle at the conclusion of the lease term if the lessee does not purchase the vehicle.

I have even seen several car manufacturers audacious enough to advertise no-money-down lease deals, and then require the payment of an acquisition fee. If you can't negotiate it away, and most often in manufacturer-sponsored deals you can't, by all means figure it into your total cost. And take another look at buying the same vehicle. After all, if a big benefit of leasing is the small amount of cash required, why pay a substantial acquisition fee?

The flip side of the acquisition fee is the *disposition fee*. This charge comes at the end of the lease, when you are required to make the payment if you don't purchase the car you've been leasing. Look for this charge in the fine print and negotiate it away if you can.

If you decide you want to get rid of the car before the end of the lease term, you have to pay a substantial fee, the *early termination charge*. Don't lease for a term longer than you plan to keep the vehicle. If you do, you'll pay hundreds of dollars to get out of the lease or, even worse, you'll be responsible for the entire balance of the lease payments.

Yet another pitfall is your *gap liability*. If your leased car is totaled in an accident or is stolen and disappears, the insurance you are required to carry as part of your agreement will pay for the vehicle at or near its true value. But that figure might be far less than you owe on the lease, and you signed a contract to pay the money owed on the lease. To protect yourself from this dire predicament, when you lease you should acquire *gap insurance* or deal with a finance company that builds gap coverage into its overall pricing structure. Ask your insurance agent and car salesperson about this coverage. Check with the salesperson about the types and amount of insurance required by the lease. Most leasing companies require that you carry a high (and expensive) level of coverage.

Finally, be realistic about the miles you will drive over the course of the lease agreement. If you exceed the mileage cap, you will pay a per-mile penalty that can add up quickly. As you negotiate the terms of the lease, you might be able to up the mileage cap, or at least buy some additional miles at a lower rate than you'd pay at the conclusion of the lease.

The Lease/Buy Acid Test

I wish it were simpler to decide whether to buy or lease, but a car acquisition is one of the most complicated financial deals most of us will make. Since each of our individual financial circumstances differ, so does the right answer to this important question. The following quiz will help you decide whether leasing or buying your next vehicle is the best decision in your individual situation.

Answer these simple yes and no questions, giving yourself either one point or no points as indicated. When you have answered the questions, total up your score. A total of **four or less** indicates you should lease your next vehicle. A total of **five or more** indicates you should buy.

1. Is it important to you to get a new car or truck every two to three years?
   Yes (0 points) or No (1 point)

2. Do you have at least 10 percent of the purchase price of the new vehicle in cash or in equity in your current vehicle that you are willing to use as a down payment on your next vehicle?
   Yes (1) or No (0)

3. Does the reputation or word-of-mouth about the vehicle you are currently considering cause you concerns about its reliability or dependability?
   Yes (0) or No (1)

4. Will the vehicle you are considering require a larger monthly payment than you would be able to afford using a conventional car loan?
   Yes (0) or No (1)

5. Have you ever owed more on a vehicle than it was worth when you wanted to trade it in to acquire another car?
   Yes (0) or No (1)

6. Is the manufacturer of the vehicle you'd like to acquire currently advertising a specific lease payment on a model that has the equipment you want?
   Yes (0) or No (1)

7. Do you drive more than 12,000 miles per year?
   Yes (1) or No (0)

8. Would you like to be free (eventually) of monthly car payments?
   Yes (1) or No (0)

9. Do you plan to keep the vehicle you'd like to acquire longer than three years?
   Yes (1) or No (0)

10. Do you have any plans to modify or customize the vehicle?
    Yes (1) or No (0)

The Lease-t You Need to Know

➤ You can initiate a lease with no down payment or a low down payment.

➤ Leasing generally offers lower monthly payments than the purchase of the same vehicle over the same term.

➤ The key advantage of purchasing your vehicle is building ownership (equity) in a valuable asset.

➤ You generally pay extra overall for the convenience of leasing.

Chapter 17

Side-by-Side Comparison: Leasing Versus Buying

In This Chapter

➤ Up-front payments

➤ The lease fine print

➤ Cap cost and residual

➤ Lease rate

➤ Direct comparison

Now that you've seen the essential differences between leasing and buying, let's take a look at two similar vehicle acquisition transactions in this chapter to illustrate the nuances of the two transactions and how they differ.

Leo and Edith both have their eyes on a brand-new Gleamus EQ400 with an MSRP (sticker price) of $21,500—about average for a new car right now. Being frugal individuals, neither Leo nor Edith want to pay the "list price" for the car, and since the model they like isn't one of the hottest on the market, they should be able to make an agreement with the dealer to pay less.

Even though they like the same model, Leo and Edith come into the bargaining process with different financial circumstances. Leo doesn't own a car (he's getting sick of riding the bus), but he has scraped together $2,000 in cash. On the other hand, Edith just sold her previous car for $3,000 and has another $1,000 in the bank to put toward her car purchase.

When they go to the dealership, both Leo and Edith negotiate a purchase price of $20,000 for the car they want, using the tips and techniques you've read about earlier in this book.

The Initial Payments

Edith decides she wants to buy the new car. She knows that to get a conventional auto loan the financial institution will require a down payment of 10 to 20 percent. This protects the institution if she suddenly decides to quit her job, front a grunge band, and blow off the monthly payments. Since Edith is toting $4,000 in cash, 20 percent of the purchase price, she's ready to rock.

> ### Bet You Didn't Know
>
> The reason most financial institutions require a down payment is that it allows them to hedge against the possibility you won't repay the loan. If that happens, the financial institution must repossess the car and sell it to recover its money, but the down payment you put up gives them a head start in the game.

Leo, on the other hand, with just $2,000 in his pocket, is on the ragged edge of not qualifying for a conventional car loan. Since license fees and state sales taxes could add another $2,000 to the total transaction, he might be out of luck. If he wants to buy a car he might have to look for a less expensive model—or consider leasing.

Edith moves ahead to purchase her Gleamus, and she puts $4,000 down on the car. Two thousand of that goes to state license fees and sales tax, while the remaining $2,000 is applied against the car's purchase price. In other words, after the fees and taxes are paid, she has paid $2,000 in cash for $2,000 of ownership (equity) in the new car.

Leo is trying to figure out what to do. His dealer tells him he can qualify for a car loan, but, because he's a high-risk borrower, it will be at 12 percent APR. With only $2,000 to put down, he can only pay for license fees and sales taxes, so he must finance $20,000. At the 12 percent rate on a 3-year loan, he'll have to come up with $664 each month. Even if he finances the car over five years, he'll still have to pay $444 each month.

Leo is bummed in a major way and ready to stick with the bus, but the salesman is not about to let this fish swim out of the pond. With his most sincere grin, he suggests that Leo *lease* that shiny, new Gleamus instead. With $2,000 down, the salesman assures him, he can drive for three years for just $334 a month.

Leo, being the sound financial strategist he is, immediately signs up for the three-year lease. If you ask him, he'll tell you that he's saving 50 percent by leasing rather than buying over three years. After all, his monthly payment is $334, about half the $664 he would have paid if he'd bought the car.

A Look Behind the Lease

Leo, of course, has fallen into the car buyer's most common trap—looking at just the monthly payment. By now, we all know that the monthly payment is just one element of the transaction, and an element that's open to serious manipulation.

Edith's situation is much more straightforward. She must borrow $18,000 to complete the purchase transaction. Shopping around by comparing the rates of her bank, credit union, and dealer's financing, she finds that because she's a good credit risk, she can get a much better rate than Leo got: 10 percent APR. (APR, of course, stands for annualized percentage rate.) At that 10 percent rate, if she finances the car over three years (36 months), she'll have a monthly payment of $581. That payment, plus the added cost of insurance for her new car, fits into her budget, so she makes the deal.

When you compare the monthly payments, Leo's three-year lease does seem like a great deal. And maybe it is, particularly for guys like Leo. But take a closer look at what Leo and Edith have done, and then decide which scenario you'd like to follow.

First, let's see how the dealer arrived at Leo's monthly payment of $334. This requires a short explanation of leasing, which, in simple terms, is the agreement to rent over an agreed-upon period of time. Over the course of his three-year lease, Leo, the lessee, agrees to pay $334 each month to the lessor (probably a finance company) for 36 months.

In addition, he also agrees to maintain the car in reasonable fashion, insure it to the lessor's satisfaction, and drive it no more than a specified number of miles a year, usually 12,000 or 15,000 miles. Leo isn't buying anything but the use of the car over a three-year period.

How does the dealer arrive at the $334 monthly payment? It's good you asked, because the answer is not nearly as straightforward as a conventional car loan transaction, which I explained in an earlier chapter. To arrive at the monthly payment, we must start with the purchase price, which in a lease deal is usually referred to as the *capitalized cost* or, simply, cap cost. This is the price the lessor will pay to purchase the car from the dealer. In Leo's case, as in Edith's, the purchase price is $20,000.

Unlike Edith, however, Leo is only purchasing use of the car for a portion of its useful life (in this case, three years). So how does the lessor figure what Leo should pay for this? Well, it must determine approximately how much of the car's value Leo will use up over three years; or, in accounting terms, it must figure out how much the car will depreciate in three years. Several widely recognized industry firms track this data and publish estimates of depreciation for each individual model after one, two, three, four, and five years. The figure is usually expressed as a percentage of the MSRP.

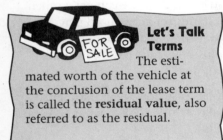

Let's Talk Terms
The price at which the financial institution is buying the car from the dealer in a lease transaction is called the **capitalized cost**. Equivalent to the cash purchase price in a conventional purchase, it's commonly referred to as the "cap cost."

In Leo's case, using the industry-recognized tables, the finance company believes that after three years the car will be worth 60 percent of its original sticker price. The original sticker price was $21,500, so 60 percent of that is $12,900. That number is referred to as the *residual value* or, simply, the residual. That's what the finance company estimates the car will be worth at the end of the 36 months Leo drives it. And, in most lease contracts, Leo will have the right to purchase the car at that price after the lease term ends.

Let's Talk Terms
The estimated worth of the vehicle at the conclusion of the lease term is called the **residual value**, also referred to as the residual.

So part of what Leo will pay each month is a simple division of the depreciation—the purchase price minus the residual value—by the number of months in the contract. In Leo's case, the total depreciation is $20,000 (the purchase price) minus $12,900 (the residual value) which equals $7,100. Divide that by 36 months, and you get $197 per month.

Figuring the Lease Rate

But that isn't all Leo must pay, because for Leo to lease the car, the finance company has to buy the car from the dealer. (Very few dealers actually finance their own leases.) To make its profit, the finance company charges interest for the use of its money in the transaction. Leo must make this interest payment as well as paying off the depreciation.

This is where complication can set in. Most financial institutions use what is referred to as the *constant yield* method to determine this additional monthly charge. To figure this *lease rate* or financing charge, add the purchase price to the residual, and then multiply this number by the *money factor*.

What's the money factor? It's an algebraic expression of the interest rate used to compute the monthly finance cost on a lease. Luckily, without being a Nobel laureate, you can determine the money factor simply by expressing the interest rate in term of a decimal (10 percent = .1) and then dividing that number by 24. Conversely, you can take a money factor and determine the interest rate it represents by multiplying it by 24 and then converting that decimal to a percentage. (Don't be confused thinking the number varies by the length of the loan or anything else; it's always 24.)

Another complication that arises: Some finance companies use alternate methods of determining their lease rates. However, the calculations and overall results are similar, so you can see if you're being treated fairly. Simply go through the mechanics of the transaction using the constant yield method I just described, and then see how the monthly payment you arrive at differs from the monthly payment you are quoted. A difference of more than a few dollars a month means you deserve an explanation.

In Leo's case, the salesman offers him a lease at an interest rate of 10 percent (though he most likely won't tell him what the interest rate is; why clutter his head with numbers?) This translates into a money factor of .0041666, which is .1 divided by 24. Adding the purchase price ($20,000) to the residual ($12,900) gives us a sum of $32,900, which is then multiplied by the money factor (.004166), giving us $137. By adding that $137 to the $197 depreciation charge we get a total monthly lease payment of $334.

Actually, Leo's salesperson took it easy on him. Naive as Leo was, he might have bitten on several profit-building gambits by the dealer—acquisition fees, disposition fees, and the like. What the salesperson has going for him is the fact that many car buyers are only concerned with the monthly payment, and leasing virtually always guarantees a lower monthly payment than a traditional car loan. That's as it should be, since the consumer is only purchasing part of the car's life, not the entirety of that life.

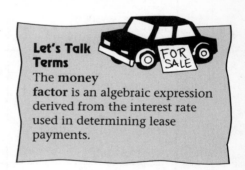

Let's Talk Terms
The **money factor** is an algebraic expression derived from the interest rate used in determining lease payments.

Comparing Edith's Purchase to Leo's Lease

Edith's situation is straightforward. Over the course of her three-year loan she will pay a total of $20,916 in monthly payments. Add that to the $4,000 she gave as a down payment, and she will have paid $24,916 for her three years of driving.

Leo, in comparison, will have made 36 monthly payments of $334 for a total of $12,024. To which we must add the $2,000 he spent on license fees and sales taxes when he initiated the lease. His total to drive the car over three years is $14,024.

But when Edith makes her 36th payment, she can celebrate, because she now owns her car free and clear. She can sell it without paying off the loan, trade it in on a new car or, perhaps best of all, she can keep and drive the car for years to come for just the cost of gas, oil, maintenance, and insurance. No monthly car payment! She owns a valuable asset that's probably worth about $12,900. Maybe more.

In contrast, when Leo makes his 36th payment, he's under the gun to get another vehicle. True, he can buy the car for $12,900. But, since he's not likely to have that kind of money in cash, he'll have to finance it. He'll need at least 10 percent of the purchase price in cash, and then he'll have to take out a conventional car loan on the balance, very likely paying a higher interest rate than he could have obtained when the vehicle was new. Even if Leo has the $12,900 in cash, he'll still pay $26,924 ($12,900 plus the $14,024 total of his monthly payments) to own the same car Edith paid $24,916 for.

Edith and Leo's Comparison Worksheets

Buy		Lease	
MSRP	$21,500	MSRP	$21,500
Purchase price	$20,000	Capitalized cost	$20,000
		Residual value	$12,900
Down payment	$4,000	Acquisition fee	0
Amount financed	$18,000	Monthly depreciation	$239
		Disposition fee	0
License fees	$500	License fees	$500
Sales tax	$1,500	Sales tax	$1,500
Loan term (months)	36	Lease term (months)	36
Interest rate	10%	Interest rate	10%
		Money factor	.0041666
Monthly loan payment	$581	Monthly lease payment	$334
Total monthly payments	$20,916	Total monthly payments	$12,024
Total of all payments	$24,916	Total of all payments	$14,024
Equity at conclusion of loan	$12,900	Equity at conclusion of lease	0
Total payments minus equity (cost)	$12,016	Total payments minus equity (cost)	$14,024

Get the Information You Need

The biggest mistake car buyers can make is only looking at a piece of the transaction instead of the whole deal. This is especially true for leasing. Remember when the salesman told Leo he would have to pay $664 a month if he wanted to buy that Gleamus with a three-year loan? Well, how do you think Leo might have responded if he was told he could lease that same car for three years for $398 instead of the $334 he was quoted? Do you think he'd go for it? I do. But if Leo had gone for it, he would've been making a bad deal.

"Really?" you may be thinking—an extra $64 per month doesn't seem all that bad. But to arrive at that payment, the capitalized cost for the Gleamus EQ400 would be $22,000, although we know that model had an MSRP of $21,500. What this means is, in this lease transaction the car is being purchased for $500 more than sticker price and $2,000 more than Edith paid for the identical model. Of course, Leo wouldn't know this because he never asked about the capitalized cost, and the salesperson wasn't legally required to tell him.

Because of Leo's laxity, a salesperson could hit the home run of his life—a gross profit on the vehicle that could be as high as 20 percent. In Edith's case, in contrast, the gross profit was more like 5 percent. Now there's nothing wrong with dealers making a profit—they need profit to stay in business—but we want to help the market work for you, not against you.

To keep from repeating Leo's mistake, ask the salesperson for all the information you need to make intelligent decisions. In a lease transaction, you need to know the *capitalized cost*, the *residual value*, and the *interest rate* (represented by the lease rate in addition to the length of the agreement and the monthly payment). In a purchase transaction you need to know the *purchase price*, the *interest rate,* and the length of the *loan term*. Ask your salesperson for these figures. If he won't provide them, take your business elsewhere.

The following blank worksheet will help you construct your own lease/buy comparison to see how each transaction measures up against the other.

Buy or Lease Comparison Worksheet			
Buy		**Lease**	
MSRP		MSRP	
Purchase price		Capitalized cost	
		Residual value	
Down payment		Acquisition fee	
Amount financed		Monthly depreciation	
		Disposition fee	
License fees		License fees	
Sales tax		Sales tax	
Loan term (months)		Lease term (months)	
Interest rate		Interest rate	
		Money factor	
Monthly loan payment		Monthly lease payment	
Total monthly payments		Total monthly payments	
Total of all payments		Total of all payments	
Equity at conclusion of loan		Equity at conclusion of lease	0
Total payments minus equity		Total payments minus equity	

Tips for the Best Lease Deal

If you decide to lease, the following tips will help you make the best deal possible:

➤ Negotiate the cash purchase price of the vehicle down from the Manufacturer's Suggested Retail Price (MSRP) and then make the lease deal. Be certain the cash price you agreed to is listed as the capitalized cost.

➤ Demand to see the interest rate you're paying on the lease. It should be very close (within one percentage point) of the going auto loan rate (see Chapter 12). Don't rely on the monthly payment to determine if you're making a good financial deal. Remember, if you lease you're only purchasing the use of the car over a small portion of its life, and you're gaining no equity. The monthly payment should be much, much lower to reflect this.

➤ Never lease for a term longer than the manufacturer's warranty on the vehicle. Otherwise, you could be stuck dipping into your pocket to fix a car you don't own.

➤ Be realistic with yourself about the number of miles you drive in a year. Most leases have annual mileage caps of 12,000 or 15,000 miles, and you pay dearly at the end of the lease if you exceed them.

➤ Be on the lookout for manufacturer-sponsored special lease deals. Television and newspaper ads touting a specific monthly payment are an obvious giveaway that the manufacturer is putting the car on sale. But remember: The deal is no good if it's on a model you don't want.

The Least You Need to Know

➤ Leasing offers added convenience but you'll pay extra for it.

➤ Leasing is a good alternative for those with little cash for a down payment.

➤ Be certain to get all the information you need to make a good financial decision.

➤ Don't think a low monthly payment means you got a good deal.

Tactics at the Dealership

In This Chapter

➤ Defining goals and making crucial decisions

➤ Your negotiating skills

➤ The "cheat sheet"

➤ Buying from inventory versus factory orders

➤ The negotiation three-step

➤ Decision time

All right, the homework is over. You've done your research on the various vehicles and your own financial capabilities. You've shopped several dealerships and test-driven a number of vehicles to get a well-defined idea of what you want and where to get it. You've also shopped for financing, so you have a handle on the going rates, and you've decided whether leasing the vehicle rather than buying it makes sense in your special situation. Finally, you have a very good idea what your current vehicle is worth whether you decide to sell it or trade it in.

You've come a long way, baby. And now is the time to put all that hard work to use in negotiating the best deal you can for yourself. This chapter gives you a leg up.

Define Your Goals

Only you can decide exactly what you want to achieve in your new-vehicle acquisition process. It's up to you to come to terms with the factors that are most important to you. This may seem silly or self-evident, but if you don't define your goals clearly you can't expect to achieve them.

Do you simply want the cheapest vehicle in its class? Do you want price to be the deciding factor between one or more vehicles? Do you want the lowest price on a specific vehicle equipped a certain way? Do you want to buy from a specific dealer?

While I don't expect you to adopt the vehicle-acquisition goals I'm suggesting blindly, I believe that they do make sense for a large majority of consumers who will buy or lease a vehicle. Those goals are:

1. Obtaining a well-built vehicle that meets my needs.

2. Obtaining that vehicle at a price I can afford.

3. Obtaining that vehicle at a price that I believe gives me a very positive amount of value per dollar spent.

4. Obtaining that vehicle in a transaction that I fully understand and feel comfortable with.

With these goals or a list of your own goals in mind, you should apply the fruits of your due diligence.

Your research and shopping efforts should have given you all the information you need to arrive at the choice of a vehicle, equipped with specific options, that meets your needs and desires. That vehicle should also pass the test of affordability based on your financial status and of value per dollar spent based on your standards.

With these factors in mind, your goal in the acquisition phase of your new-vehicle quest is to structure a transaction that allows you to acquire the vehicle, equipped as you would like it, under terms that you understand fully and feel comfortable with.

The Decision Tree

You are nearly ready to go into the dealership to acquire a new vehicle. But before you do, I strongly urge you to make firm decisions on several very important issues. If you fail to make these decisions before you enter the dealership to negotiate your acquisition, they will create indecision that could cause you to lose focus, prolong the process, and come to an unsatisfactory conclusion.

In order, these decisions are:

1. **What vehicle?** You should decide on make, model, and trim level, even color if it makes a difference to you. Some experts suggest that you negotiate seriously on several different makes and models at the same time, finally choosing the vehicle that seems like the best deal. I recommend against this, because I believe it can muddy the waters and because I believe most people, in their heart of hearts, have a strong first preference.

   It's important to have focus, and that's difficult if you're pursuing both an apple and an orange. Choosing a vehicle up front eliminates impossible quandaries, and if it takes some serious price-shopping to arrive at your model-of-choice, so be it. If you're going fishing, you don't pack a deer rifle, and if you're hunting deer, you don't pack a fishing rod—but if you don't know what you're doing, it doesn't matter what you pack. And you can quote me on that.

2. **What equipment?** You should get very specific here. Choose the engine and transmission. Specify if you want antilock brakes, air conditioning, a CD player, leather upholstery, power windows, power door locks, heated seats—every last thing you want and don't want. Why? For the same reasons I mentioned above. You have to stay focused.

3. **Cash purchase, financing, or leasing?** Sure, it's nice to have choices, but it's better to make as many choices as you can *before* you get down to negotiating with the dealership. After reviewing the material in Chapters 16 and 17, you should be able to tell where you fall on the lease-buy continuum.

4. **Disposal of current vehicle?** Are you going to sell it yourself or trade it in to the dealer? To maximize your financial position, you'll probably be better off selling it yourself, but there is the downside of inconvenience and even potential danger when you do that. If you fail to make this choice before you enter the dealership to start the negotiation process, it's just another area that can lead to confusion and a poor decision.

Assessing Your Negotiating Skills

Another important thing to do before you go into the dealership is take a long look at yourself. How well-honed are your negotiating skills? Are you cool under pressure or do you get flustered? How do you respond when a large amount of information (or disinformation) is thrown at you in a short span of time?

If you're like most consumers, you don't negotiate deals every day, and when you buy a car you'll be going up against a team that does. Most often that team is well-organized, and it has a systematic approach to fall back on. Salespeople and managers want to take control of the deal and consummate it their way. They may use several different approaches, from nearly overzealous sweetness to intimidation. Some will play their version of good cop/bad cop, while others will attempt to bond with you like a long-lost brother.

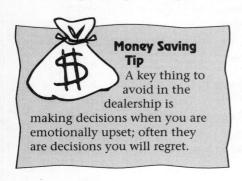

Money Saving Tip
A key thing to avoid in the dealership is making decisions when you are emotionally upset; often they are decisions you will regret.

Before you walk into the caldron, picture your response to these scenarios. If a salesperson is trying to pressure you, sweet-talk you, or simply BS you, what will you do?

At the risk of harping on an old theme, your best defense against anything a dealership throws at you is your ability to walk out the door. You are a rare and extremely valuable commodity to any dealership—a qualified consumer ready to purchase or lease a vehicle. If, at any time, you feel you're not getting the respect or attention you deserve, exercise your shoe leather. Like beautiful girls and city buses, another car deal will be along in a couple of minutes.

Developing Your Negotiating Plan

With this as a backdrop, you should develop a negotiating plan. You've already chosen the make, the model, and the equipment. Write it all down along with both the Manufacturer's Suggested List Price and the dealer invoice price for the vehicle and all the options you want. If you know of any incentives on the model you want, be it special financing, cash-back, subsidized leases, or factory-to-dealer cash, jot that down, too. In addition, write down the best current finance terms in your area, and your estimate of your current vehicle's wholesale (trade-in) and retail value. This is your "cheat sheet." Refer to it whenever you feel confused about the information that's being thrown at you.

As another part of your plan, decide which dealerships you plan to visit. By now, more than likely, you've gotten some "good vibes" from some dealerships and "bad vibes" from others. It makes sense to go to two or three of the good ones first and either eliminate the bad ones or save them for a worst-case scenario when and if none of the good ones has the vehicle you want.

New-Vehicle Acquisition Cheat Sheet			
	Description	Dealer Invoice Price	Manufacturer's Suggested Retail Price
Make, model, trim			
Option package			
Option package			
Option package			
Option			
Option			
Option			
Option			
	Destination Charge		
	Subtotals		
Subtract:	Factory-to-customer cash		
Subtract:	Factory-to-dealer cash		
	Dealer net cost:		
Financing source:		Rate: Term:	
Current vehicle retail value:			
Current vehicle wholesale (trade-in) value:			

Getting Respect at the Dealership

Every customer deserves respect from every member of a dealership's staff, from the dealer principal to the cashier to the porter. Sadly, not every customer gets respect, and even more sadly, many dealerships still have a long way to go in giving respect to women and members of minority groups.

This book won't cure the social ills that ail us as a nation, but I do urge you to use your right to refuse to do business if you're not getting the treatment you deserve. New vehicles and new-vehicle dealerships are everywhere. If you look, you will find dealerships and salespeople more than willing to treat you with dignity.

Further, you can enhance the respect with which you are treated by behaving with dignity yourself. Like you, the salesperson deserves respect at least until she or he proves unworthy of it. Extending kindness and courtesy toward the salesperson can go a long way to building a businesslike rapport, which will enhance the quality of the buying experience.

Still another way to get respect, perhaps the best way, is to quickly demonstrate that you know what you're doing. Of course, with the knowledge you've gained in the research and shopping phases of your quest, you do know what you're doing, so this shouldn't be too difficult to demonstrate.

The Negotiating Scenario

There is no right or wrong way to negotiate a satisfying new-vehicle acquisition. The following scenario is one straightforward method that will gain you instant respect and has the potential to net you a very good deal. At the same time, feel free to adapt it to meet your special circumstances.

1. Choose the dealership where you will make your first visit.

2. If you have become familiar with a helpful salesperson at the dealership, ask for her or him.

3. Early in the conversation with the salesperson, make it clear that you mean business and that you're not merely window shopping.

4. Quickly establish if the dealership has a vehicle in stock that meets your requirements. This is discussed in the next section.

5. Negotiate a firm cash purchase price.

6. Negotiate a firm financing deal or use your pre-arranged financing.

7. Negotiate a firm price for your current vehicle.

8. Shop for other offers if the current deal doesn't satisfy you acquisition goals.

The rest of this section will cover each step of the scenario in greater detail.

Steps 1–3: Zeroing In on Who to Work With

When choosing a dealer to work with, step 1, you have two choices, as I see it. If one dealer stood out in your shopping visits, you might return to that dealership and see if it can satisfy your goals. Or you might want to be strategic by visiting number two first. A firm price from this dealer will give you something to shoot for when you visit number one. After you select the dealer, step 2 is to ask for a specific salesperson, if you have one you want to work with. 'Nuff said about that.

To set the tone for the negotiations and demonstrate that you mean business, step 3 in the negotiation scenario, drop in these salient points:

1. You know the model, color, and equipment you want.

2. You have pre-qualified for financing, but you're willing to listen to the dealer's financing terms before you make up your mind (if that's true).

3. And, you will buy the vehicle today or in the next day or two if you get the right deal.

All this will immediately separate you from the crowd that walks in every day. "Hallelujah!" the salesperson will think. "Here's a person who actually knows what they want; here's a person who's ready to buy!"

Step 4: Buy from Stock or Order from the Factory?

Before we go onward in the negotiation scenario, here is a little digression on an important issue. Should you buy from the dealer's inventory or order a vehicle from the factory?

Well, if you're buying an import (or even domestically built vehicles with import brand names), you can forget about a special order. The factories are too far away and the transportation between them and your dealer are too slow to make this practical. (The only exception to this is a luxury car ordered for delivery in Europe.) On the other hand, a proportion of domestic car buyers cannot conceive of anything but sitting down with a salesperson and checking off option boxes until they've specified exactly the vehicle they want. They're willing to wait as long as two months before they can drive their dream car.

> **Money Saving Tip**
> Optional equipment offered by dealers is often available from other sources after the vehicle purchase for less money. Examples of this are stereo and CD players, alarm systems, and even sunroofs. Shop around and you might be able to save a considerable amount of cash.

Though this option is available, however, domestic manufacturers don't do much to encourage it these days. Increasingly, they are grouping options in packages rather than allowing them to be purchased individually. This makes for better build quality—and higher profits.

Additionally, the economics favor purchasing from dealers' inventory. For one thing, dealers have money invested in their inventory—money they'd like to recoup by selling a vehicle here and there. For another, many dealers finance their inventory, meaning they are paying interest (called *flooring charges*) on the vehicles they have in stock; further meaning that if they had their druthers, they'd rather sell one in stock than a factory order.

In this instance, the manufacturers line up with the dealers, because they would rather sell cars they've already built than cars they might build in the future. For cash-flow reasons, the overriding desire of all manufacturers is to keep their factories operating, and it doesn't make much sense to build new cars if you haven't sold the cars you've already built. Because of this, the vast majority of manufacturer incentives are good only on vehicles purchased from dealer inventories. Since the right incentive can save you hundreds, maybe even thousands of dollars, cast another vote for buying from dealers' stocks.

Bet You Didn't Know

A factory that's not manufacturing vehicles is extremely expensive for an automobile company since building and equipping a modern factory can cost as much as $500 million. Think of the monthly interest on that mortgage, huh?

An argument could be made for special ordering hot-selling vehicles that are in short supply, such as the Dodge Viper. In this instance, you might get the dealer to okay a lower price than he would demand if you took delivery off the showroom floor. But here, he's gambling that the demand for the vehicle will cool by the time your special-order unit arrives.

This presents another potential pothole—if demand doesn't lessen, you might come in to take delivery of your new Zowiemobile only to find—guess what—the dealership just sold it—"by mistake," they claim. Oh, they'll be happy to refund your $1,000 deposit that they've been holding for the eight weeks you cooled your heels waiting. Or they'll put you on the list for the next one that comes in. In theory, you could sue them, but they're betting that you won't.

The advice here is: Buy a vehicle from the inventory the dealer has on hand. Failing that, ask the dealer to obtain the model with the equipment you want from another dealer. Swaps like this are done all the time. Order from the factory only if you're dead set on getting a model with equipment that just can't be found on a pre-built unit.

Steps 5–7: The Negotiations Continue

Once you establish that the dealership has a vehicle that meets your requirements, and you make certain it is what you want, you are ready for some serious negotiations. To complete step 5 of the negotiating scenario, the number you want to arrive at is the "cash price." If the salesperson mentions a trade-in or financing, tell her or him, politely but firmly, that those issues aren't on the table. You want to negotiate one item at a time, and right now you are concentrating on the purchase price of the new vehicle.

At this point, the salesperson might offer some minor discount off the sticker price to get the negotiations rolling. One way to take charge of the give-and-take is to counter this with an offer of a hundred bucks or so above the dealer's invoice cost minus any factory-to-dealer incentive money. This will immediately mark you as a customer to be reckoned with.

It's doubtful that this offer will be accepted. (If it is, move on to the other areas you want to negotiate, like financing and your trade-in.) One tactic many dealerships use could be called "intimidation by delay." When you make a offer, the salesperson will tell you she or he has to "take it to the sales manager," then disappear, often for half an hour. Now, it doesn't take half an hour to look at the offer—you're not proposing to buy the Hope diamond; you just want a car. What this does, in many cases, is break down a consumer's sales resistance.

Your time is too valuable to let the salesperson play that game. If they say they have to check your offer with the dealer principal or sales manager, simply tell them, "Time is money to me; if you're not back in five minutes, I'll have to go to another dealer." Another ploy you can use is: "Oh, I thought you could okay a deal; if you can't, I want to speak to someone who can." This last line might earn you a trip to the sales manager, which generally will speed up the process considerably.

By this point, the salesperson knows you have a good handle on their costs and the new-vehicle incentives. When the salesperson gives you a counter-offer, take time to ponder it, then counter with a new offer of your own, perhaps adding two hundred dollars or so.

> **Money Saving Tip**
>
> It's not productive to make a purchase offer of less than the dealer invoice unless the model is about to be replaced by a newer model or there is a factory-to-dealer incentive that will allow the dealer to make a gross profit when selling at less-than-invoice. This will simply mark you as naive.

This is the time to be a good poker player. Make your offer, then keep quiet and let the salesperson respond to you. Unlike most poker games, you always have the ace-in-the-hole—your ability to walk away and take all your money with you.

Very likely, after a few rounds of offers, you'll either arrive at a cash purchase price that you feel is appropriate or you'll realize that you and the dealer are worlds apart. You may get the salesperson to agree to a very palatable sales price at this stage, hoping that the dealership can build additional profit in the financing, trade-in, and after-sale portions of the transaction.

Once you arrive at an agreement on the cash price, move on to step 6 of the negotiating scenario, telling the salesperson you may be interested in financing through the dealership if their deal is competitive. At this point the salesperson might continue to handle your deal or you might be passed on to the sales manager or F&I (Finance and Insurance) manager. No matter whom you're dealing with, be straightforward in spelling out the length of loan term you'd like (in most cases, no more than four years) and let them know that you've been pre-approved by a specific financial institution at a specific annualized percentage rate. The dealership representative will immediately tell you whether or not they can offer you a better deal.

In a surprising number of instances, the dealership can give you a better financing deal. Often, there are special manufacturer-sponsored financing offers designed to make individual models more attractive buys. In addition, working with the manufacturer-owned captive finance company, the dealer may be able to get you a lower rate to keep you in the brand.

Once you've come to an agreement on financing, you can move on to step 7 of the negotiating scenario, and begin to negotiate on your trade-in. This presents the dealership's last opportunity to turn what has been developing as a low-profit deal into a "home run," so be careful at this stage. The dealership might try to give you a very low offer for your current vehicle. But you've walked in the door armed with good information about its value, so if they scoff at your figures, don't let self-doubt build.

Money Saving Tip
If things aren't going the way you'd like, one good motivator is to pack up your things and get up from the table. Take it from me, no salesperson wants to see a hot prospect walk out the door.

Many consumers collapse at this stage, figuring, "They're the experts. What do I know about used-car values?" Well, before you did your due diligence you didn't know anything, but now you do. Stand up for your assessment of the car's value, and if you can't come to a mutually satisfactory agreement at this stage, be prepared to walk away from the entire deal. Remember, that low cash price you've negotiated is no good if the dealer is greatly undervaluing your trade-in.

Step 8: Making Your Final Decision

With luck and through the skills and professionalism you've brought to the negotiations, you will come to an understanding of the dealer's terms on all the points of the deal—cash purchase price, financing and trade-in value. Now it's decision time.

This is where you need to make a studied assessment of how those terms match your goals for the transaction. Often, they will match your goals exactly, but if they don't, are the differences ones you can feel comfortable with?

At this stage some experts suggest that you take the dealer's final offer to another dealership to see if they can beat it. My reaction to that advice is mixed. Certainly, you have the right as a consumer to use this tactic to get yourself a better deal. On the other hand, if the dealer has bargained with you in good faith, treated you with dignity and respect, and the deal meets all of your goals for the transaction, I suggest that the dealer deserves your business.

Of course, if you're uncomfortable with any aspect of the transaction offered you by the dealer, by all means go elsewhere. Use the techniques outlined in the last few pages to arrive at the second dealership's final offer.

Still uncomfortable? Go to a third dealer and do the dance again. After that, well, I have a saying, "If three people tell you you're sick, lie down." What it means in this context is, if three dealers can't meet your acquisition goals, then I don't think any dealership will. You should adjust your thinking on cash price, financing, or trade-in value or decide that now isn't the time to buy that new vehicle.

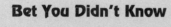

Bet You Didn't Know

Statistics show that a substantial proportion of new-vehicle buyers shop only one dealer before they purchase their vehicle.

More often than not, though, after visiting three dealerships, you will have reached an agreement to buy a vehicle that you can not only live with, but that you can feel proud of. In fact, you will probably have earned the grudging admiration of the dealer personnel you've dealt with. Certainly, they don't want 100% of their customers to be like you, but you have bargained with dignity and in good faith.

Of course, there are always other ways to skin the cat. For those of you who want alternatives, tune in to the next chapter.

The Least You Need to Know

➤ To achieve your new-vehicle acquisition goals, you must define them before you enter the dealership.

➤ Look at your negotiating skills honestly and decide if you can deal with the confrontational nature of car-buying.

➤ Put together a "cheat sheet" that includes all the data pertinent to your vehicle acquisition. Your negotiating position is strong because you'll be dealing from knowledge.

➤ It's usually more advantageous to buy from dealers' inventory than to factory-order your new vehicle.

➤ Negotiate the cash price of the new vehicle, then the financing terms, then the trade-in value of your current vehicle.

➤ Shop around for other deals if any aspect of the offer made by the first dealer does not match your goals and expectations.

Other Negotiating Alternatives

"If you want something done right, you have to do it yourself." You've certainly heard that old saw over the years, usually when someone is picking up a mess created by others.

Here's how that relates to the vehicle-acquisition process: With skills you can hone and knowledge that is readily available, you can negotiate a very good deal on a new vehicle, a deal that will meet all of your acquisition goals. That's exactly what we saw in the previous chapters. But there is no doubt that some time and effort is involved, and there is also no doubt that we live in a society that doesn't like to spend time or effort.

This has led to the establishment of alternative car-buying and leasing methods, the subject of this chapter.

Who Needs Middlemen?

Like cars, they come in various colors and sizes—auto brokers, buying services, negotiating advisors, leasing agents, warehouse buying clubs, and computer and telephone referral outfits. The thing that they all share, since none of them performs its service for free, is that they get their money from you, the buyer, from the dealer, or from both.

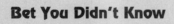

Money Saving Tip
If you know what you're doing, you can negotiate an overall deal that's as good or better than a broker or buying service could get for you—when you include the broker or buying service fee.

They act as a middleman (middleperson?) in the deal, and they get paid for it. Nothing wrong with that. Hurray for capitalism and the USA!

This does, however, have ramifications. Whether the middleman fee is charged to you up front or charged to the dealer as one of his costs of doing business (as if the middleman were an outside salesperson), it affects your overall deal. For example, if a middleman negotiates a low cash price for your purchase but charges you a fee for the service, you must add that fee into the equation as part of your total costs. And you should ask yourself, could you have negotiated the same purchase price for yourself and saved the fee?

Bet You Didn't Know

Between 10 and 15 percent of new vehicles bought last year were purchased through an alternative buying or referral service.

Even more insidious are those brokers and services which charge you a low fee or no fee, and make the bulk of their money from the dealer who sells or leases you the vehicle. You have to wonder if these entities are bargaining in your best interest, when some or all of their fee comes from the dealer.

On the other hand, many people just can't stomach the idea of walking into a dealership. They don't want to talk to salesmen, and they don't want to negotiate the price. For them, the services brokers, agents, and referral outfits provide can offer genuine value.

Soliciting Bids by Phone, Mail, or Fax

Hate to negotiate? Do you despise the idea of sitting across a desk from a dealership salesperson trying to hammer out a deal? Do you like gladiator movies? (Oops, how did that sentence get in there?)

Well, if you hate the idea of a negotiation session with the dealer, you can act as your own auto broker. By now you already know the model you'd like to acquire, the equipment you want, and the color you prefer. Just put all that information into a letter that you will then mail, fax, or send by overnight delivery to several dealers.

Bet You Didn't Know

When you solicit dealer bids, sending the request via fax or overnight delivery are your best bets because they add "immediacy," influencing the dealer to act quickly.

The communication should be addressed to the sales manager or the fleet sales manager at each dealership. (Calling each dealership to get that person's name is a wise move.) As shown in the sample in this section, in the request you should say very bluntly that you are ready to buy a vehicle within the next week, you are contacting a number of dealers, and you will buy it from the dealer who offers you the best cash price. Ask them to get back to you in a timely fashion, either by phone, fax, or overnight delivery, with their best price for the vehicle you describe. Again, fax or overnight are best because then you have the offer in writing.

The goal here is to get a number of dealerships to compete actively for your business. Of course, this tactic works best if you are unencumbered with a trade-in—it's impossible for the dealer to assess your current vehicle via fax—and if you're planning to use your pre-arranged financing source. You can solicit their best financing rate as part of your inquiry, but this often complicates the issue.

When the dealers' bids come back, hold them up to the standards of your vehicle-acquisition goals. If one or more meets those standards, pursue them quickly.

While this technique should generate some responses from dealers, it is not fool-proof. Some dealers will respond with an attractive offer, but when you waltz in to finalize the deal, the vehicle you want to buy has suddenly disappeared. It's the old bait-and-switch with the twist being you helped bait yourself.

In addition, this technique won't eliminate all negotiation. No doubt you will still get an audience with the F&I manager (I'll discuss that in detail in Chapter 20), and, if you want to trade in your current vehicle, you will have to negotiate that portion of the deal in person. But this technique does offer a good way to gauge the market price of the vehicle you want to buy simply and quickly.

Sample Bid Solicitation Letter

Mr. Sal Manager, Fleet Sales Manager
Potash of Nebbishtowne
Nebbishtowne, USA

Dear Sal,

I plan to buy a new vehicle within the next week. I am currently soliciting cash-price offers from several area dealerships on this specific vehicle:

Model Year: 1997
Make: Potash
Model: Manatee
Trim Level: BF
Color: Green
Engine: 2.5-liter V-6
Options: Option Package A (Automatic transmission, air conditioning, leather upholstery)

Option Package C (Antilock brakes, power sunroof)

Optional CD Player/changer

I intend to buy my next vehicle from the dealership that gives me the best price and service.

Please send me your price quote, including add-ons such as dealer preparation fee and dealer advertising assessment, to me at 555-1234 (my fax number). Or you may call me at 555-4321.

I look forward to hearing from you at your earliest convenience.

Sincerely,
Jack Nerad

Shopping by Phone

In years past, dealers shunned those who called looking for prices. "Come on in to the dealership," they'd say, "I can't give you a price over the phone."

Well, that was then and this is now. Those dealers who won't deliver information over the phone are in danger of losing business to those dealers who will. One way to let your fingers do the walking is by calling the sales manager or fleet sales manager and giving her or him an oral presentation of the letter outlined above. Say very directly that you intend to buy within the next few days, and you would like a firm cash price quote on a specific new vehicle. Ask if the dealership is prepared to give you a price quote. If it's not, thank him or her for their time and dial up the next dealer. If the dealership is willing to give a price quote, describe in detail the vehicle you would like to buy. Be as specific as possible, right down to the interior color and the wheelcover style.

Now that some dealers have Internet sites, you can use a similar tactics with your computer. Log onto the dealer's Web site, find the appropriate address, and make your request for a price quote. Or call the dealership, learn the fleet sales manager's e-mail address and e-mail him the letter outlining your request.

Of course, these techniques are subject to the same bait-and-switch downsides as their fax/mail counterpart. Dealer personnel can prevaricate in an attempt to get you into the store.

However, using these techniques marks you as a very sophisticated buyer, so dealers are less likely to try to pull a fast one than if you were the typical rube off the street.

Car-Buying Services

If all this seems like too much for you, there are several nationwide services that may be of help in making your car acquisition. The following mentions are not an endorsement of these services. Having not used them personally nor interviewed their users, it's impossible for me to recommend them or to recommend against them. However, I'll present the services in this section to help you make up your own mind. Table 19.1 explains how to get in touch with each service.

Money magazine has cited three car-buying services as among the best in the nation. They are: Seattle-based AutoAdvisors, Cincinnati's Automobile Consumer Services and California-based CarSource. Each of them charges a fairly substantial fee to search out the vehicle and negotiate the deal. You simply show up at the dealership they designate with check in hand to pick up your new vehicle.

CarBargains, operated by the not-for-profit Center for the Study of Services, performs a function not unlike the bid-solicitation techniques described earlier in the chapter. For a flat fee significantly lower than the fee charged by the previously cited services, it gathers price quotes from several dealers in your area and submits them to you. Each dealer agrees to stand by that price for a specified period of time.

Auto-by-Tel is a free (read dealer-subsidized) service that promises to provide you with low-price quotes from one of its 1,800 affiliated dealers nationwide. As with CarBargains, these quotes are good for a specified period of time.

Table 19.1 Auto Buying Services

Service	How to Contact
AutoAdvisors	800-326-1976
Auto Insider	800-446-7433
Automobile Consumer Services	800-223-4882
CarBargains	800-475-7283
Car Source	800-517-2277
Consumer Car Club	800-227-2582
Auto-by-Tel	CompuServe (Autobytel)
	Prodigy (Auto-by-tel)
	Internet (http://www.autobytel.com)
AutoVantage	America Online
	CompuServe
	Prodigy

Auto Insider is a free-to-the-public dealer-referral service that will provide you with a list of dealers in your area who agree to provide discounts. (Without seeming too cynical, what dealer doesn't provide discounts these days?) It does not provide price quotes, however. You must contact the dealer for that information.

Consumer Car Club is a fee-based service that assigns you to a "vehicle buyer" when you have decided the specific make, model, and equipment you want. After finding out from you how far you are willing to travel to purchase your new vehicle, that buyer negotiates a deal for you with a dealer.

AutoVantage, which does business on America Online, CompuServe, and Prodigy, charges a "membership fee" that entitles you to various services, including price negotiation with one or more of 1,000 affiliated dealers. If you like, you can place your vehicle order over a toll-free telephone number.

Be aware that some of these services may be serving two masters—you and the dealer you are buying the vehicle from. When you make the call, ask that question pointedly. Then it's up to you to decide your comfort-level with the response.

Are Auto Brokers the Answer?

Auto brokers are third parties who negotiate a purchase or lease for you for a fee. In addition to the nationwide buying services, auto brokers of one sort or another are doing business in most major metropolitan areas across the country, except in the few where they are prohibited by law.

Auto brokerages can be large organizations, participating in the sales of thousands of vehicles per year, but most of them are relatively small operations. They live off the fact that many consumers are poor negotiators or just don't want to negotiate their car deal. Consumers perceive the broker as "being on their side," their hired gun in the shoot-out with the dealer. But is that perception accurate?

In some cases, of course, it is. But in others, the broker is likely to receive greater compensation from the dealer he steers the buyer to than from the consumer who hired him. Now, there's nothing wrong with "networking"—using your contacts to help your consumer client. But there's a whole lot wrong with purporting to represent the consumer while secretly serving the other side.

If you are considering the use of a broker, put this question to him or her up front. And let them know you will be scrupulously scrutinizing the deal they come back with.

In all cases, the proof is in the deal itself. Using a referral, buying-service or broker in no way eliminates your need to do your homework. If you've done your research, you will be in a good position to assess the quality of the deals offered by these services. If you haven't, you run the risk of lining the pockets of not only your local dealer but of a buying service or broker as well.

Bet You Didn't Know

Why do dealers sell vehicles through brokers when they have their own sales staffs? The answer is the "incremental sale." Some dealers feel they can reach buyers who would never enter their dealerships through brokers.

Are You a Good Candidate to Use a Broker or Buying Service?

To answer this question an honest assessment of your needs and desires is in order. If your goal is to negotiate a vehicle acquisition at the absolute lowest cost, then stay away from brokers and buying services. In the simplest terms, they add another mouth to feed. If you are diligent, you can get just as good a price as a broker or buying service, and in the process you'll save the fee.

On the other hand, if you are willing to trade some cash to gain convenience, the use of a broker or buying service could be for you. If your goal is a good deal, not the Mona Lisa of all car deals ever made, a good broker or buying service can help speed you on your way. You might not have the time to contact half a dozen dealers to solicit bids, so why not pay someone to do it for you?

Still, I must remind you again, hiring a third-party helper does not remove the necessity to perform your due diligence. If you fail to do your homework, you can get a lousy deal through a broker or service just like you can if you negotiate the deal yourself.

How Do You Find a Good Broker?

Finding a good broker is one of the most difficult tasks around. Even if a broker comes well-referred, those referrals might be worthless. Here's why: Since many car buyers leave thousands of dollars on the table when they conclude their transaction, they might think that a broker who saves them $500 is a miracle worker. And often when they talk about the money a broker saved them, they're speaking about dollars off the MSRP. Now, you and I know that in most instances, it doesn't take Houdini to get a dealer to come down a significant amount off the MSRP.

Again, the proof is in the deal, and you're not going to see the deal a broker can make for you until you hire her or him. My best advice is: Have a frank discussion with the broker *before* you engage his or her services. If you like what they say, and you feel taking a chance on them is worth their fee, give it a shot. Otherwise, keep your cash in your pocket and do it yourself.

The Least You Need to Know

➤ The consumer's reluctance to spend time and effort in the vehicle acquisition process, and their distrust of dealers, has led to the establishment of car-buying services and auto brokerages that act as middlemen for a fee.

➤ You can act as your own broker, soliciting bids from several dealers using phone, fax, computer, or mail.

➤ Car-buying and car-referral organizations offer an array of services.

After You Think You Made a Deal

At the conclusion of Chapter 18, you and the salesperson reached agreement on a deal. After some strenuous but always dignified negotiations, you came to an understanding on the cash purchase price, the financing arrangement, and the price for your trade-in. When you shook hands, you probably breathed a sigh of relief, thinking your work was done.

Well, believe you me, at this stage your work is far from done. You still must square off against two of the dealership's heaviest hitters—the sales manager and the F&I manager. So you still have some work to do, and this chapter will help you do it better. Or, as Paul Newman said as Fast Eddie Felson in *The Hustler*, "It's not over till Fats says it's over."

Stupid (Costly) Dealer Tricks

Let's hark back for a second to the dealer's most basic goal—maximizing the profit on his 1.1 sales per day. How does he do it? Every way he can think of.

As you move through the process, confusion is the dealer's friend and your worst enemy. By now you think you have a deal, and, if you're smart, you asked the salesperson to write down everything you agreed to. For good measure, you've noted on your "cheat sheet" the exact terms for cash purchase, financing, and trade-in. Where many deals go terribly wrong is in getting this information, this "done deal," on a sales contract where it counts.

One typical gambit is for the salesperson to disappear with your paperwork to get it "okayed by the sales manager." After several rounds of negotiations, you might think this is just a formality, but that's not the case at all. This is probably a last-ditch effort to pry more money from you.

Odds are your salesperson will come back, head shaking, and say, "I can't believe it; he said I went too low." Then, looking at you with puppy-dog eyes, the salesperson will ask, "Can you help me out by going up $25 a month? If you do, I'm sure we can get him to say yes." Can *you* help the *salesperson* out? *What's going on here? Have you suddenly become blood brothers?*

The salesperson is actually working two scams on you at once. First, she or he is imposing on a supposed relationship between the two of you, a relationship that didn't exist before today and most likely won't exist tomorrow. And, worse yet, this ploy has made you concentrate on the monthly payment, rather than the big picture. Sure, $25 a month doesn't seem like much, but over the course of a four-year loan, that's $1,200—a fairly large last-second alteration in the deal, if you ask me.

The Encounter with the Sales Manager

If the salesperson tries to run a scam on you like the one just described, you have two alternatives. One is walking out the door (something you're perfectly justified in doing). The other is demanding to speak immediately to the sales manager. The second option is a doubled-edged sword because the sales manager didn't get to be the sales manager because she or he swept up the back room so well. The sales manager is often the dealership's most adept salesperson and its resident "closer," who finalizes deals.

On the other hand, the sales manager in most dealerships has the authority to okay the deal. (In many small dealerships the dealer principal is also the sales manager.) Speaking to him or her can save valuable time and allow you to cut to the chase. If you have an agreement with the salesperson about cash price, financing terms, and trade-in allowance, tell the sales manager exactly what your agreement consists of. Then ask him if his dealership is willing to back up that agreement or if it has just wasted an hour or so of your time.

Listen to his answer. If it's not the answer you want to hear, get up and walk out. Remember, you're not losing anything. You never really had a deal, just empty promises. If the sales manager says he will okay his salesperson's offer, ask him to put it in writing in the form of a sales agreement. But even if he agrees, you must be wary at this stage as well.

In yet another effort to extract money from your pockets, the sales manager may confront you with a panoply of additional, unforeseen charges, which he will characterize as being "routine" or "standard practice." Among them are:

> ➤ Vehicle preparation fee, what we used to call "dealer prep."

> ➤ Document preparation fee.

> ➤ Dealer advertising association fee.

> ➤ Vehicle inspection fee.

> ➤ Loan origination fee.

Money Saving Tip
Dealers don't expect to get the same level of profit on every sale. They hope to offset low-profit deals (like yours) with "home run" deals made with other buyers.

Your basic response to all these gambits should be no. Each of these "costs," if indeed there is a real cost involved, is a part of the dealer's everyday business. The dealership should absorb these costs as part of the purchase price. After all, does your grocery store put a surcharge on the price of a quart of milk to cover its advertising costs?

If the sales manager won't budge on these charges, you suddenly have a very different deal, a deal that could cost you $500 to $1,000 more than the deal you agreed to. Again, it may just be time to exercise your shoe leather. Most sales managers will be very reluctant to let you walk out at this late stage unless their only hope of profit lies in the add-ons you're saying no to.

With any luck, though, you and the dealer will be able to come to a mutually acceptable agreement. You may well have to suck up and accept at least some of the add-on charges. Perhaps you can rest easier knowing that most dealerships will do pretty much the same thing. Then the final purchase price that you and the sales manager agree on will make it onto the appropriate line of the dealership's sales contract. You're nearing the finish of your new-vehicle quest, but you have one more hurdle to jump.

The Encounter with the F&I Manager

"F&I" in the F&I manager's title stands for finance and insurance. Now, that sounds properly innocuous and unthreatening. Well, don't be fooled. The F&I manager is another of the dealership's soldiers in the war to maximize profits.

Quite likely, you will be ushered into the F&I manager's office, "to put the finishing touches on the paperwork," according to the salesperson or sales manager. You should know that most F&I managers are very skilled commission salespeople, and they have a mission—extract as much after-sale cash as they can.

One way they can do it is by altering the financing deal slightly from what you agreed to. A common ploy is to suggest, "Hey, how would you like your monthly payment to be $75 lower?" Well, who wouldn't? But you can bet he's not going to lower the interest rate. With your okay, he's going to lengthen the term, something that could cost you $1,000 or more. Of course, financing is just one of the F&I manager's bailiwicks. Another prime profit opportunity is selling insurance.

"Insurance?" you may be saying, "Who buys their car insurance from their dealer?" The answer is no one, if by "car insurance" you mean "car-accident insurance." But auto dealers sell millions of dollars of car-related insurance each year, primarily three types—credit life insurance, health and disability insurance, and extended warranties. Let's look at each one.

Credit life insurance is designed to help your survivors pay off your car loan in the event of your death during the loan period. This might have made some sense back in the old days of the "family car," where the surviving spouse might not have been able to handle the loan payments if the breadwinner in the family came up dead, leading to the tearful repossession of said vehicle. If you have proper life insurance coverage, you need this add-on like an elephant needs spats.

Health and disability insurance isn't a bad idea in these days of outrageous medical costs, but the auto dealership isn't the place to get your best bargain on this coverage. If you really need health and disability coverage, contact several local insurance agencies and/or sign up for coverage through your employer, union, or other affinity group.

Finally, there is the *extended warranty*. Many people don't even look at it as insurance, but that's exactly what it is. Essentially, you are betting that your vehicle is going to break down and require costly repairs and the insurance company is betting that it won't. The complicating factor is the fact that virtually all new vehicles sold today are backed by substantial manufacturer-backed warranties. With the minimum coverage on most vehicles three years or 36,000 miles, whichever comes first, you have to ask yourself, how much longer than three years will I be driving this vehicle? Add to that the even longer powertrain warranties that are prevalent these days, and you have to wonder how many car buyers actually benefit from buying extended warranty coverage.

Bet You Didn't Know

You don't have to buy extended warranty coverage when you buy the vehicle. Usually you can purchase such coverage any time during the first year of ownership before you car has turned 12,000 miles.

Yet, millions do every year, spurred on by the sales pitch of the F&I manager. Often the purchase will be presented like this: "For just $20 a month, you can be fully protected for six full years." However, over the course of a four-year loan, that $20 a month will total $1,000—and your extended coverage won't begin to protect you until the end of three years or your 36,000th mile.

Of course, that $1,000 will seem cheap if your engine explodes at 40,000 miles. And that could happen, but the insurance company that collects your premiums, backed up by their highly paid statisticians, are betting it won't.

It all comes down to the goals of your purchase. If you intend to drive your new vehicle for a period longer than three years, it could make sense to consider an extended warranty. If you do consider one, keep these factors in mind:

1. Consider only a manufacturer-backed warranty. In the past decade several independent warranty companies have gone belly-up, leaving their policy holders with no coverage.

2. Remember the price is negotiable, and there's a lot of room for negotiations.

3. Take time to understand exactly what is covered, what isn't, and what the deductibles (the cash that comes from you pocket in the case of a repair) are.

Say No to Add-Ons

In addition to finance and insurance, the F&I manager is also in charge of selling so-called after-sale items.

One prime after-sale add-on is sold as "paint sealant," "finish protector," or something along those lines. In most instances the many coats of high-tech paint that go on today's vehicles will do just fine without this treatment, which most often amounts to a $70 wax job that could cost you $300. A close cousin of the "paint sealant" gambit is the "fabric protector" or "interior protection package," which is claimed to guard your seats from spills, spots, and even sun damage. Again, the cost is usually high, the benefits low.

Lemon
After-sale corrosion protection can void the manufacturer "rust-through" warranty.

Particularly in the eastern half of the U.S., undercoating is a heavily marketed item. The claimed benefits—corrosion prevention and sound-deadening. Well, today's vehicles are engineered and built with the latest rust-preventative techniques and many come with a warranty against rust-through. And they are wind-tunnel tested to be as quiet as possible. Bottom line—little value here.

With very rare exceptions, the after-sale items presented to you by the F&I manager either have dubious value in the first place or could be purchased cheaper elsewhere. As Nancy Reagan might advise you, just say no.

Analyzing the Purchase Agreement

After you have your meetings with the sales manager and F&I manager, you will be given a document to review and sign. This is the sales agreement, otherwise known as the sales contract. It's important that you take the time to review it carefully. If you don't think you can do that in the hubbub of the dealership, ask to take it home to review. This piece of paper is a contract to purchase or lease a very expensive asset.

Look at the document carefully and get any questions you have resolved by the dealership. Check each individual charge and do the math to make certain the total cost you are approving is the total cost you agreed to. Even at this late stage, some dealers will try to slip one by you, plus there is always the possibility of honest clerical error in putting the papers together. When you are certain that all of the papers are in order according to your understanding of the deal, you are ready to take delivery. But don't sign the contract or hand the dealer your check yet. You still need to do a thorough inspection of the vehicle, which is described in the next chapter.

The Least You Need to Know

➤ The sales manager may present you with a laundry list of add-on charges—after you thought you had a deal. You can negotiate many of these charges away.

➤ The F&I manager is most often a commission salesperson. Most of the items offered by F&I managers are high-cost, low-value.

➤ Look at your plans for your new vehicle before you buy an extended warranty.

➤ Review the sales contract carefully and get any discrepancies remedied.

Chapter 21

Taking Delivery

In This Chapter

➤ Checking it out

➤ Exterior and interior checklist

➤ The pre-delivery test drive

➤ What if it's not what you thought?

Taking delivery of a new car, truck, sport utility, or van should be a joyous time. Of course I'm prejudiced, but I think vehicles are a lot of fun and new vehicles perhaps the most fun of all. Obtaining one in a transaction you can feel proud of is a significant achievement.

It's not time to drop your guard yet, however. You still have to take delivery of that expensive combination of steel, glass, rubber, and plastic, and there is still time to fumble the ball even though you're very close to the goal line.

Of course, excitement is building and your adrenaline level is up, but you have to stay calm. Remember, that vehicle isn't yours until you sign the sales contract and hand over your check. Until then, that's the way you want it, because you want to do your final inspection, as detailed in this chapter, while the dealer still owns the vehicle.

Performing the Inspection

These days many dealerships, usually at the recommendation of manufacturers, are turning the delivery process into a ritual. A contingent of the dealership's personnel get together, the salesman hands you the keys to your shiny new Whatzitz BM, and you get a standing ovation for being such a smart shopper. That's all well and good (if you don't mind a cheap standing-O), but this is not what you need in a delivery process. What you need is the unfettered opportunity to take a long look at the vehicle, inside and out, plus a chance to test drive it, before signing that old John Hancock and handing over the check.

Lemon
Perform your pre-delivery inspection in daylight. It's amazing how much you might miss under lights at night or in inclement weather.

The goal here is to find any and all defects while the dealer still owns the vehicle. If you do find defects, you can either wait to get them rectified to your satisfaction or (and I know it's tough with that attractive new vehicle saying, "I'm yours") to walk away from the deal.

The first thing to do is to let the salesperson know this is how you intend to take delivery. You want some time with the vehicle, perhaps as much as an hour.

While not jumping for joy, the salesperson should have no problem with this and will help you schedule your delivery appointment.

Inspecting the Exterior

It might sound simplistic, but you should start with the big picture. Is this the vehicle you thought you were about to buy? Is it the same vehicle you inspected and did your test drive on?

It's amazing just how often dealers present unsuspecting customers with the wrong vehicle. Oh, the general particulars may be right—same model, same color, similar level of equipment—and I'd like to think it's usually a case of honest mistaken identity. But if I put in the time to do a thorough test drive and I thought that was the specific vehicle I was buying, I'd be more than a little perturbed if another one was offered to me on delivery day. (One way to assure this is to jot down the vehicle identification number—VIN—when you do your test drive.)

Once you establish that the vehicle in front of you is the right one, inspect the exterior of the vehicle carefully. Use the checklist in this section to remind you of which items to check, and make notes about what you find. Look for scratches, dents, and dings. Check body panels for unusual gaps and poor fits. Examine chrome, badges, and rub strips for misalignment and looseness. Open and close each door, the hood and the trunk lid, making certain they all function properly.

Pre-Delivery Checklist—Exterior		
Item to Inspect	**OK**	**Needs Attention**
Scratches, dents, dings		
Chrome, badges, rubstrips		
Doors		
Hood		
Trunk lid		
Radiator cap		
Cooling system reservoir		
Windshield solvent reservoir		
Engine oil		
Brake fluid		
Automatic transmission fluid		
Headlights		
Tail lights		
Brake lights		
Back-up lights		
Side warning lights		
Front turn signal indicators		
Rear turn signal indicators		
Tires (brand, model and size)		
Wheels, wheel covers		
Wheel locks, wheel lock keys		
Body damage		

When looking under the hood, check the radiator cap, the cooling system reservoir and its cap, and the windshield solvent reservoir and its cap to make certain they are all in place and in good condition (no cracks or discoloring). At the same time, check the engine oil, brake fluid, and automatic transmission fluid levels to see they are where they should be.

Ask the salesperson to help you check the function of all exterior lights—headlights, tail lights, brake lights, back-up lights, side warning lights and front and rear turn signal indicators.

Check the tires to make certain they are all the same brand, model, and size. Inspect the wheels and wheel covers for nicks, scratches, and chips. If you've ordered wheel locks, make certain they have been installed and that keys for the locks are in the vehicle.

In your inspection, be on the lookout for body damage. A surprising number of new cars are damaged in transit from the factory, and whether the damage occurred on a ship, train, or truck, it can be difficult to fix properly. The paint may look okay now, but will it match the rest of the vehicle months or years down the road?

In fact, even if the body is not damaged, significant damage to the paint surface can be difficult to repair since matching can become a problem.

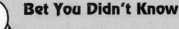

Bet You Didn't Know

According to J.D. Power and Associates, problems with body panel fit-and-finish are the most prevalent exterior problems in new vehicles.

Inspecting the Interior

Once you give the exterior of the vehicle a thorough going-over, it's time to dive into the interior of the car. Again, the checklist in this section can help. First, slip into the front seat and check the odometer reading. It should be very low, well under a hundred miles, reflecting only a test drive or two. (Hopefully you put a number of those miles on the vehicle yourself in your own test drive.)

If the mileage is higher than that, something odd has happened. Could be that once you put the car on hold, the dealer or salesperson has been commuting in it for the past several days. Or the dealership has run several test drives on your "sold" vehicle. Whatever the reason, you deserve an explanation.

While still behind the wheel, inspect the dashboard and steering wheel for fit and finish. Make certain all the optional equipment you ordered is on the vehicle and that it all works. Ask the salesperson to help you understand the controls for the air conditioner, sound system, sunroof, convertible top, remote-control side mirrors, remote filler cap opener, remote hood opener, remote trunk or hatch release, heated seats, and everything else you ordered.

If you ordered power-operated seats, ask the salesperson to teach you how to adjust them. If the power seats have a memory feature, learn how to use it and make certain it works correctly.

Go to each seating area and check the upholstery for stains, tears, and ripped or un-sewn seams. Check the carpeting for fit, stains, and looseness. Check the headliner above each seating area for stains, rips, tears, and droops.

Check the operation and fit-and-finish of the glovebox and the center console. Do the doors open easily? Is the glovebox light working?

Check the sunvisors for quality, fit, and finish. Is the fabric torn or frayed? Does the light for the vanity mirror work?

With each door open, check the weather-stripping around the doors for rips, tears, and looseness. Do the same around each window frame with the windows lowered. (Poor weatherstripping can cause leaks and irritating wind noise.)

Open the trunk or cargo area and check the operation of the trunk light and the accessibility of the spare tire. Make certain that all the tire-changing tools, including lug wrench and jack, are in their proper places. Check the trunk weatherstripping for possible problem areas that could cause leaks.

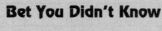

Bet You Didn't Know

According to J.D. Power and Associates, electrical and accessory problems are the most prevalent problems in new vehicles overall.

Pre-Delivery Checklist—Interior		
Item to Inspect	**OK**	**Needs Attention**
Odometer mileage		
Dashboard		
Steering wheel		
Air conditioner		
Sound system		
Sunroof, moonroof		
Convertible top		
Remote-control side mirrors		
Remote filler cap opener		
Remote hood opener		
Remote trunk, hatch release		
Heated seats		
Power-operated seats		
Memory seats, mirrors		
Seat upholstery		
Carpeting		
Headliner		
Glovebox and glovebox light		
Center console		
Sunvisors		
Vanity mirror and vanity mirror light		
Dome light		
Reading Lights		
Weatherstripping on doors, windows, and the trunk lid		
Trunk, cargo area carpeting		
Trunk, cargo area light		
Spare tire and tire-changing tools		

The Final Test Drive

As I mentioned in Chapter 9, during the test drive, you want to concentrate on the driving dynamics of the vehicle. If you test-drove the same vehicle previously, you don't have to make this test drive as lengthy or drive on various road types. What you are looking for this time are any differences between the way the vehicle rode and drove previously and what it's doing now. Of course, if there are big differences, it's a sign of a problem and/or abuse.

Here are some areas you should analyze (you can use the checklist in this section to make notes):

Ride comfort Is the ride soft, harsh, or somewhere in the middle? Does the vehicle develop unusual ride characteristics like bucking, weaving, or hobby horsing? Does it develop vibrations over unusual surfaces?

Quiet Is it quiet in the cockpit of the vehicle? Is there an objectionable amount of wind noise, tire noise, engine noise, or exhaust noise? Are there squeaks and rattles from the dash, glovebox, or other areas?

Acceleration Does the vehicle accelerate smoothly and strongly as the accelerator pedal is pushed? Does the vehicle seem powerful or weak? Are there "dead spots" when you begin to accelerate or as you accelerate? Pay particular attention to the action of the transmission. If it's an automatic, do the gears change effortlessly without noticeably affecting the vehicle's motion, or do they thunk and clunk? If it's a manual, do the gears engage smoothly and does the clutch pedal operate smoothly and with little effort?

This is the time to test the operation of the cruise control. Does it keep the car at a steady speed? Does it engage easily or does it work in fits and starts?

Braking Does the vehicle slow smoothly as you apply the brakes? Does the braking action seem progressive, that is, more braking the harder you push the brake pedal? Are there objectionable vibrations through the brake pedal? Is the car's steering affected by braking?

Handling Does the vehicle seem easy to maneuver? Is the steering too light, too heavy, or just right? Does the vehicle respond quickly to turns of the wheel? Does it respond too quickly (it feels jumpy) or too slowly (it feels lethargic)?

Bet You Didn't Know

According to J.D. Power and Associates, squeaks and rattles afflict 10 percent of new cars and 15 percent of new trucks based on owner-reported problems.

Delivery Test Drive Checklist		
	OK	Unacceptable
Ride Comfort		
Quiet		
Squeaks		
Rattles		
Acceleration		
Transmission		
Cruise Control		
Braking		
Handling		

If It's Not What You Thought You Bought

At the conclusion of the exterior inspection, the interior inspection, and the test drive, you will find yourself back at the dealership in front of a salesperson who will be scratching his or her head, because he or she has never seen a delivery process this extensive. No matter. You deserve to have this multi-thousand-dollar machine right—before you buy it.

With any luck it will be right. Everything will check out, and you'll be happy to hand the salesperson the check and drive off into the gathering dusk.

But what if it isn't? Well, if you ask me (and I guess you did), it depends on the severity of the problem(s). I classify the problems into four categories:

1. Problems so minor they can be fixed on the spot.

2. Problems so minor you can trust the dealership to fix them at a later date.

3. Problems that must be fixed before you take delivery of the vehicle.

4. Problems so major they cause you to reject the vehicle.

The first level of problems can be fixed by the addition of a little elbow grease, the turning of a screwdriver, or the addition of some fluids (into the car, not you.) They are basically no-brainers.

The second level presents a different problem, because once the vehicle is yours the dealer has much less motivation to fix problems quickly. Here you have to judge how responsive the dealer personnel seem. If I was going to err in this judgment, I'd err on the side of "not too responsive." In other words, I'd accept very few category-two problems. Instead, I'd insist that the dealer fix the problem on the spot or I would drop them into category three.

Category-three problems are a bear because just when you're all psyched up to take delivery, you have to delay that gratification until the vehicle is fixed to meet your satisfaction. Because of this, many buyers blow off problems that should have been addressed. The lesson to be learned is: If you have loose chrome, bad weatherstripping, or a faulty dashboard warning light, you should not take delivery until the dealership has rectified the problem.

Finally, the most vexing problems are category fours. You worked hard, put together a good deal, and now you must turn your back on it. It's hard. But if the vehicle has body damage, a deep paint scratch, or some other problem that you believe can never be fixed to your satisfaction, the time to cut your losses is now.

The Least You Need to Know

➤ You must perform a thorough inspection of the new vehicle before you take delivery to protect yourself and your investment.

➤ Look closely at all areas of the interior and exterior of the vehicle, noting areas that need to be fixed.

➤ Check the vehicle's odometer mileage; if the mileage is more than 100 miles and the vehicle wasn't a demo, demand an explanation.

➤ If the vehicle checks out to your expectations, accept delivery; if it doesn't, you must be prepared to walk away from the deal.

If Things Go Wrong

I have a motto—you could call it Nerad's Law—that says, "Nothing is as easy as it should be." I don't know why it's true, but I do know that it *is* true, and it applies to the process of acquiring an automobile.

You can choose the brand, model, and equipment level right. Pick the dealer right. Do the deal right. Do the preliminary test drives right. Do the pre-delivery inspection right. Heck, you can do it all right. Yet when all is said and done, you can still get yourself a bad vehicle, and this chapter can help you deal with such a situation.

I can't promise you that even if you buy one of the new car or used car best bets mentioned in the appendices of this book, you won't have trouble with your vehicle. Cars and trucks are very complicated machines—too complicated to operate perfectly all the time.

Odds are you will have some trouble. According to J.D. Power and Associates, the industry average of new-car problems in the 1996 model year was 100 problems per 100 cars. You don't have to be calculator-equipped to figure out that means an average of one problem per vehicle. And that's in the first 90 days of ownership!

Bet You Didn't Know

Trucks have more problems than cars, at least according to the most recent data from J.D. Power and Associates. In the latest survey, the problem incidence per truck was 1.23 versus 1.0 per car.

Sure, some car owners didn't report any problems with their cars, but they were far outnumbered by those who did. Face it, somewhere along the way you're going to have a problem or two with your new wheels. The question is, what to do about it?

How to Complain to Your Dealer and Get Results

With the high visibility of customer satisfaction data these days, especially the much-quoted J.D. Power and Associates Customer Satisfaction Index, dealers are not quite so quick to dismiss their customers' complaints as they once were. Since the CSI is based on vehicle quality and dealer service, manufacturers are getting pretty insistent that their dealers don't drop the ball on servicing people with complaints. The fact that many manufacturers also grant extra perks to dealers with high CSI scores lights additional fire under them to be more responsive than in the past.

Another factor in your favor if something goes wrong—new-vehicle warranties are both lengthy in time and lengthy in coverage. The average bumper-to-bumper new-car warranty these days is three years or 36,000 miles, whichever comes first.

This doesn't assure that getting the problem fixed is a walk in the park. Dealers still make more money performing regular service and maintenance than doing warranty work, but the difference is far less significant than when the item wasn't covered by a warranty at all. However, if you do have a problem, you may need to follow all the steps in the Consumer Complaints Chain, described throughout this chapter, to get satisfaction.

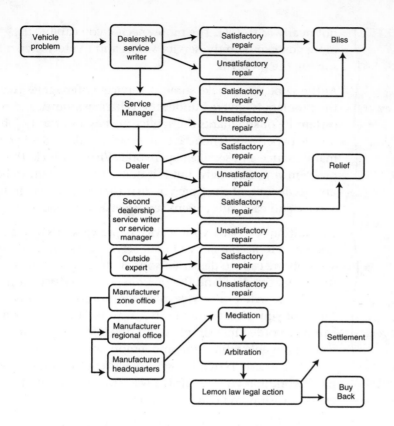

The Consumer Complaints Chain.

If You Have a Problem

If (should I say when) you have a problem with your new vehicle, it's in your best interest to help the dealer solve the problem quickly. It's also in your best interest to determine whether the problem is covered under the vehicle's warranty, and, if it is, get it into the warranty system immediately.

Start by scheduling an appointment with the service department of the dealership where you purchased the vehicle. This will give you the most leverage, though, under factory warranty terms, you can take the vehicle to any authorized service facility.

When you meet with the service writer, describe in as precise terms as you are able what the problem is. If the hood won't open or there's a water leak at the top of the windshield on the passenger's side, that's pretty easy to describe, but if the problem is less-well-defined, say a hesitation on acceleration or a clunky gear shift when the car is cold, that's

Lemon
Most dealership service writers are not technicians or mechanics; they are commission salespeople whose job is to sell you service and maintenance.

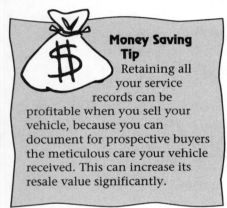

Money Saving Tip
Retaining all your service records can be profitable when you sell your vehicle, because you can document for prospective buyers the meticulous care your vehicle received. This can increase its resale value significantly.

not nearly as simple. The more specific you can be, the more you can help the service writer and the technician in solving the problem.

At the same time, make sure the service writer agrees that the problem is covered under the vehicle warranty and be certain he or she marks the service visit as a warranty job on the paperwork. Then save that paperwork, and all your maintenance and service paperwork. With any luck, the problem won't get ugly, but if it does, it's important to be able to document the time you first took the vehicle in for service and each subsequent service visit you made.

In addition to saving your service paperwork, it's also a good idea to keep a diary of your service appointments and your phone calls to dealer personnel. Record what was discussed, the date, and the outcome of each discussion. If the service writer or service manager promises you any relief for your situation note that as well. This diary, which can be recorded in a simple steno notebook, will serve you well in possible arbitration and lemon law legal action. Also, make certain that the service writer notes on the paperwork that your repair is a warranty item on each and every occasion you come in for service.

Part of your job in helping solve the problem is being smart and flexible about your visit to the service department. For instance, if your vehicle has trouble starting on cold mornings, it's not the wisest thing to take your car in for service at noon on a warm, sunny day. It's far better to leave the vehicle overnight, so the dealer technician can duplicate the conditions in which you're having trouble the following morning.

By taking an intelligent approach to automotive service—and by keeping up with your vehicle maintenance schedule—most problems can be fixed quickly and painlessly.

Problem Problems

On the other hand, some vehicle problems just don't seem to go away. These problems are maddening to both customer and dealer. Dealers call them "comebacks." Comebacks come in several varieties. There is the maddeningly inconsistent "intermittent problem." Sometimes the cars starts right up; other times it won't start at all. Or the vehicle will suddenly cough and die right in the middle of the expressway, but when the customer tries to duplicate the problem under the technician's watchful eye, it proves to be impossible.

Then there are the subjective problems, like wind noise or brake squeal. The car's shape is its shape, and if the engineers messed up in the wind tunnel and the development engineers didn't pick out the source of the wind noise in the development rides, there's darn little a mechanic can do about it now. Of course, the stock answer, "They all do that," will do little to calm the irate consumer.

Let's Talk Terms
A customer with an unresolved problem who returns to the service facility is referred to as a *comeback*.

Then there's the problem of simple incompetence. There is a crying need for well-trained, highly skilled auto technicians today. Because of this, some problems aren't solved the first time or the second time, or the twentieth time.

Finally, there are the problems the manufacturers know about but don't want to do anything about. Sad to say, but somewhere along the way many manufacturers make the "business decision" not to fix certain known problems that occur again and again, usually the result of a design or manufacturing defect. They figure that it would cost more money to fix the problems than they would lose by alienating the customers whose vehicles have the problem.

Taking Complaints Beyond the Dealer

Let's assume for a moment that you took your vehicle in for service, but when you got back it was not repaired to your satisfaction. What do you do?

The first thing to do is to take it back to the service department and speak to the service writer that handled your job in the first place. Most often, after a short discussion, the dealership will make another attempt to fix your problem, again at no charge since the problem is covered under warranty. If, after this second attempt, the problem persists, speak with the service manager. At this point, she or he will probably assign the department's best technician to your vehicle to give the repair another shot.

If the problem still remains unsolved after this third visit, you have two choices. You can return to the dealership again and speak to the dealer principal if you're getting no cooperation from the service manager or you can take your vehicle to a second dealership of the same make. Sometimes the service department at the dealership where you purchased the vehicle just won't have the technical expertise that another service department will have. (Just as some surgeons are better than others, so are technicians.)

If the problem persists after retrieving your vehicle, you should take it to a third dealership service department. By this time, you will probably have heard one of two things about your vehicle. Either "they all do that" or "we can't seem to find anything wrong with it." Neither is a good thing.

Bet You Didn't Know

Some manufacturers have recently instituted a policy of "dealer self-authorization" on warranty claims, giving dealers wide latitude to fix customer problems without a specific factory okay.

At this stage, I recommend taking the vehicle to the best independent shop in the area that specializes in the type of repair your vehicle needs, even if you have to pay for their diagnosis. For example, if your transmission is acting up, ask around to find the best transmission shop in the area. Often the seasoned veterans at these independent businesses can give you a clear picture of what the problem is, including letting you know if the problem is a manufacturing or design defect.

If it is such a defect, the dealership service departments were correct when they said, "They all do that." It also means that the manufacturer might be "stonewalling" the problem—refusing to admit it exists and refusing to pay for fixing it.

Consumer Remedies from the Manufacturer

If you've made several visits to your dealer's service department and visited one or more additional same-make service departments, it's time to speak directly with the manufacturer's zone or regional office. In most instances, the zone and/or regional offices and their telephone numbers are listed in the owner's manual that accompanies your new vehicle. (Most owner's manuals also spell out the dispute-resolution process in detail.) By this point, your dealer probably has spoken to the zone or region as well, because it is the zone or region that authorizes payment for the warranty work. With a recurring problem, your vehicle has long since passed the threshold of what the manufacturer is usually willing to pay for the repair, so the dealer must get additional work authorized by the region or zone office. Sometimes this isn't too difficult. Other times it's darn near impossible.

A discussion with the region/zone customer service manager or general manager may get you some action. Additional work can be authorized and, by this time, the factory service department might have come up with a solution if the problem you are experiencing is also occurring in other vehicles.

If the problem still is unresolved after all this, you can also take the problem to the manufacturer's national office. Write or call the highest-ranking member of the organization's customer satisfaction and/or service department. (A phone call to the CEO of a giant car company will generally net you exactly nothing.) Describe your problem precisely in as unemotional a manner as is possible under the circumstances, and ask her or him what the company is going to do about it. Listen carefully to the answer, because it can give you hope or let you know, diplomatically, that the manufacturer isn't going to do anything at all about the problem.

Mediation, Arbitration, and Consumer Groups

If the manufacturer service/customer satisfaction department gives you the impression the company is ready to let you twist in the wind, immediately seek professional mediation of your issue. You can do this by contacting the region/zone office and requesting information about filing for mediation or by contacting a local consumer advocacy group. (Local radio and television consumer reporters are good sources for information about these groups.)

In mediation, a third party or independent panel will attempt to help you reach an agreement with the manufacturer. You will present your story, backed up with all your accumulated service records, correspondence, and notes about conversations documented in your diary. Then the manufacturer will present its story. The third party will attempt to work out some sort of arrangement or compromise, based on what they've heard. Of course, you are under no obligation to accept this compromise.

If you don't accept the suggestion of the mediator and find it impossible to come to an agreement with the manufacturer, you can request arbitration. Again, your local consumer group can tell you how to enter this process.

In arbitration, you and the manufacturer present your sides of the story. The arbitrator will hear both sides, then give a ruling. If you have agreed to "binding" arbitration, you must abide by this ruling. If not, you still have the option of taking legal action.

Lemon
One resource for consumer-protection information is the Center for Auto Safety, 2001 S Street NW, Washington, DC 20009, 202-328-7700.

State Lemon Laws

A majority of our 50 states have adopted what are commonly known as "lemon laws" in an attempt to protect consumers who have purchased certifiably awful vehicles. Though specifics of the lemon laws vary widely by state, they apply only to the worst of the worst of vehicles.

Under the terms of the vast majority of these laws, a vehicle must have a recurring problem that cannot be fixed and the customer must have made numerous attempts to obtain the proper repair. Many of the laws also specify that the vehicle must have spent a proscribed number of days in the service department and the consumer has been without his or her vehicle for a proscribed number of days before the lemon law provisions apply.

Resorting to a state's lemon law is a worst-case scenario and should only be done after you have exhausted all the remedies discussed previously. When necessary, however, the proper pursuit of a lemon law case can result in the manufacturer buying back your problem vehicle.

To get more information about your state's lemon laws, contact your state attorney general's office or contact a local attorney specializing in lemon law litigation through your state or local bar association.

The Least You Need to Know

➤ Most problems can be resolved with one trip to the dealer's service department.

➤ If you have a recurring problem, take your vehicle to another dealer service department or visit an independent shop that specializes in a specific system or repair.

➤ You can take unresolved problems to mediation or arbitration.

➤ State lemon laws are a last-resort solution for only the worst recurring problems.

Glossary of Automotive Terms

acquisition fee   A fee charged to the lessee to initiate a lease, in some ways equivalent to a down payment.

active safety devices   Devices that aid the driver in controlling her or his vehicle but require some form of driver participation. Antilock brakes are an example.

all-wheel-drive   A system in which all four vehicle wheels are powered at all times, alternatively called full-time four-wheel-drive.

antilock brakes   A sophisticated braking system that senses impending wheel lock and reduces braking effort to eliminate the locking of one or more wheels, effective in helping retain steering under hard or emergency braking.

auto mall   A collection of several dealership operations on one site.

capitalized cost   The price at which the financial institution buys a vehicle from the dealer in a lease transaction. Equivalent to the cash purchase price in a conventional purchase, it is commonly referred to as the "cap cost."

captive finance company   A finance company that is owned by an auto manufacturer. Examples are Ford Motor Credit, Chrysler Credit, and General Motors Acceptance Company.

closed-end lease   A lease the specifies the residual value of the vehicle at the conclusion of the lease term

closer   The member of the dealership's staff who usually concludes new-vehicle transactions. In simpler language, the person who closes the deal.

collateral   Assets you own that document your ability to pay back borrowed money and that may be seized by the financial institution if you fail to pay.

comeback   A customer with an unresolved problem who returns to the service facility.

comparison test   A magazine or newspaper article that compares two or more vehicles of the same type. Also called a "shoot-out."

dealer invoice price   The price the dealer paid the manufacturer or distributor for an individual vehicle before holdback, special reductions, and incentives.

depreciation   The amount an item decreases in value over time. In automotive terms, the difference between the price you paid for the car and the price you get when you sell it.

disposition fee   Fee charged to the lessee to dispose of the vehicle at the conclusion of the lease term if the lessee does not purchase the vehicle.

early termination charge   Fee charged to lessee if lessee decides to quit the lease before the conclusion of the lease term.

float   The time interval that occurs between the writing of a check and the moment that check is redeemed by the financial institution.

holdback   The dollar amount refunded to the dealer by the manufacturer after a vehicle is sold. Most often holdback represents a percentage of the Manufacturer's Suggested Retail Price.

incentives   Cash or special financing offers usually offered by vehicle manufacturers, designed to induce consumers to purchase or lease the vehicles.

installment loan   A loan repaid in separate increments, usually monthly.

interest   The price you pay to borrow money, generally expressed as a percentage of the amount borrowed. For example, if you borrow $100 at 10 percent interest, at the conclusion of the loan period you will pay back the $100 plus an additional $10 in interest.

lessee   The person making the payments on a leased vehicle.

lessor   The entity (usually a financial institution) that purchases ownership of a vehicle and contracts to provide it to another entity or consumer for a proscribed period of time.

line of credit   A loan amount that is approved by a financial institution but has not yet been used.

Manufacturer's Suggested Retail Price   The price the manufacturer suggests that the dealer charge for the vehicle. By law the manufacturer cannot enforce a retail price.

mileage cap   The contractually imposed limit on mileage in a lease. Exceeding the mileage cap leads to a per-mile penalty that can add up quickly.

money factor   An algebraic expression derived from the interest rate, used as a mathematical shortcut in determining lease payments.

open-end lease   A lease that assigns no residual value to the vehicle. The residual value in an open-end lease is determined at the conclusion of the lease term.

opportunity cost   The potential advantage that could have been realized by using resources in one way that were not gained because the resources were used in another way.

optional equipment   Equipment or features that are not included in the sticker price, but are available for an extra charge and can be ordered individually or as part of a package.

passive safety devices   Devices designed to help protect vehicle occupants that require little or no effort from driver or passenger. Airbags are an example of a passive safety device.

resale value   The amount an owner receives in payment for a vehicle he had purchased previously.

residual value   The estimated worth of the vehicle at the conclusion of the lease term. Also called the "residual."

retail price   The price a consumer pays a dealer to acquire a vehicle.

salesperson   (Facetiously speaking) someone who was doing something else six months before and will be doing something else six months from now.

sticker price   The Manufacturer's Suggested List Price. Also referred to as "the dealer sticker."

term loan   A loan repaid in a lump sum with interest at the conclusion of the loan period.

trade-in value   The amount the dealer pays to buy your current vehicle when you acquire a new vehicle. Also called "trade-in allowance."

transplant   A vehicle designed by a company based in one country and built by a factory in another country.

trim levels   Sub-models within a model line, usually differentiated by equipment differences and an alphabetic designation. For example, if the brand is Doofus and the model is Goofus, the various trim levels might be the low-line Doofus Goofus DX, mid-level Doofus Goofus RA, and the top-of-the-line Doofus Goofus BLT-NO MAYO.

upside down   Being in the position of owing more money on an asset than the current worth of that asset. Buyers who purchase using small down payment and loans of relatively long duration frequently find themselves upside down in the middle of the loan term. Also referred to as having "negative equity."

wholesale price   The price a dealer pays to acquire a new or used vehicle.

Jack's Best Bets

New Vehicles

The following are my personal recommendations of vehicles in 11 different vehicle categories, both new and used. I call them "Best Bets" because I believe that these vehicles offer the best combination of quality and value in each category. The vehicle models are listed in descending order of preference (my favorite on down), but, in my estimation, each of them will provide above-average overall value. These "Best Bets" are based on my many years as a vehicle reviewer, augmented by secondary research from the Consumer Research Bureau and other pertinent sources of vehicle information.

Family Cars

Honda Accord	Ford Taurus	Nissan Maxima
Toyota Camry	Chevrolet Lumina	

Small Cars

Honda Civic	Mazda Protege	Toyota Tercel
Geo Prizm	Subaru Impreza	

Sports Cars

Honda Prelude	Acura Integra	Mazda MX-5 Miata
Toyota Celica	Saturn SC	

Large Domestic Cars

Buick LeSabre	Buick Park Avenue	Ford Crown Victoria
Mercury Grand Marquis	Oldsmobile 88	

Domestic Luxury Cars

Cadillac DeVille/Concours	Lincoln Town Car	Lincoln Mark VIII
Lincoln Continental	Chrysler LHS	

Import Luxury Cars

Lexus LS400	Mercedes-Benz S-Class	Lexus SC300/400
Infiniti Q45	Volvo 960	

Compact Sport Utility Vehicles

Ford Explorer	Geo Tracker	Isuzu Trooper
Toyota 4Runner	Honda Passport	

Full-Size Sport Utility Vehicles

Toyota Land Cruiser	Chevrolet Blazer/GMC Yukon
GMC/Chevrolet Suburban	Ford Expedition

Minivans

Honda Odyssey	Nissan Quest	Mercury Villager
Toyota Previa	Dodge Caravan	

Compact Pickups

Ford Ranger	Chevrolet S-10	Mazda B-Series
Toyota Tacoma	Nissan pickup	

Full-Sized Pickups

Toyota T100	GMC Sierra	Chevrolet C/K
Ford F-Series	Dodge Ram	

Used Vehicles

When buying a used car you are generally best-advised to purchase the most recent model year vehicle you can comfortably afford. This is less important, however, if you don't plan to re-sell the vehicle in the future. A vehicle's condition is the overriding factor—much more important to your driving comfort and safety than mileage or model year. Again, these are listed in descending order of preference.

Family Cars

Honda Accord (1988-current)   Ford Taurus (1993-current)

Toyota Camry (1988-current)   Subaru Legacy (1990-current)

Nissan Maxima (1988-current)

Small Cars

Toyota Corolla (1988-current)   Toyota Tercel (1988-current)

Honda Civic (1988-current)   Mazda Protege (1990-current)

Geo Prizm (1990-current)   Subaru Impreza (1993-current)

Sports Cars

Honda Prelude (1988-current)   Acura Integra (1990-current)

Toyota Celica (1989-current)   Saturn SC (1992-current)

Mazda MX-5 Miata (1990-current)

Large Domestic Cars

Buick LeSabre (1993-current)   Buick Park Avenue (1993-current)

Mercury Grand Marquis (1993-current) Oldsmobile 88, 98 (1994-current)

Ford Crown Victoria (1993-current)

Domestic Luxury Cars

Lincoln Town Car (1993-current)   Lincoln Mark VIII (1993-current)

Lincoln Continental (1994-current)   Chrysler LHS (1995-current)

Cadillac DeVille/Concours (1994-current)

Import Luxury Cars

Lexus LS400 (1990-current)   Infiniti J30 (1993-current)

Mercedes-Benz S-Class (1995-current) Volvo 960 (1993-current)

Lexus SC300/400 (1992-current)

Compact Sport Utility Vehicles

Toyota 4Runner (1990-current)

Ford Explorer (1993-current)

Isuzu Trooper (1992-current)

Honda Passport (1994-current)

Isuzu Rodeo (1993-current)

Full-Sized Sport Utility Vehicles

Toyota Land Cruiser (1991-current)

GMC/Chevrolet Suburban (1994-current)

Minivans

Honda Odyssey (1995-current)

Toyota Previa (1991-current)

Mercury Villager (1993-current)

Nissan Quest (1993-current)

Dodge Caravan (1994-current)

Compact Pickups

Ford Ranger (1993-current)

Toyota (1990-current)

Nissan (1988-current)

Mazda B-Series (1989-current)

Chevrolet S-10 (1993-current)

Full-Sized Pickups

Toyota T100 (1993-current)

Chevrolet C/K (1993-current)

GMC Sierra (1993-current)

Ford F-Series (1993-current)

Dodge Ram (1994-current)

Index

RAP

12-16-98

GAYLORD FG